AF262545

Sign Painting

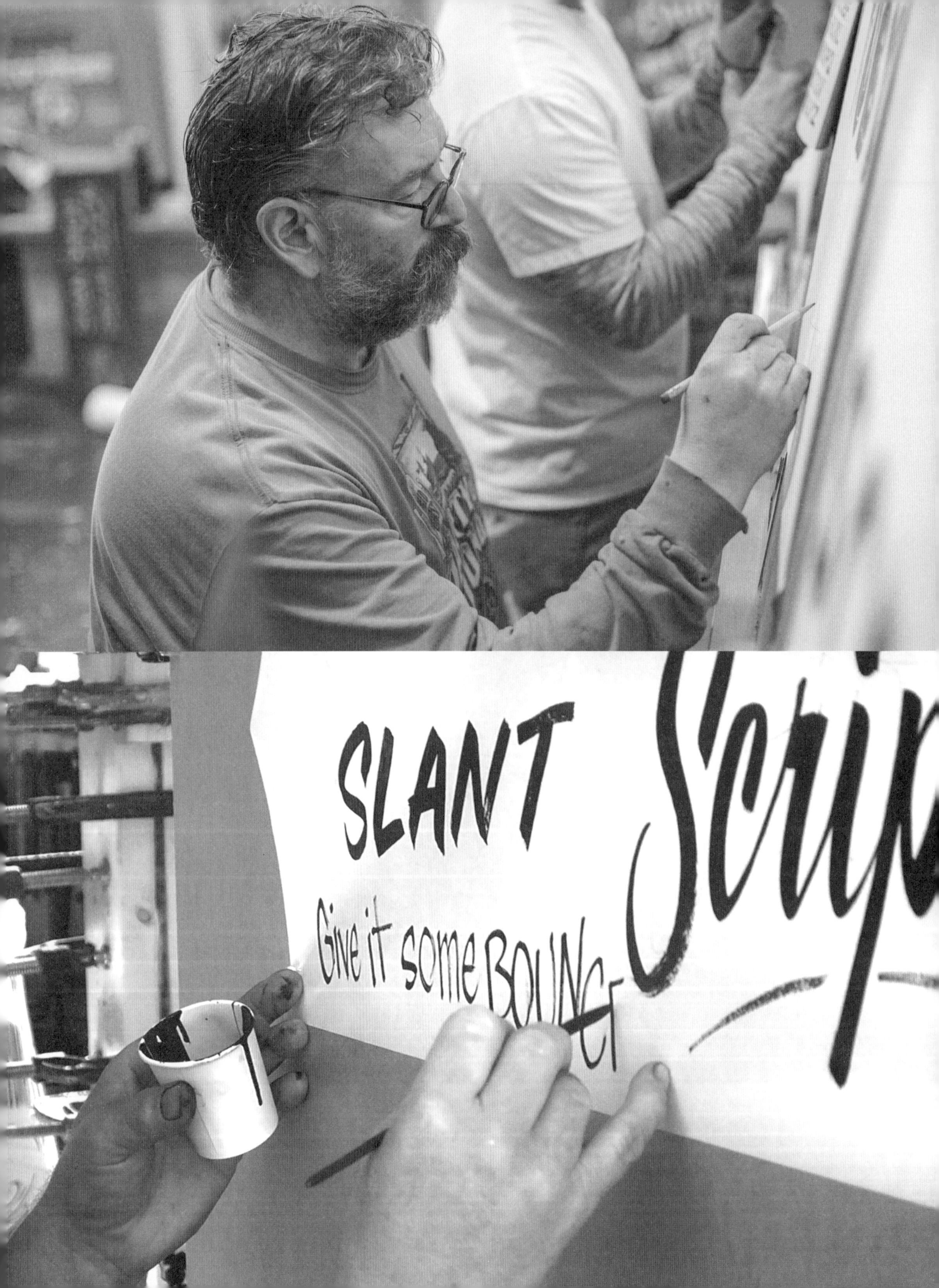

SLANT
Give it some BOUNCE
Scrip

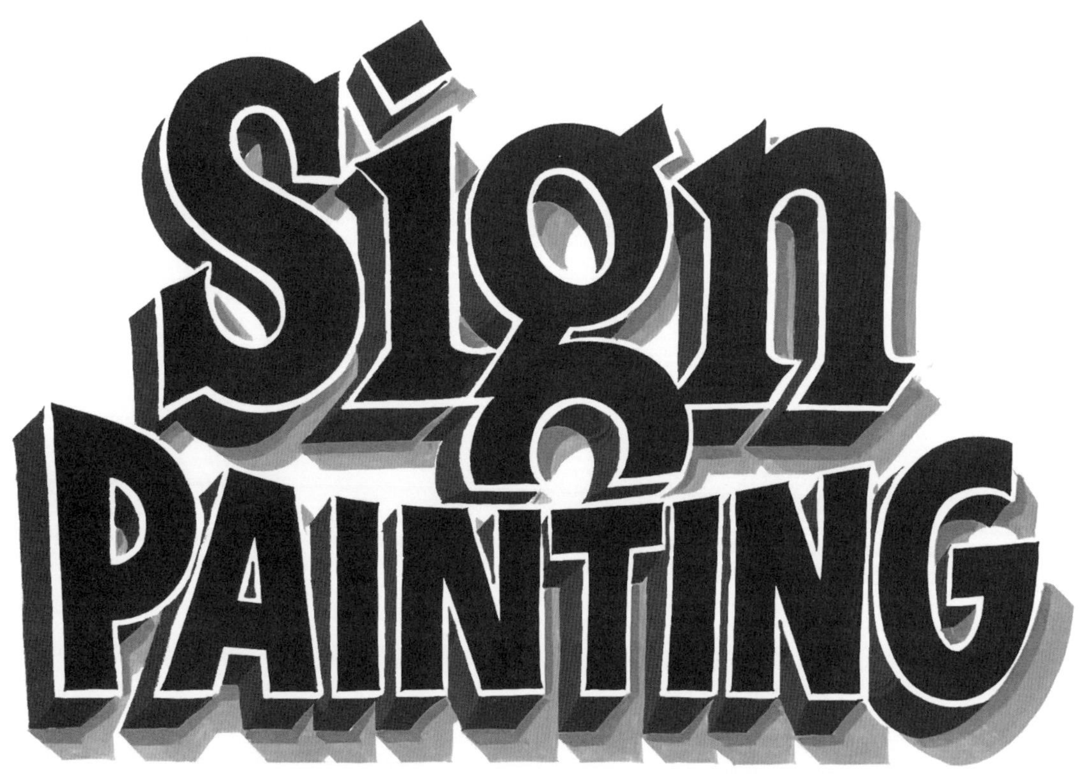

A PRACTICAL GUIDE TO TOOLS, MATERIALS, AND TECHNIQUES

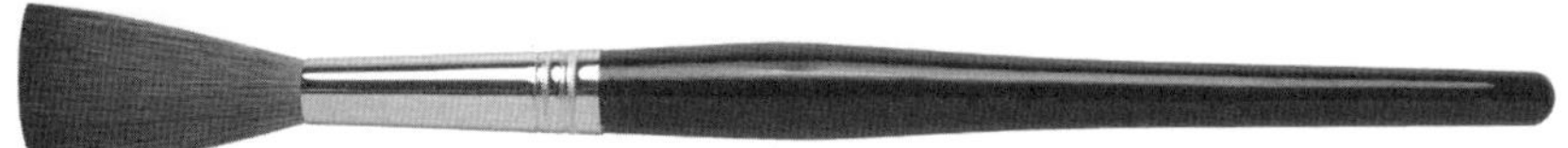

Mike Meyer & Friends
Better Letters

Laurence King Publishing

LAURENCE KING

Published in Great Britain by

Laurence King Student & Professional
An imprint of Quercus Editions Ltd
Carmelite House
50 Victoria Embankment
London EC4Y 0DZ

An Hachette UK company

The authorised representative in the EEA is
Hachette Ireland, 8 Castlecourt Centre, Dublin 15,
D15 XTP3 (email: info@hbgi.ie)

Reprinted in 2025

Copyright © Text and step-by-step drawings 2020
Mike Meyer, Sam Roberts, and Jasper Andries.

The moral right of Mike Meyer, Sam Roberts, and
Jasper Andries to be identified as the author of this
work has been asserted in accordance with the
Copyright, Designs and Patents Act, 1988.

All rights reserved. No part of this publication
may be reproduced or transmitted in any form
or by any means, electronic or mechanical,
including photocopy, recording, or any
information storage and retrieval system,
without permission in writing from the publisher.

A CIP catalogue record for this book is available
from the British Library

TPB ISBN 978-1-78627-692-6

Quercus Editions Ltd hereby exclude all liability to
the extent permitted by law for any errors or omissions
in this book and for any loss, damage or expense
(whether direct or indirect) suffered by a third party
relying on any information contained in this book.

10 9 8 7 6 5

Design: Blok Graphic
Cover design: Alexandre Coco, lettering by
Mike Meyer

Printed and bound in China by C&C Offset Printing Co., Ltd.

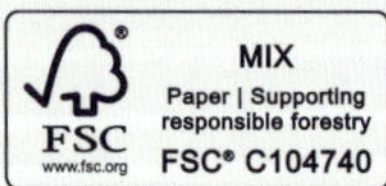

Papers used by Quercus are from well-managed
forests and other responsible sources.

Contents

Foreword by Sam Roberts **6**
Introduction by Mike Meyer **7**

A   **The Sign Painter's Toolkit** 9

Paint 10
Health & Safety **10**
Composition of Paint **10**
Types of Paint & Uses **11**
Storing Paint **15**
Preparing & Mixing Paint **16**
Oil-Based Paint Additives **17**
Water-Based Paint Additives **20**

Brushes 23
Brush Anatomy **23**
Brush Markings **23**
Ferrules & Fillings **24**

Brush Types 28
Chisel-Edge Writers 28
Pointers 29
Flats 29
Liners 30
Lining Fitches/Slant Liners/Cutters 30
Fitches 31
Rollers 31
My First Brushes 31

Brush Care 32
Storage **32**
Brushes for Oil-Based Paints **33**
Brushes for Water-Based Paints **36**

Tools & Their Uses 37
Sign Kit **37**
Brush Boxes **37**
Paint Handling **38**
Palettes & Dippers **38**

Brush Care **40**

Marking-Out Tools **40**

Pouncing Materials **43**

Rests **45**

Application Tools **46**

Tapes **46**

Clips & Fixers **47**

Blades **47**

Abrasives **48**

Hardware **49**

Basic Starter Kit **52**

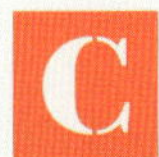 Core Techniques **53**

Preparing & Finishing Substrates **54**

Timber **54**

Aluminum **57**

Walls: Brick, Concrete, & Plaster **58**

Glass **60**

Vehicles **61**

Paper & Card **62**

Fabric & Vinyl Banners **62**

Setting Out **63**

Transferring Designs **63**

Pouncing **64**

Pressure Transfer **66**

Projecting **67**

Vinyl Mask **68**

Using Tape **70**

Copying **70**

Direct Markup **70**

Painting **76**

Posture and Positioning **76**

Rests **78**

Paletting **79**

Brush Strokes **80**

Block & Thick 'n' Thin **80**

Casual **85**

Script **89**

Summary **91**

Your Learning Journey **92**

The Alphabets **95**

Artist Profiles **178**

Glossary **182**

Stockists **186**

Further Reading **188**

Index **189**

Acknowledgments **192**

Photography Credits **192**

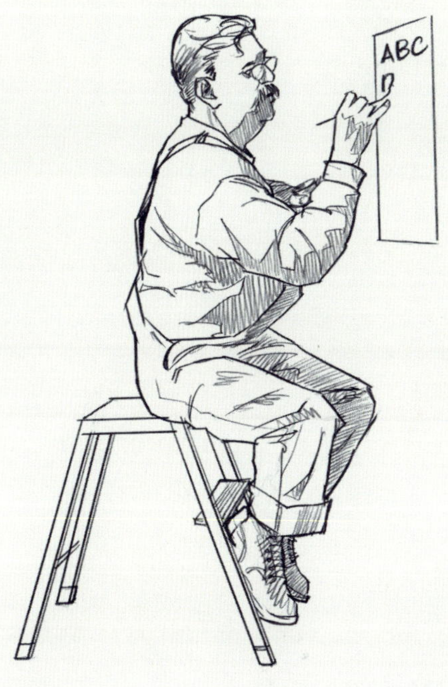

In his element: Mike Meyer, his brush, and 26 friends.

Foreword by Sam Roberts

In 1984 Bill Stewart wrote of "the renaissance of the crafts-man" in his book, *Signwork*. This continued a tradition of books remarking on the current state of sign painting. Those at the early stages of their career when Stewart was writing, including Mike Meyer, have seen a fall and rise in demand for the sign painter's craft: In the last ten years or so we have truly witnessed a resurgence. This appears to have been driven by business and consumer desire for a human touch in their interactions, something that comes naturally from a hand-painted sign, less so from a digital screen.

It is encouraging that so many newcomers are seeking to learn through workshops, Letterheads events, and by sharing resources online. This book supports their efforts with technical information and alphabetic inspiration.

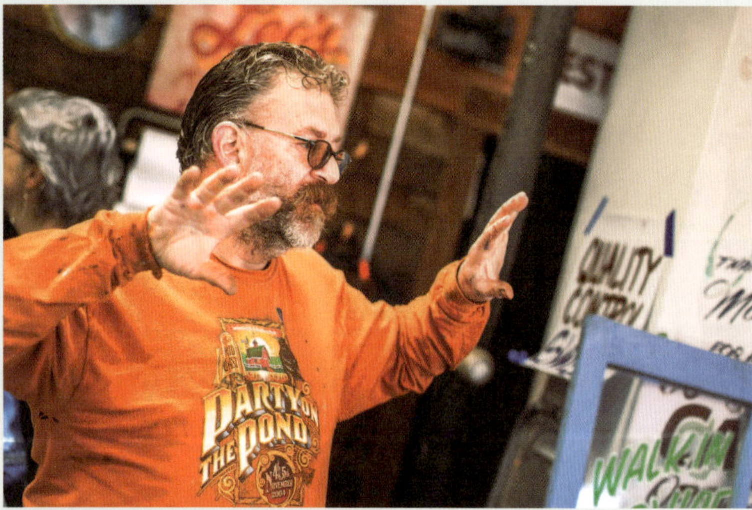

Mike teaching at his shop in Mazeppa, Minnesota.

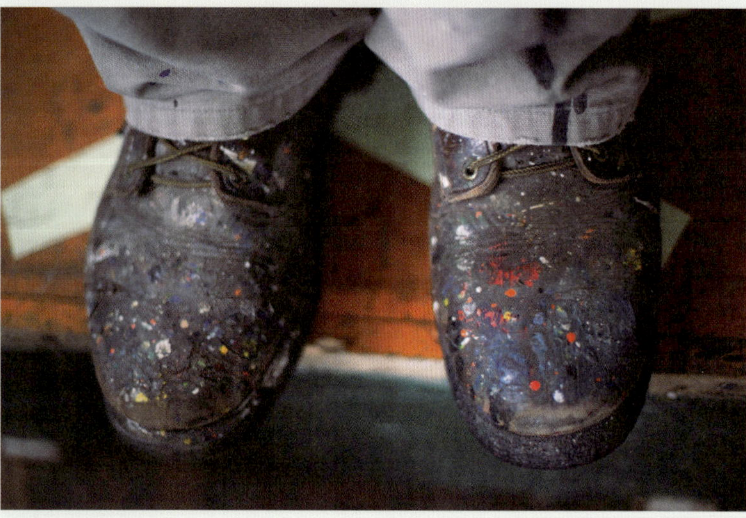

Mike's customized Red Wing boots.

Introduction by Mike Meyer

This book was written following many requests from curious people who are striving to learn the fascinating craft of sign painting. In the pages that follow I have tried to set out some of the essentials for getting started, with the aim of providing a solid foundation for you to build upon. In this introduction I want to talk about some of my core beliefs about sign painting and being a sign painter. These have been formed over my many years in the trade, and have stood the test of time.

As a sign painter you will experience many successes and failures—this is the way life goes, and it is the same for everyone. Whenever you think that someone is more successful or better than you, remember that they too have experienced, and will experience, failures and setbacks along the way. What's important is that you learn from your experiences and carry this learning with you into the future.

Hard work and dedicated practice of both creativity and business will form the backbone of your career. I believe that there is no other business that connects the owner to their community as much as that of a sign painter. Whatever size shop you are running, you will serve many clients, and your resourcefulness will be called upon in many ways. If you have a passion for your craft, you will ultimately find happiness and fulfillment in your work. Some people consider sign painting "just a job," but we know better!

Keep in mind that the purpose of signs is to create the best possible impression for your clients. Your signs should help them attract customers, generate profit, and prosper. In turn they will become silent salespeople for you and your work, and through this you will build your own reputation.

Letting others speak for your work will help to keep you humble, and I believe that humility is an important characteristic to nurture in yourself. You should always take pride in your work, but don't pound your chest about it. However good you think your latest creation might be, there is always something, or someone, better. Don't be boastful, and always strive to improve what you do.

Signs can be taken for granted in everyday life, but their words and directions have been essential to societies all over. Remember that readability is your top priority. It is no good creating the most amazing decorative lettering and sign work if it can't be read easily by the people who need to read it. I have traveled to towns and cities all over the world and everywhere readability separates good signs from bad.

To understand what works, and what does not, it is important to develop the constant habit of observation. Take note of everything you see, not just pretty lettering. What does the lettering do? Is it directional? Does it identify something (buildings, vehicles, consumer goods, etc.)? Does it advertise?

Consider why a sign is effective and why it impresses you—or not. Is it the lettering style? Is it the choice of colors? Is it the placement? Is it the wording? And, of course, ask yourself whether you can easily read and understand it.

Through this process you will improve your understanding of effective signs and lettering and be able to apply this to your own work. There is so much that can be learned through the simple process of questioning observation.

You should also apply this attitude to your own work and remember that in signs, if it looks right, it is right. The impact of a sign comes from its presentation and the spontaneity that arises from creative lettering choices, the use of color, punctuation, effects, and even images.

As you go about learning and developing as a sign painter, I think it is important to remember what I refer to as the three Ds: desire, dedication, and discipline.

Desire is something you probably already have if you are holding this book. You have a curiosity about signs and lettering, and a desire to learn more. Nothing will happen without this.

Sometimes this desire doesn't go any further but, with dedication, it can power your sign-painting journey. You must be dedicated to your future as a sign painter and take actions that will

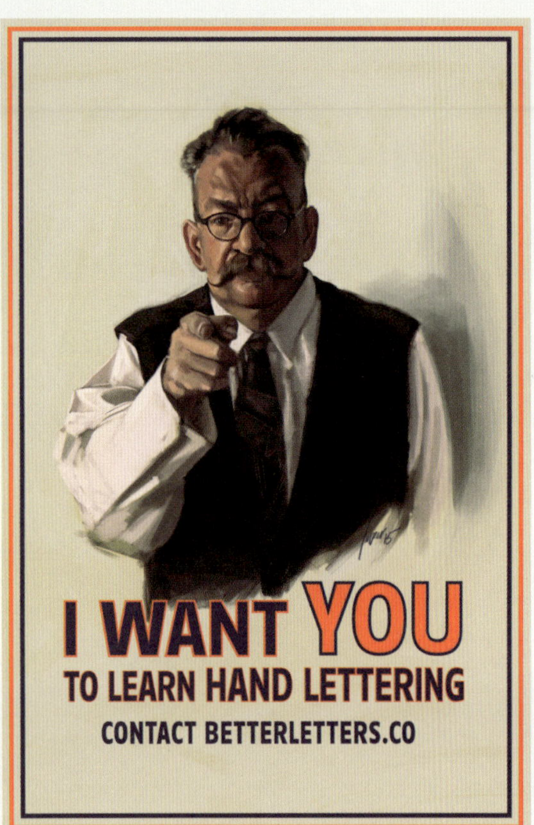

Poster by Jasper Andries (2015), after
Alfred Leete.

help you get there. These include some of the
points mentioned earlier—observing, focusing
on your client, remaining humble, etc.—but also a
commitment to meeting others and learning from
them. Your dedication is also a promise to yourself to keep going when things get tough.

Finally, you will need discipline to practice
and improve your skills. At times this will feel
difficult, even boring, but the more you practice,
the better you will get. Sometimes discipline
means getting up and going when you feel tired
in the morning, sometimes it means missing
out on some other activity to do your work,
but ultimately it will build your focus and
skill to lead your life as a sign painter.

The three Ds are something I share with
attendees at my workshops, and I am always
amazed by the experience. Those who come
clearly have the desire, but they often start out
feeling intimidated. Over our days together we
develop as a group, gaining confidence and

forming a bond with each other as we learn.
Sometimes this ends with tears (of joy) but always
with people moving one step closer to the goal of
becoming a sign painter, while making new friends
and developing a support network along the way.

I was taught at an early age to use envy as a
tool to drive me to become more knowledgeable and
build my awareness of why making nice lettering
makes me feel so satisfied. This is something I try
to pass on to my students. Don't feel bad if someone
else is ahead of you. Learn from their work and use
it to push your own forward. Also, let someone know
if you like what they are doing. Show others appreci-
ation, and it will be shown to you.

In my workshops I focus on the structure of
letters and working with a brush to create them, and
less on some of the technical aspects—such as tools,
materials, and preparatory techniques—that are covered in this book. I want students to get addicted the
way I am to an array of intoxicating letter styles, get
drunk on color contrasts, and overdose on shadows
and outlines. We all occasionally need to check into
"layout rehab" to prevent crowding out the edges
of a sign, or making one completely in ornate Old
English capitals! But, ultimately, this is a fun, and
relatively safe, addiction to develop.

Who is an instructor of lettering, and what
determines a good instructor, is in the eye of the
student. In the later years of my career I realize I
was an instructor all along. People who were curious
about proper techniques and brushes and paint and
asked me questions about them were early students.
I will forever remain a student as well. If you stop
asking questions and seeking solutions, you stop
growing and halt your own creative development.

And finally, a note on this book and its contents.
If you gave the job of writing this book to 100 different sign painters, you would get 100 completely
different books. What you have in your hands is my
way of presenting the craft, which I hope you, the
reader, find useful. I know that I have learned a lot
from the process of putting it down in book form,
and I know that there are things that other people
will disagree with. At this stage it is probably worth
remembering an unwritten law in the sign business:
In signs, the rule is "There are no rules."

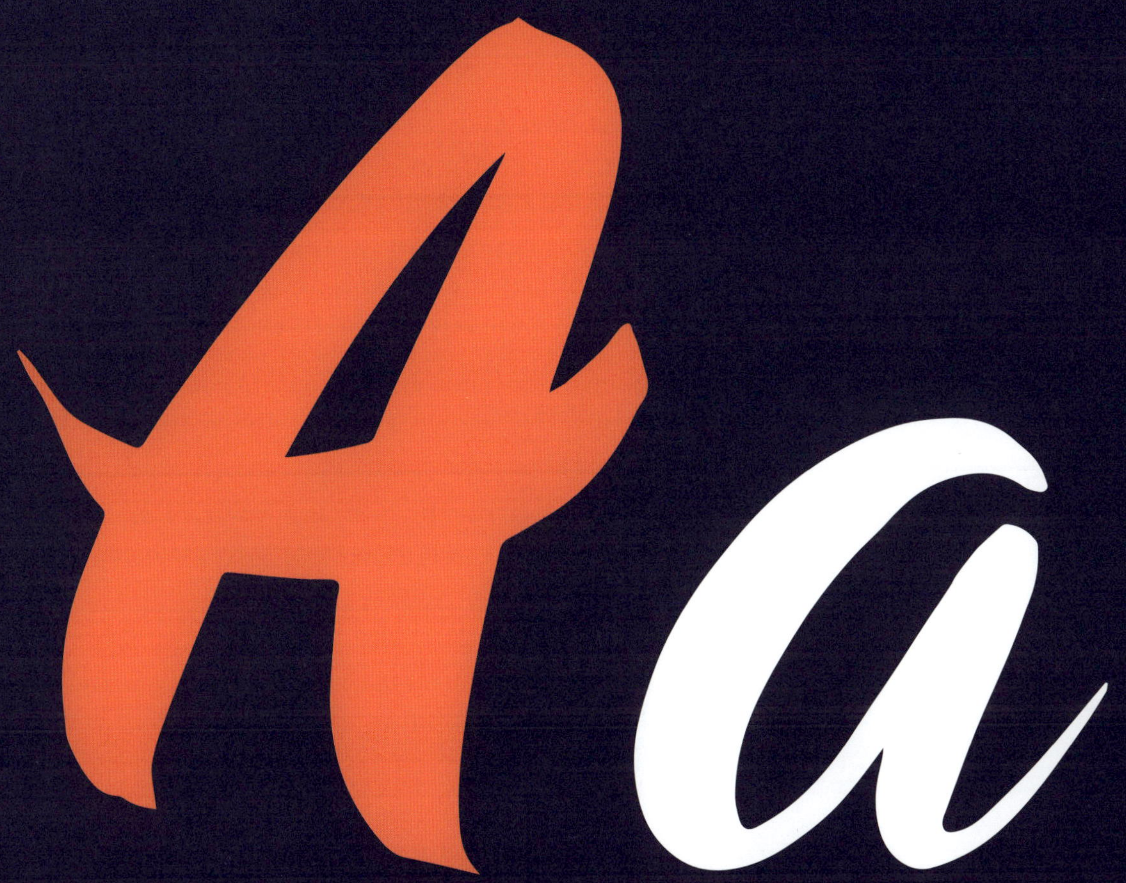

The Sign Painter's Toolkit

Lettering by Carla Hackett, Fruity Script, see page 114

Paint

In sign painting you will use a lot of different paints to prepare and letter a variety of surfaces (substrates).

Health & Safety

Many of the paints and additives used in sign painting are toxic and/or flammable. This toxicity applies to water-based as well as oil-based paints. For your own safety, always read the label, and follow these general rules to protect your own health.

– **Work in well-ventilated spaces, ideally with air circulating to the outside. Consider a filter mask in spaces where ventilation is limited.**

– **Wear latex gloves, especially if your skin is sensitive. Toxins in paints and additives can pass through skin, and extreme or ongoing exposure can be dangerous.**

– **Always wash your hands thoroughly before handling food or placing them anywhere near your mouth. If you ingest paint or additives, seek immediate medical assistance.**

– **Keep paints and additives away from your eyes. Seek medical assistance if you accidentally get anything in your eyes.**

– **Keep naked flames, heaters, cigarettes, and any other heat emitters well away from paints and additives.**

– **Allow rags/tissues that are damp with paint or solvent to dry before disposing of them, especially in hot temperatures. Placing them in confined spaces such as a bin can result in heat building up and spontaneous combustion.**

– **Store and work with paints and additives out of the reach of children and animals. They are less able to protect themselves from accidents.**

It is important to have a basic understanding of the main types of paint you will be using and, as it can be quite an expensive material, how to look after your stock.

Composition of Paint

Paint is any form of liquid that cures (dries) to form a solid film after application to a substrate for decorative and/or protective purposes. This includes non-pigmented liquids such as varnishes. Paint consists of the following four components: binders, solvents, pigments, and additives. In the past, sign painters made their own paint by mixing these components together, but these days most will use industrially manufactured products.

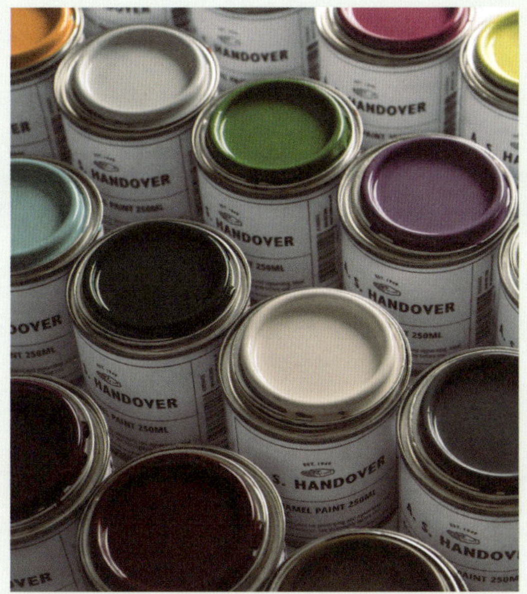

Mike's Tip

Most red, maroon, and purple pigments fade more quickly than other colors, especially on external signs with high levels of exposure to the sun. Take this into consideration at the design stage and make your client aware that a repaint might be needed sooner when using these colors.

Binder (Film Former)

Binder is the film-forming part of the paint that becomes solid once the paint has cured (dried). It is the backbone of the paint and provides a number of qualities including gloss, durability, flexibility, and weather resistance. The main types of binders used in sign painting are oils, alkyds, and acrylics. These are too viscous (thick) to be used alone, and so they are thinned using a solvent. Each type of binder requires a specific type of solvent.

Solvent (Diluent or Thinner)

Solvents are liquids used to dilute the binder and make it possible to apply the paint by thinning it, allowing the paint to transfer effectively from brush to substrate and helping it to flow. Solvents are only a temporary part of the paint mixture; they evaporate during the curing process, leaving the binder (and pigment, if present) behind. The solvent used will depend on the type of binder found in the paint. Common solvents include, among others, turpentine for oil-based paints and water for water-based paints.

Pigments (Color)

Pigments are solid particles added to paint to color it. "Hiding" pigments are added in small quantities to less opaque colors to improve their opacity (without detracting from their color) and to give protection from ultraviolet (UV) light. Pigments can be natural or synthetic, and have varying levels of naturally occurring opacity, toxicity, and longevity.

Additives

Small amounts of other substances can be added to paint to improve its working properties, such as flow and curing speed. Additives can also be used to change the gloss level and otherwise affect the final appearance of the paint. Others enhance UV resistance and pigment stability.

Types of Paint & Uses

There are many different types of paint, and not all of them are suitable for sign painting. For example, regular artists' watercolors will not hold up well against moisture in an exterior environment, while pure oil paints are far too slow drying to be commercially viable for a working sign painter.

Paints can broadly be divided into oil-based (sometimes called solvent-based) and water-based (or waterborne). In oil-based paints, "oil" refers to the binder, which is a drying oil such as linseed oil. This, and the pigment, are what remain when the thinning solvent has evaporated and the paint cures. In contrast, the water in water-based paints refers to the solvent itself, with the binder diluted within the water. The binder and pigment then remain after the water has evaporated. Many water-based paints also contain small quantities of solvents that are more commonly associated with oil-based paints, such as mineral spirits.

The processes for working with oil-based and water-based paints differ, especially the thinners and additives used. The type of paint used also affects the way that brushes are cleaned and cared for. If you use both oil-based and water-based paints, I always recommend having two sets of brushes, one for each type of paint. While it is possible to use a brush in oil-based paints after it has been used with water-based paints, moving from oil- to water-based can cause big problems if oil in the brush contaminates the water in the paint—remember, oil and water don't mix!

The following are the main types of paint used for sign work, and should be enough to get you going in the trade. Some specialist applications require paints outside of this list; talk to suppliers and other sign painters to discuss these needs as and when they arise in your work.

Sign & Lettering Enamels

The most common type of paints used in sign painting are enamels. The word *enamel* itself refers to the hard, typically glossy finish that these paints provide, similar in appearance to but distinct from that of metal enamel signs. The toughness and resilience of these paints makes them well suited to outdoor applications.

Most sign enamels are made from oil-modified resin (alkyd) binders, but there are now increasingly more water-based products described as enamels. It is important to know the nature of any enamel paint that you buy, so that you can use the right types of brushes, thinners, and other additives for their application.

As the solvent in the paint evaporates, the (oil) binder is exposed to oxygen in the air, causing a chemical reaction (oxidization) that hardens it. Paint cures from the outside in, so while the surface may harden relatively quickly and feel "touch dry," the inside can take much longer. It is therefore important to allow sufficient curing time between coats to avoid wrinkling, crazing, lifting, and/or potential surface defects.

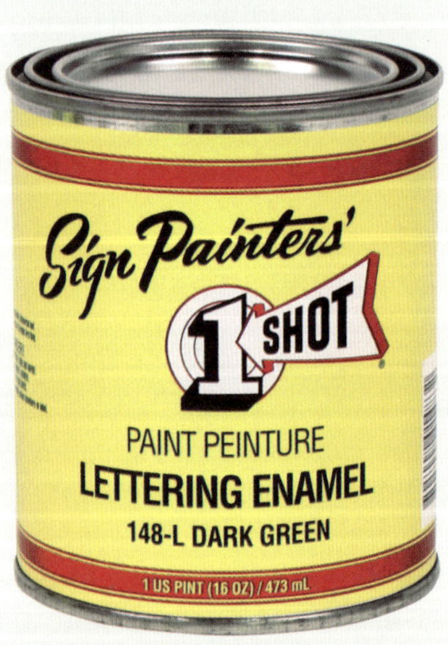

1 Shot oil-based lettering enamel.

Use oil-based enamel paints for:

– **Shopfronts, either wooden or metal (both the topcoat and lettering).**
– **Vehicles (with hardener added to increase gloss and resilience to washing).**
– **Billboards (you can also use bulletin colors; see below).**
– **Permanent window pieces.**
– **Indoor murals that are likely to be touched regularly.**

Currently on the market are a variety of sign and lettering enamel paints. The most well-known and widely available is the range from 1 Shot. In North America, Ronan Paints and Alphanamel from Alpha 6 are also available, while in Europe A.S. Handover and Craftmaster Paints both offer their own brands of sign-painting enamels. Try the brands that are available to you and talk to other local sign painters about what they use and why.

Bulletin Colors

These sign and lettering enamels are formulated differently for temporary billboard work. They usually contain high quantities of flowing agents and less pigment, which affects their application (they are less viscous) and longevity (they fade and degrade quicker).

Poster Paints

These are often called Japan colors, or flats, and they dry quickly to a matte finish. (They differ from distemper or tempera, which are also often referred to as poster paints.) They are usually made by increasing the quantity of driers in enamel paint, which speeds up the curing time and takes away the gloss finish. This means that they can be worked with in exactly the same way as sign and lettering enamels, using the same brushes and additives.

Use poster paints for:

– **Paper and card signs.**
– **Indoor menus.**
– **Anything indoors where a matte finish is required.**
– **Practicing on paper (I use kraft paper in my lettering workshops and it works perfectly with poster paints).**

As with the enamels, 1 Shot offer the most widely available poster colors, while Ronan Paints manufacture a line of Superfine Japan Colors for the North American market.

13

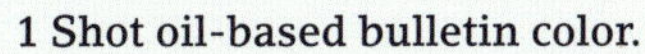

1 Shot oil-based bulletin color.

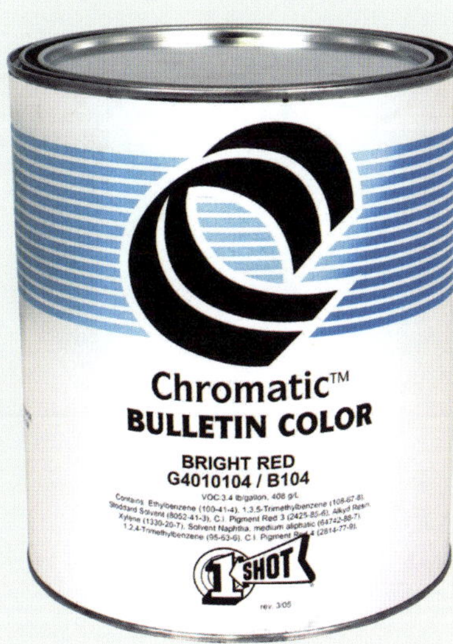

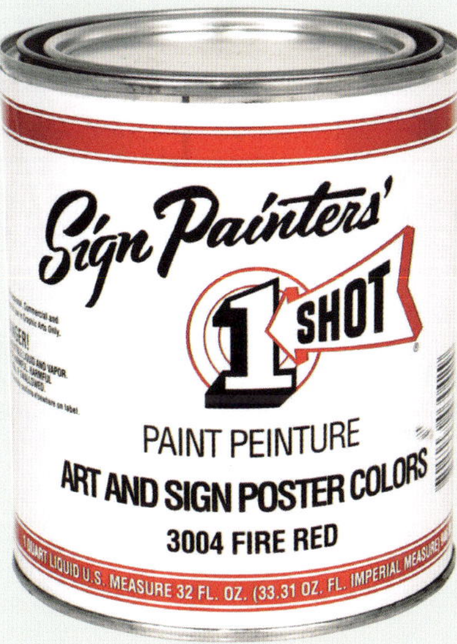

1 Shot oil-based poster paint.

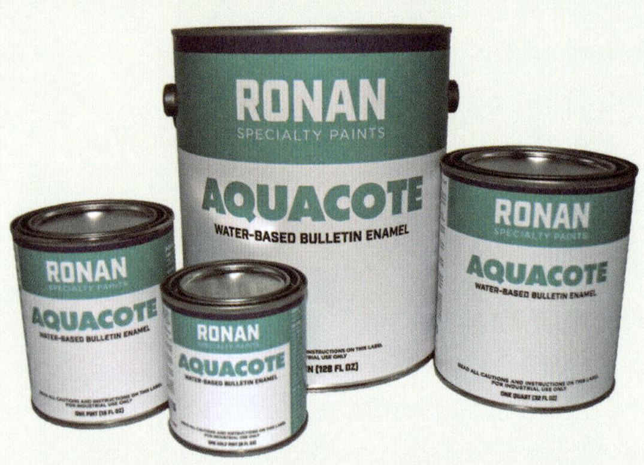

Ronan Aquacote water-based
bulletin enamel.

In Europe, A.S. Handover offer their own brand of Japan
fast-drying flat oil colors.

Latex & Acrylic (Emulsion) Paints

Latex and acrylics (also called emulsion paints) are fast-drying water-based paints formed from pigment suspended in an acrylic polymer emulsion (the binder). The emulsion is enabled by the use of added chemicals (emulsifiers) that prevent the otherwise incompatible components from separating.

Latex and acrylic paints are water soluble, and so water is used as the solvent. As the water evaporates after application, the polymers soften and bond to form a solid film. Once the paint has cured, the resulting film is water resistant and elastic, and cannot be re-dissolved in the solvent that originally carried it. Exterior latex paints contain additives that toughen them and provide greater UV protection.

A wide variety of mixtures can be found on the market to suit various needs and budgets. Paints made with 100% acrylic resins are the most durable and most expensive types of water-based paints. The use of vinyl (e.g. Polyvinyl acetate or PVA) in combination with, or in place of, acrylic reduces the cost of the paint but also its durability. Always ask for exterior paints for outside work, such as murals.

Latex and acrylic paints are especially suited to materials that expand and contract or that need to breath (e.g. brick walls). Their elasticity also makes them ideal for flexible surfaces such as vinyl and fabric.

Use latex and acrylic paints for:

- **Exterior murals.***
- **Vinyl banners.**
- **Awnings, canopies, and tents.**
- **Clothing, including leather.**
- **Temporary window pieces.**
- **Priming wooden signs and walls.***

** Ensure that the paint specifies that it is for exterior use.*

In North America the main brands of water-based paints for sign work are Ronan Aquacote and Nova Color. Alpha 6 also have a line of acrylic paints. Elsewhere in the world I would recommend talking with your local supplier about what is available and its suitability for the job at hand. It is also worth testing samples for flow before investing in stock.

14

Emulsion & Latex

An emulsion is a mixture of two liquids that under normal circumstances do not blend, for example oil and water. The word comes from the Latin *emulgere*, which means "to milk out"; milk is a naturally occurring emulsion of fats blended with water. A vinaigrette salad dressing, mixing olive oil and vinegar, is another common emulsion. In British English the word *emulsion* is used to describe what Americans call latex paints, which, oddly, don't contain any latex (rubber) at all.

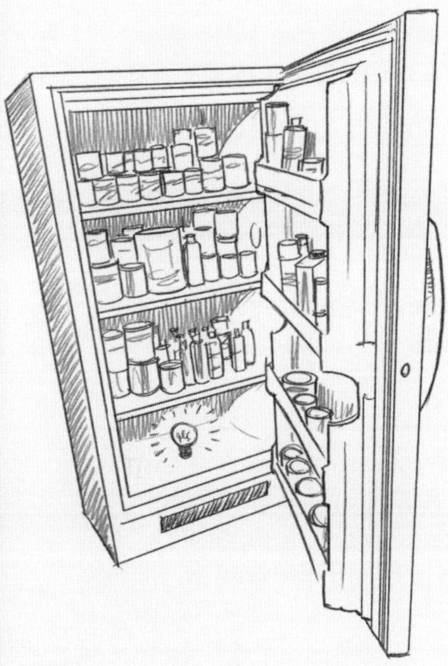

Mike's Tip

Where I live in Mazeppa, Minnesota, it gets extremely cold in the winter, and I've lost a lot of paint to freezing temperatures. A neat solution that I've found is to acquire old refrigerators and wire up a 40W bulb inside each of them, which is plugged into the mains socket. All the paint is placed inside and, because of the insulation in the structure of the fridges, the bulbs maintain a slightly warm temperature that stops the paint from freezing.

Primers

Primers are a special category of (usually) latex paints that are manufactured to seal substrates effectively and ready them for the application of further layers of other paints. They are clearly labeled as primers, but take care to ensure that you buy a product suitable for the substrate that you are working on (walls, wood, aluminum, etc.).

Storing Paint

Specialist paints, especially sign enamels, are expensive and you can save a lot of money by storing them well for use again on future jobs.

The main objective when storing paint is to minimize its exposure to air, heat, and cold, each of which can damage the paint or cause it to partially or fully cure (dry). Keeping the paint in an environment that does not experience extremes of hot and cold is the most straightforward thing to do. This means avoiding outhouses, sheds, garages, and other places that are not heated in winter, and places that are exposed to direct sunlight or that get very hot (e.g. lofts) in the summer. Closing lids properly so that they are fully airtight will prevent air from reaching the paint.

It is important to mix paint really well before you start using it for the first time, and each time after that. This ensures an even distribution of all the constituents of the paint, especially the pigment, and the best possible results when applying it to signs and lettering.

Some stores will have a paint shaker in-house, and you can request a good shake-up when you buy it. If that is not an option, there are electrical shakers and stirrers that you can buy to keep in your shop. Something that helps, whether you are using a mechanical shaker or shaking the paint yourself, is placing a couple of bolts, nuts, or large ball bearings inside the paint tin. These will agitate the pigment that tends to solidify at the bottom, helping it come loose and spread evenly throughout the liquid.

When storing your paint, it is really useful to mark the top of the container with a dab of the color that is inside. This will help you quickly find what you are looking for as your collection builds up over time.

If you find your paint has "skinned over," or cured on the top, all is not lost. There is still liquid paint underneath. Using a knife or screwdriver, cut around the edge of the skin until you can pull it out of the tin, ideally in one piece. Mix the remaining paint well, as if you had bought the tin new.

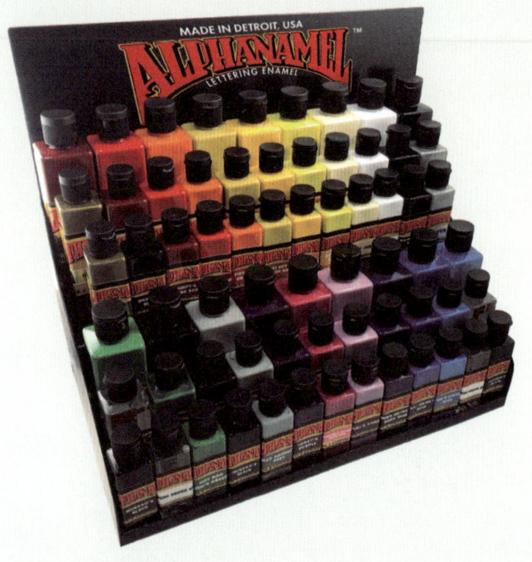

Alphanamel oil-based enamels in squeezy plastic containers.

Mike's Tip

To store smaller quantities of paint, including colors that you have mixed and may need again for touch-ups or corrections in the future, use small jars or plastic vitamin containers that seal airtight. Mark the top with the paint color, and the client or job name if needed.

Preparing & Mixing Paint

Transfer paint between a tin and a smaller container, such as a paint cup, using a palette knife or large stir stick (tongue depressors are the perfect size). Hold your paint cup above the container and dunk the palette knife into the paint. Pull it out relatively quickly and push it down against the inside rim of the cup, forcing the paint that has been picked up on one side into the cup, while any drips are caught by the tin. Repeat until you have filled the cup enough to work with. Using this technique will help keep the rims of your paint tins clean, allowing the airtight replacement of the lid.

Some manufacturers (e.g. Alpha 6) produce their paints in squeezy plastic containers that are both practical to use and help to reduce paint wastage. If you buy your paint in tins, decant it into squeezy bottles purchased from catering merchants, or artists' paint tubes, to gain similar benefits.

Mixing Colors

When mixing your own colors from those supplied by manufacturers, first make sure that all the paints are compatible. Mixing incompatible paints can have a variety of negative side-effects and should be avoided. The most straightforward way to avoid these problems is to only mix colors from a single manufacturer. If in doubt, talk to your paint supplier or manufacturer.

When mixing colors you will quickly learn that dark colors are "stronger" than light colors. For the best results, start with the lighter color and gradually add the darker color, stirring well until you reach the tone that you want: for example, to make orange, start with yellow and add red. If you start with red (the darker color) you will likely end up having to add huge quantities of yellow (the lighter color), and making much more orange that you actually need. That said, it is worth mixing a little more than you need, and keeping some stored after a job, in case you are asked back to fix something. It is virtually impossible to replicate a color you have previously mixed, unless you have done it in a very measured, scientific way.

It is also worth remembering that colors will not dry to the same tone that you see in your paint cup or tin—typically they will dry darker. For this reason, it is often advisable to test a color before going ahead and working with it. This can add time to a job, but is especially useful when clients are very specific about their color requirements for branding or other reasons.

Clients may give you Pantone® references for particular colors. If you are buying in larger quantities from a store, you can take the Pantone® reference and have the color made up. However, most specialist sign-painting paints are not sold by Pantone® color, so you will need to explain to your client that it is not possible to buy that exact color but you will match it as closely as possible. Experimenting with color mixing, testing, and refining is the only way to handle this, and over time you will gain the experience required.

If you are using 1 Shot paints, the company has created a tool on their website that allows you to enter a Pantone® reference number and receive a formula for their paints that approximates that color.

In Europe many paints are sold using the RAL color standard, and you can request this information from clients so that you get exactly the colors they want. If you have a Pantone® reference but are buying in RAL, there are websites that offer approximate equivalents.

Oil-Based Paint Additives

Paint is not always ready to use straight out of the container. In addition to mixing well, you may also want to add things to help with flow, curing times, and the final finish. Here are some useful additives for oil-based paints.

17

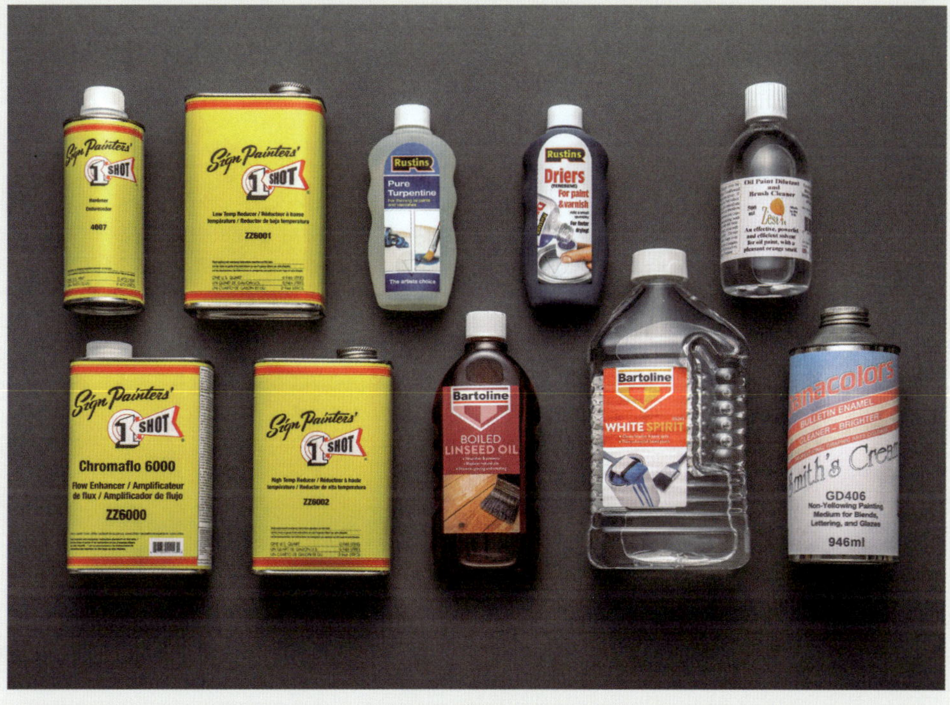

Additives for oil-based paints.

Thinners

Paint can be too thick to work with, even when it has been well mixed. Thinners will help decrease the viscosity (thickness) of the paint and improve the flow when painting. However, thinners will also reduce the ratio of pigment to solvents, so only use the minimum required to get the level of flow you want. For absorbent surfaces such as paper, you will want more thinner than you do for very smooth surfaces such as glass, where the paint is more likely to run.

My preferred thinner is turpentine, stored in a squeezy bottle to help control the quantity that I'm adding. Alternatives include bespoke products such as 1 Shot ChromaFlo Flow Enhancer. For practice it is fine to use mineral spirits for thinning, but I avoid them for commercial sign work, with the occasional exception of work on paper with poster colors. There are also non-toxic products on the market now, such as Zest-it Oil Paint Dilutant and Brush Cleaner, which are worth trying, especially if you are adversely affected by the fumes from mineral spirits and other solvents.

I usually work out of a 3–4oz (c.90–120ml) paint cup and will add a few drops of thinner at a time, stirring thoroughly until the paint reaches a cream-like consistency. I test the consistency by pulling the stir stick out and watching the paint run back. If it is dripping in big blobs then it needs more thinner; if it is running more quickly, like water, then I have thinned it too much and will need to either add some more paint or start again with a new cup.

It is important to keep adding thinners as required while you are working. Over time they will evaporate and the paint will begin to thicken, causing your brush to drag. Mix in a couple more drops, and you are ready to go again. If you are using dippers, you will be maintaining the correct consistency as you work by adding thinners using your brush. This can lead to variations in the ratio of paint to thinner as you work, and affect how quickly different parts fade in the future.

In very hot and humid conditions, it is possible to thin the paint too much. With enamels, this can lead to a poor finish. Try adding some boiled linseed oil to the paint; this will act as a retarder (see below) and slow the drying time.

Reducers

Sometimes you may find yourself working in temperature extremes that cause the paint to cure either too fast (hot) or too slowly (cold). Reducers assist with the flow of the paint while also slowing down or speeding up the drying time,

High-temp reducer will slow the curing time of oil-based paints.

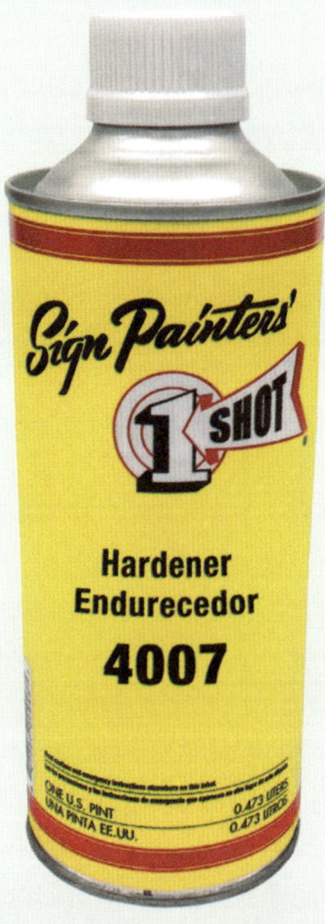

Hardener is added to oil-based enamels to provide extra toughness, especially for work on vehicles.

Mike's Tip

Hardener is very sensitive to humidity, and it is important to replace the lid immediately after use to reduce exposure to the air. Place the container inside a sealable plastic bag for extra protection and to increase the hardener's working life.

without affecting the quality of the finish. Reducers can be used in the same way as thinners, adding them to paint until the preferred consistency is reached, and then continuing to maintain that over time by adding more when required. High-temp and low-temp reducers are available from 1 Shot and Alpha 6, and talk to your local supplier about what they have available.

Hardeners

While oil-based enamels give a tough finish, there are times when additional strength is required, such as truck and other vehicle lettering. For this type of work, a hardener is recommended—add a few large drops to your paint and mix it in well. Hardeners can be purchased from most automotive paint/parts shops, or from brands such as 1 Shot and Alpha 6. I always buy hardener in the smallest possible quantity to minimize losses if it turns bad when stored.

Retarders (Extenders)

If you are working on large pictorials, or other jobs where lots of color blending is required, then extending the "open" time of the paint (during which it is still liquid and can be manipulated) is essential. Smith's Cream from 1 Shot and Jack's Cream from Ronan are both blending mediums that can be used for this purpose. Alternatives are other petroleum creams or linseed oil. These will all thin the paint slightly and so should be added before any thinners.

When I need to blend colors—for example, painting a face—I usually make a special mixture of two parts Smith's Cream and one part each of boiled linseed oil and turpentine (at Colossal Media in Brooklyn they call this mixture the "soup"!). I smear this over the area where I'm going to be blending colors. Then I paint in the main blocks of color before returning to a brush loaded with the special mixture, which helps me blend colors smoothly. It is also possible to add the mixture to the paint directly, which will achieve the same retarding effect.

Driers

Sometimes you want your paints to dry quicker than usual. Low-temp reducer is one option. Another is the addition of a drying agent (e.g. Japan drier or gold/gilding size), which speeds up the oxidation process that causes the paint to cure and a film to form. Use only very small quantities of drier: drops rather than glugs. Too much can actually reverse the effect and lead to the paint never drying.

19

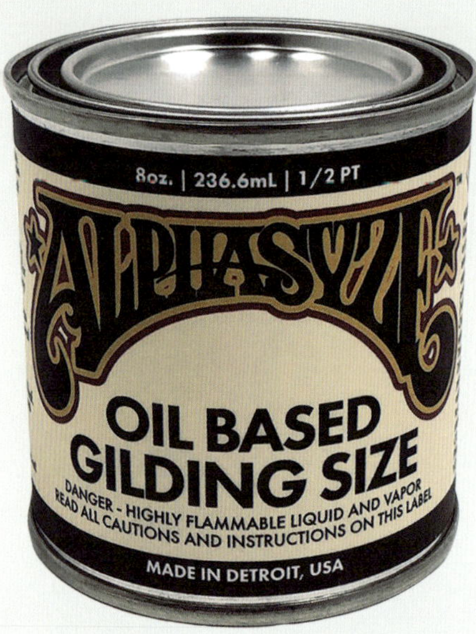

Gold size can be added to oil-based paints in small quantities to speed up the curing time.

Driers are useful when you are under time pressure and greater efficiency is required. However, I recommend planning your work to avoid having to use driers.

Water-Based Paint Additives

These additives can help with the application of water-based paints—mainly latex and acrylic (emulsion) paints.

Thinners

Water-based paints are usually thinned with water, although I prefer to use (100% acrylic) floor wax (polish). Lots of people recommend regular dishwashing soap, and there are other products (e.g. Flood Floetrol, which is similar to dishwashing soap/washing-up liquid) that have been developed especially to improve the flow of latex and acrylic paints.

Water used for thinning should be room temperature or slightly warm. Add it in small quantities, mixing as you go until you reach the consistency you want for working. Don't exceed 1 part water to 10 parts paint, as this will reduce the quality of binder adhesion. It is always a good idea to test the paint to ensure that it is not too thick or thin to work with, and that it will give a good, even finish.

Many sign painters and showcard writers working with water-based paints will "thin as they go," keeping some water nearby to constantly refresh the brush before paletting (shaping the paint-loaded brush). It is important to remember that, as with oil-based paints, thinning as you go can result in different parts of your work having different coverage, due to the varying quantities of thinner applied while you are working.

Hardeners

Water-based paints are not a good choice for jobs that usually require hardeners, for example vehicle lettering. Use oil-based paints with added hardener instead.

Retarders (Extenders)

Given the fast curing times of water-based paints compared to most oil-based paints, it is often useful to extend their curing time through the use of retarders. Nova Color sell a good-quality acrylic retarder, and acrylic scumble can be used in the same way to slow the curing process and allow time for blending.

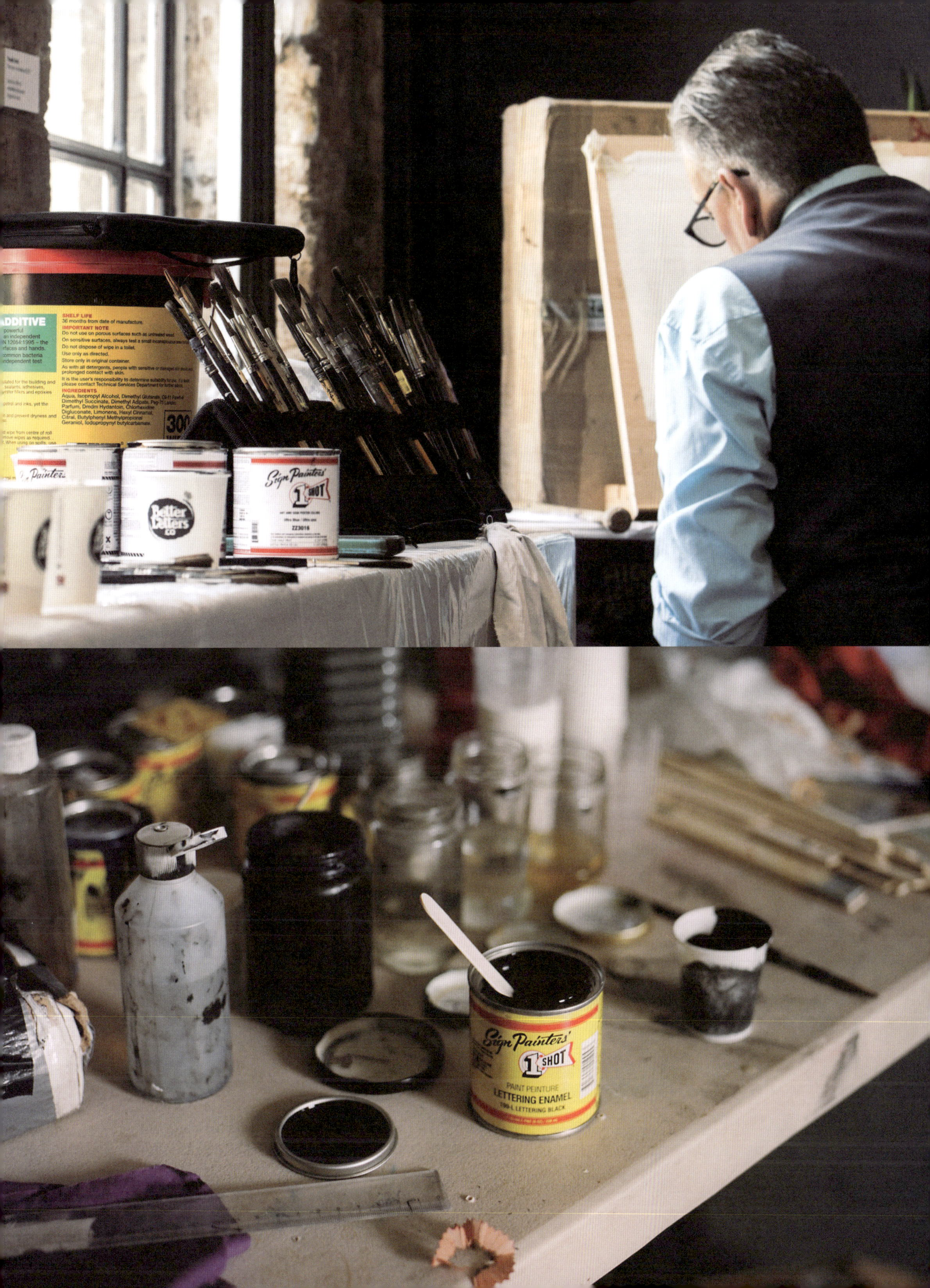

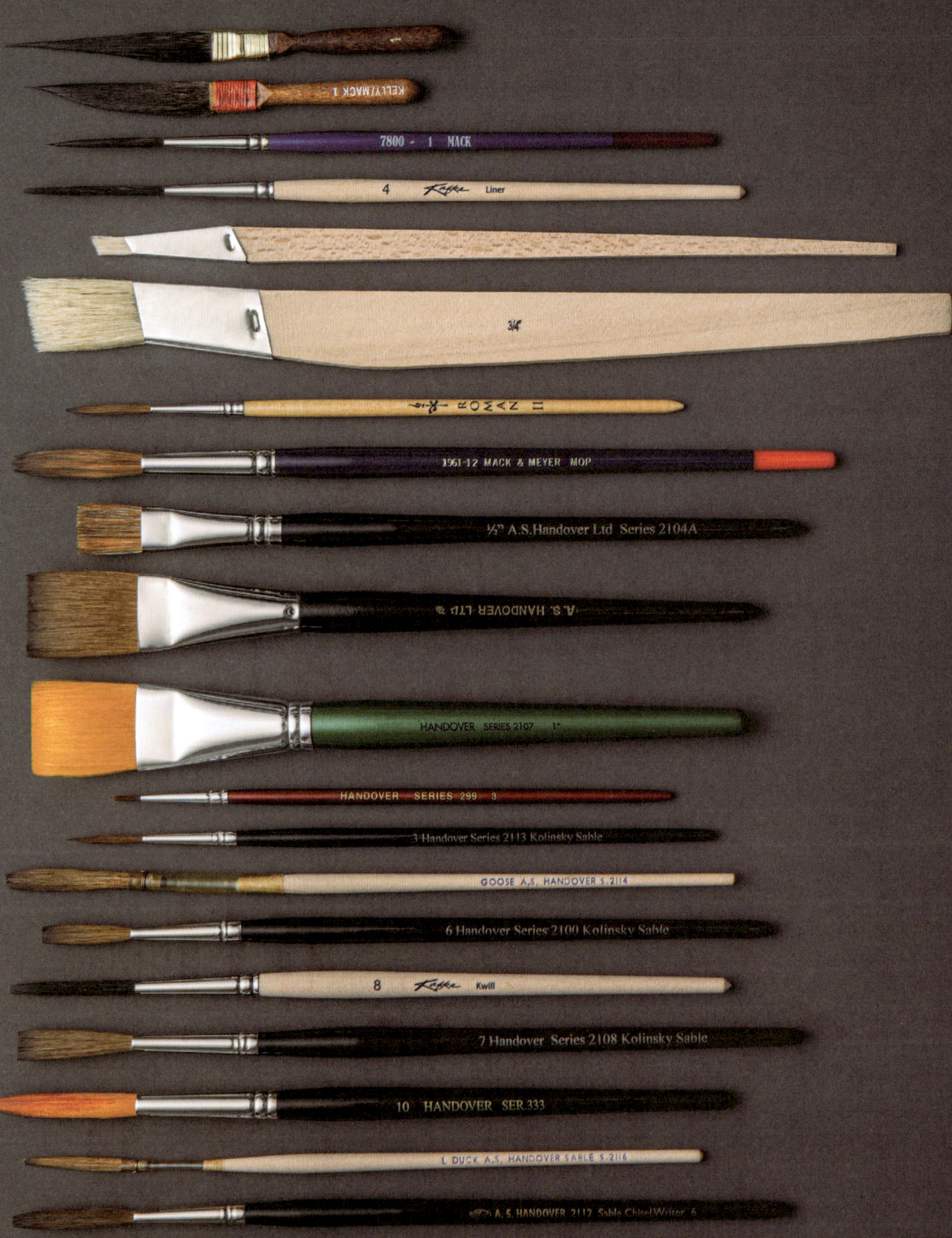

KELLY/MACK 1
7800 - 1   MACK
4   Kafka   Liner
3/4
ROMAN II
1961-12 MACK & MEYER MOP
½" A.S.Handover Ltd Series 2104A
A.S. HANDOVER LTD ¾
HANDOVER SERIES 2107 1"
HANDOVER   SERIES 299 3
3 Handover Series 2113 Kolinsky Sable
GOOSE A.S. HANDOVER S.2114
6 Handover Series 2100 Kolinsky Sable
8   Kafka   Kwill
7 Handover Series 2108 Kolinsky Sable
10   HANDOVER   SER.333
L DUCK A.S. HANDOVER SABLE S.2116
A.S. HANDOVER 2112 Sable Chisel Writer 6

Brushes

The brush is the most important tool of the sign-painting trade. Many experienced sign painters will have their favorites, but you only need a small number to get started with.

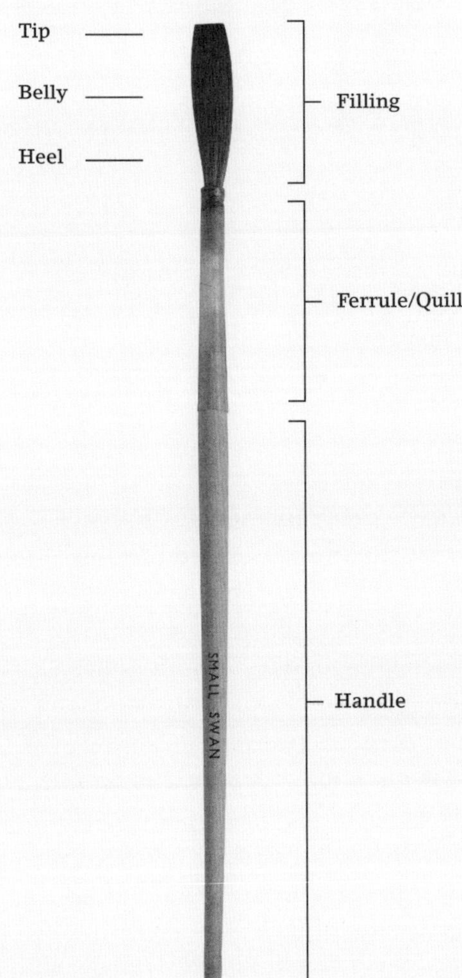

The main elements of a sign-painting brush.

Over time you can experiment with different styles, until your collection grows and you have a preferred brush for each type of job that comes in.

Brush Anatomy

A brush essentially consists of three parts: the handle, the ferrule/quill, and the filling. The handle is what we hold when painting with the brush, and the filling is made up of the hairs that hold the paint for application to the substrate. The ferrule or quill fixes the filling in position and joins it to the handle. In the past, the ferrule and filling were sold as a separate unit to the handle, and sign painters would use the same handle for multiple ferrules and fillings. These days, most brushes come complete with all three parts together.

The filling itself has three main components: the tip, the belly, and the heel. The tip is the very end of the brush and usually consists of hairs that are each tapered to a point. The belly is the main bulk of the filling and is where most of the paint is held. The heel is the area where the filling joins the ferrule. These distinctions are important for brush care and brush technique (see pages 32 and 76).

Despite this relatively simple construction, a variety of materials is used for fillings, there are different configurations of these fillings in the ferrule or quill (e.g. flat versus pointed), and different types of ferrule. This variation leads to a wide range of brush styles, some of which are more, or less, suited to particular types of work.

Brush Markings

Most manufacturers mark their brushes to give important information to customers. This typically includes the manufacturer's name, the series number/code, and the size of the brush. The series number identifies brushes of the same style, made of a particular set of materials, in a particular way, and available in a variety of sizes.

Brush sizes are given as a single number, ranging from 00 (smallest) to 12 (largest), with some series available in even larger sizes. Although less common today, traditional quills were made using an actual quill of a bird feather for the ferrule. These were then named according to the size of the bird, and therefore the feather, that the quill came from. UK manufacturer A.S. Handover still produces brushes using real bird quills. The table on the next page details the variety of brush sizes from 00 to 12, the diameter of their filling, and the bird quill equivalent.

23

Brush Sizes

Ferrule (size)	Diameter mm (approx)	Quill name
00	1.1	N/A
0	1.3	Lark
1	1.6	Crow
2	1.9	Small Duck (or Large Crow)
3	2.2	Duck
4	2.6	Large Duck
5	3.1	Small Goose
6	3.6	Goose
7	4.2	Large Goose
8	4.9	Extra Small Swan
9	5.6	Small Swan
10	6.3	Swan
11	7.1	Large Swan
12	7.8	Condor

A.S. Handover's 2112 sable chisel-edge writer in a variety of sizes.

Ferrules & Fillings

The ferrule of a brush is usually made in one of two ways. The first is the traditional way: the filling is cased in a bird's quill (although some manufacturers now use plastic), which is warmed so that it expands and then contracts around the filling as it cools. A small piece of metal wire is sometimes used to secure the quill and fillings in place. The second way uses a tapered metal ferrule; the hairs protrude from the narrow end, and the wider end is punched to fix it to the handle.

Fillings come in a wide range of materials, some natural and some synthetic. They can either be "pure" (i.e. made of a single material) or produced using a mixture of different materials. The material used in the filling of a brush will affect the quantity of paint that the brush can hold, the strength and coarseness of the brush, its "snap" or springiness, its cost, and its suitability for different types of paint and work.

The ideal filling for a sign-painting brush is a fine hair with a sharp point and plenty of spring, so that it is responsive to the sign painter's touch. It is also important that the

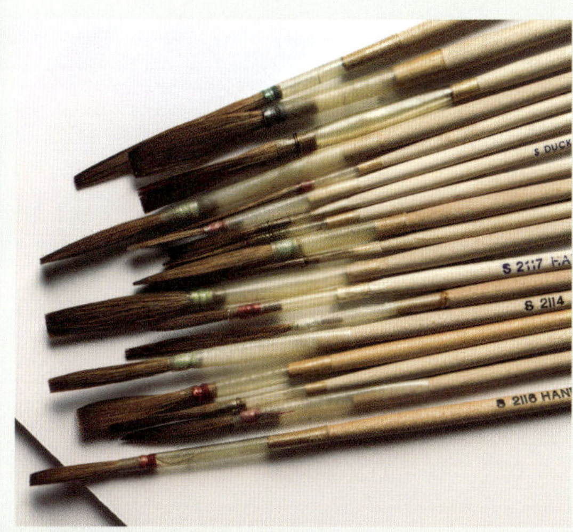

Traditional quills manufactured by
A.S. Handover.

hair holds together well, not sticking out at all angles, and that it is tough enough to resist the effects of oil-based paints and their associated solvents.

No single type of hair meets all of the criteria, while also being affordable to manufacturers and purchasers. Readily available natural hairs include hog (bristle), ox, squirrel, and sable. Bristle (from pigs), is long and tough but does not have a point, making it impossible to obtain sharp edges. Ox hair was widely used until the 1990s for rougher or larger work, as it represents a halfway house between bristle and the fine hairs such as squirrel and sable.

Squirrel and sable have been the mainstay of sign-painting brushes since the craft first developed. Squirrel hair is widely used in North America. It holds together nicely and comes to a fine point. Most British sign-painting brushes have been made with sable over the years. This hair has all the desired characteristics but is very expensive. It also needs to be cleaned and cared for extremely well if the hair is not to become brittle and break off.

In recent years, synthetic hairs have improved to the extent that they now offer a reasonable alternative for many applications. They are usually made from a form of polyester. Nylon has been largely phased out as a material these days.

Here is a summary of the main types of natural fillings used in sign-painting brushes. Experiment with different fillings and brands to learn first-hand how they feel, and you will no doubt develop favorites for different types of work. Don't be shy about talking to your supplier about what their brushes are made from, and what they recommend for work that you are planning. And, of course, other sign painters will be a great source of advice on the topic of brush selection.

Hair	Strength	Snap	Coarseness	Flow	Paint hold	Cost
Kolinsky Sable	High	High	Low	High	High	High
Red Sable	High	Medium	Low	High	High	High
Grey Squirrel	Low	Medium	Medium	Medium	Medium	Medium
Blue Squirrel	Low	Low	Medium	High	Medium	Medium
Ox	High	Medium	High	Low	Low	Medium
Hog (Bristle)	High	Low	High	Medium	Medium	Low

Pure kolinsky sable hairs before
being made into brushes.

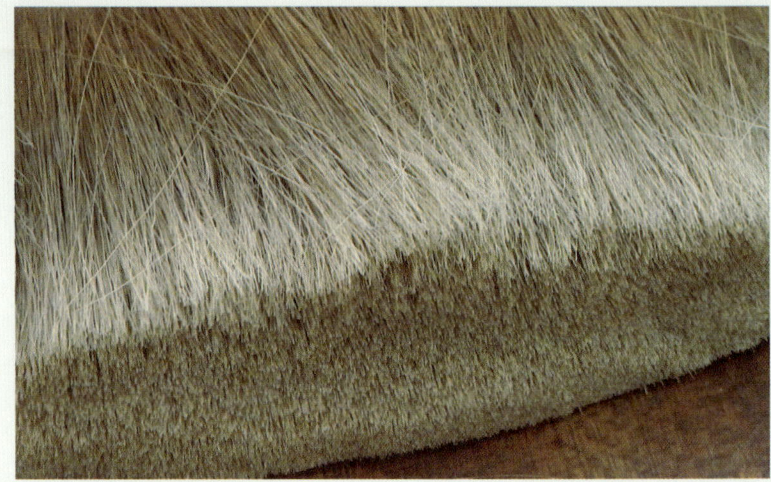

Pure kolinsky sable hairs before being made into brushes.

Mike's Tip

With all types of brushes, and especially sables, never trim the ends to reduce the length of the hairs. Tapering to a very fine point is one of the reasons these hairs are so good for lettering brushes, and trimming destroys this. If you prefer to work with shorter-haired brushes, then buy them at the size you require, keeping the sharp points intact.

Kolinsky Sable

This hair comes from the tail of the Siberian weasel (not the sable, which is another animal entirely) and is the premium-quality filling for a brush. It has the best combination of relative strength, spring, and snap, with the hairs coming to a very fine point after a bulge in the middle, which is known as the "belly." It is this belly that allows the hairs to be set in the ferrule or quill for maximum snap. The scaly surface of the hairs allows them to hold a good quantity of paint, reducing the frequency with which the brush has to be reloaded and regulating the flow of the paint from the brush. While expensive, good-quality pure kolinsky sable brushes will have a very long lifetime if cared for properly.

Red Sable

This hair usually comes from the same species of weasel as that used in kolinsky sable brushes, but from animals that live in slightly warmer climates than Siberia. As a result, the hairs have a different structure, making them straighter without the characteristic belly that gives the kolinsky sable hairs their snap. Red sable provides a more economical, yet still good-quality, alternative to kolinsky sable.

Squirrel

Blue, grey, and brown (Kazan) squirrel hairs are more readily available than kolinsky and red sable. They are fine hairs that come to a point, but have much less snap and are not as resilient as their sable cousins. Longer hairs are easier to obtain, especially from blue squirrels, and they have a very good, even flow that makes them perfect for liners and striping brushes. Grey squirrel hairs are stronger

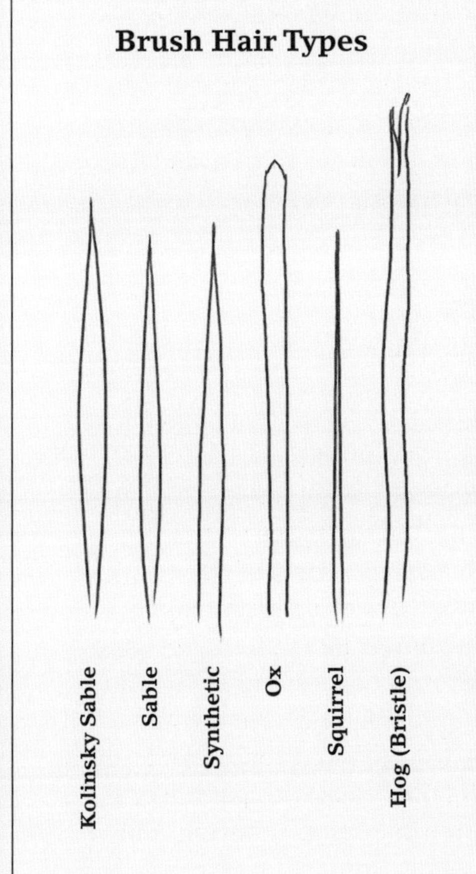

and have the most snap of the squirrel hairs, although they are harder to obtain in longer lengths, and are therefore more expensive.

Ox & Sableline

Ox brushes are made from the silky ear hairs of the animal and can originate from brown, golden, or light oxen. Those from light oxen that are dyed to look like red sable are referred to as Sableline. Ox hairs are very resilient and have some spring. However, they have a very blunt tip and do not hold a lot of paint. Ox hairs will often be mixed with other hairs in brushes to add body and resilience.

Hog (Bristle)

These are stiff hairs that "flag" (split) at the tip. They also curve slightly, although this can be limited by processes within the manufacturing of brushes. Their toughness makes hog hairs ideal for fitches and other types of coarse brushes for use on rough surfaces such as brick.

"Camel"

There are no brushes made from the hair of camels, despite the name. In the past, the term was sometimes used to label brushes made from squirrel hairs. These days, it is generic and usually used within the brush trade to refer to poor-quality hairs that cannot be sold otherwise. I would not recommend these hairs for sign work except in desperate circumstances.

Synthetic

Synthetic brushes are usually made from polyester, although nylon was once widely used. Different techniques are used when manufacturing the hairs to emulate the characteristics of natural hair, such as tapering them to a point, and adding scaly surfaces to hold more paint. These techniques are constantly improving, and are important as natural hairs become increasingly expensive, but so far the belly of kolinsky sable brushes has not been reproduced synthetically. Synthetic hairs are my strong preference when working with water-based paints, but I now use them regularly with oil-based paints too.

Brush Types

The combination of ferrule, hair length, and hair type results in a wide range of brushes that can be used for sign painting.

The selection of brushes for different types of work is very personal, and if you asked a large number of sign painters which brush they would use for a particular job, you would get many different answers. However, there are some general rules of thumb that can help you get started, and that you can use as a basis for experimentation as you learn about your own preferences.

Chisel-Edge Writers

Sometimes just called chisels, writers, or pencils, these brushes are the mainstay of the trade and consist of hairs set in a quill or metal ferrule that come to a flat edge (chisel) when pressed between thumb and forefinger. They are perfect for block lettering, Roman, casual, script, shadows, and, in smaller sizes, outlining. With practice you can execute most sign work with a small variety of sizes.

The length of the hairs in a chisel-edge writer can vary quite considerably, with shorter hairs often preferred for showcards and ticket writing. Longer hairs are harder to control, at least initially, but in the long term are more efficient as they hold more paint, allowing for longer strokes and less time taken reloading the brush with paint. Try a short-haired chisel-edge writer for casual lettering, and something longer for block and script.

The chisel shape of the brush, when correctly paletted (see page 79), allows for variations in stroke width, according to the angle that the brush is held at and the pressure that is applied. This angle can be kept constant for script lettering or twisted to create other letter forms such as block and Roman.

Mike's Tip

If you have a regular chisel-edge writer that is no longer good for lettering, trim away some of the outer hairs using a razor blade to create a small lining brush.

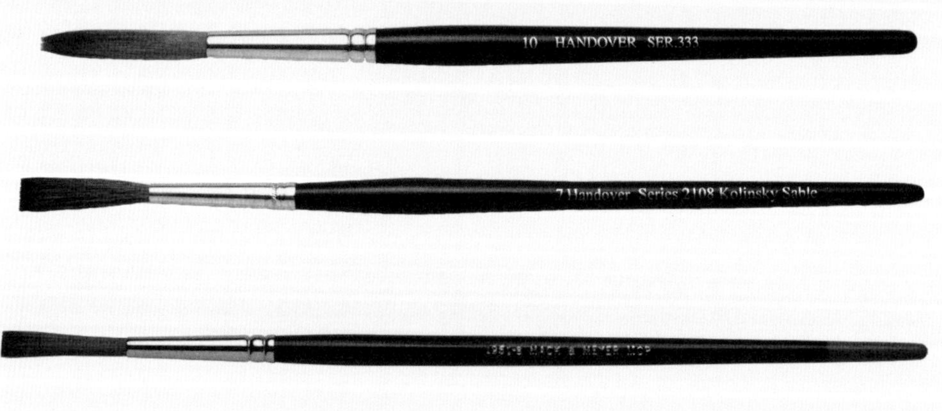

Chisel-edge writers in different sizes and with synthetic and natural hairs.

Pointers

These differ from chisels in that they naturally come to a point due to the way the hairs are tied before being fitted within the ferrule. Pointers can be used in a number of different ways, and are usually best for smaller and built-up letters. They are also used for script lettering, where the variation in stroke width comes from applying different amounts of pressure to the brush. For this reason, they are well suited to scrollwork and other flourishing techniques where thicks and thins are required. The choice between a chisel and a pointer is largely one of personal preference (my "go to" brushes are the chisels).

Pointer with sable filling, size 3.

Flats

Sometimes called one-stroke brushes, these have the hairs set in an oblong rather than circular ferrule. This means that they are naturally set in a flat shape, although some paletting can be required to ensure an even spread of hairs. Many sign painters work exclusively with flats rather than chisel-edge writers, and it is worth experimenting with both to find your own preference.

I sometimes use larger flats with (cheaper) synthetic hairs for filling in bigger letters. They are also good for executing one-stroke block and casual lettering, especially at larger sizes.

Flats in different sizes with sable fillings.

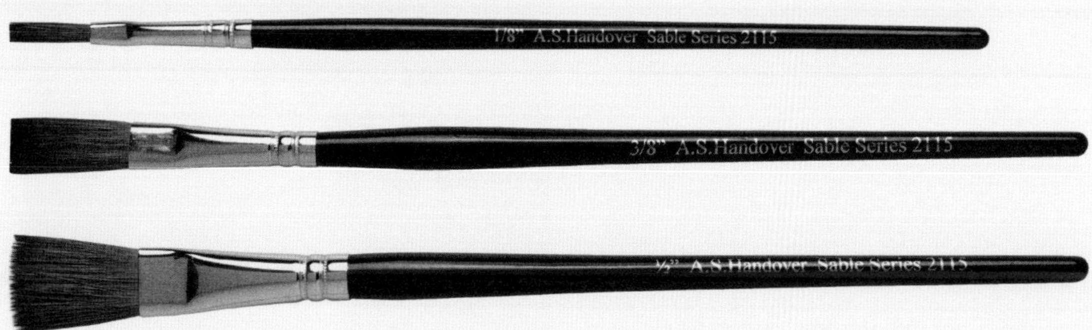

29

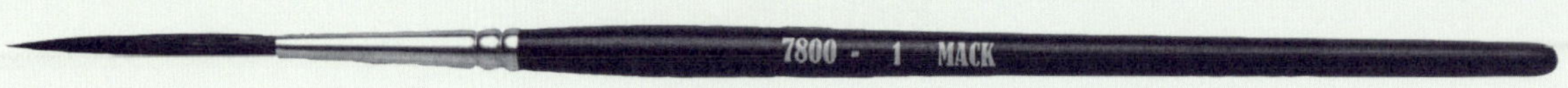

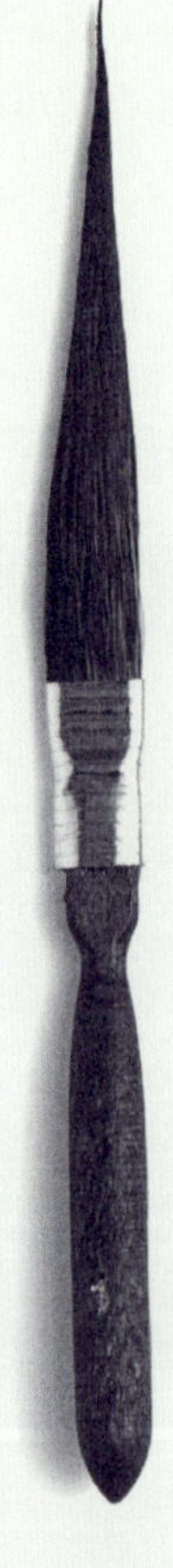

(above) Liner with mixture of blue squirrel hair and synthetic filling, size 1. (below) Sword liner with squirrel hair filling, size 1.

Liners

Liners have much longer hairs, and are not usually made from pure sable due to the difficulty in obtaining long sable hairs. The purpose of the long hairs is to hold plenty of paint so that they can be pulled across a substrate to create continuous lines, including outlines and decorative elements such as scrolls, without running out. Many painters prefer to work without the handle, or with a trimmed-down handle (e.g. 2½in or 65mm length) to provide closer control of the line.

Sword liners are a specialist brush, usually made from squirrel hair and used for pinstriping, but also good for lining on signs. When paletted the hairs taper to a point, like a knife blade, and hold a lot of paint, allowing for very long lines to be pulled. The technique of working with them is different to other sign-painting brushes; I recommend reading specialist books, and/or attending a pinstriping class, to learn more.

Lining Fitches/Slant Liners/Cutters

These brushes are usually made from coarse hog bristles or synthetic hairs, shaped into a flat, often slanting edge, set in an oblong metal ferrule. They are perfect for painting straight lines on rougher surfaces such as masonry and concrete, either for direct lettering or "cutting in" letters in reverse. Longer hairs can hold more paint, and produce longer lines, but are more difficult to control than shorter-haired brushes.

Lining fitches made from softer hairs can be used to blend colors on all types of sign work.

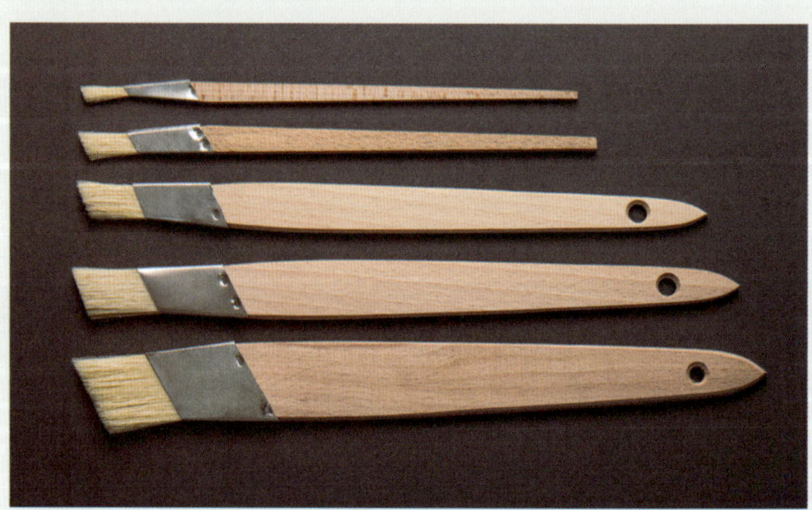

Lining fitches with hog bristle filling in a variety of sizes.

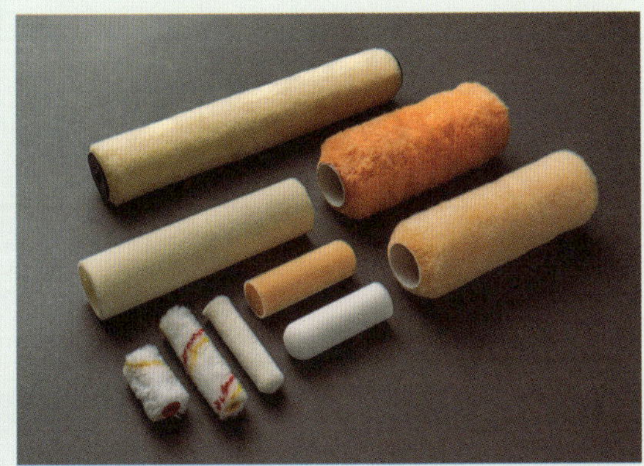

Paint roller heads including foam and nap rollers.

Fitches

These are made from hog bristles or synthetic hairs set in a round metal ferrule and shaped into either a flat or domed end. They are not often used in sign work, but they can be useful for pushing paint into crevices in carved or other signs that feature relief work. Due to the coarseness of their hairs, they will not be damaged by such use like a sable brush would.

Rollers

Rollers are good for covering large areas of substrate, either with primer or color, such as on billboards. Different types of roller are available to suit different surfaces. Where a smooth finish is required, such as when priming and top-coating sign boards, use a foam roller in a size that will allow efficient coverage of the surface. For rougher surfaces such as masonry, use a nap roller that gets into recesses more easily and reduces the amount of filling in that is required with a brush after rollering.

My First Brushes

I am often asked "What brushes should I buy to get started?" You want to balance your budget against having enough variety to begin practicing, experimenting, and learning about your preferences. The suggestions here (see box, left) will give you plenty to get going in oil-based paints. If you are only working in water-based paints to begin with, I suggest buying only synthetic brushes.

Once you have tried those out, and are serious about advancing your career in the sign-painting business, try some larger-size chisel-edge writers and experiment with flats. You can also get a liner to practice pulling lines, and a lining fitch to try out on some rougher surfaces.

After that, I should warn you that buying brushes will become an expensive, but worthwhile, addiction, and your collection will grow. You will always have your favorites, but there is also the joy of rediscovering a brush that you might have neglected for a while. They all have their roles to play, and you should always treat them with care and respect.

31

A Brush Starter Kit:

2 x squirrel or pure sable chisel-edge writers, sizes #4 and #6, perhaps trying out one in a metal ferrule and one in a quill.

1 x synthetic chisel writer, either size #5 or #6.

1 x sable or synthetic pointer in a small size, such as #2 or #3.

Brush Care

Your brushes are your most important tools. They can also be quite expensive, especially for larger sizes in good-quality kolinsky sable. It is important to look after your brushes so that they look after you when you need them to.

Good brush care ensures long working lives for your brushes, so that your old favorites stay with you for many years. The first major rule of brush care is to keep your brushes for oil-based and water-based paints well separated. Water and oil do not mix, and neither should water- and oil-based brushes. While it is possible to work with oil-based paints using a brush that has previously been used with water-based paints, going from oil-based to water-based spells disaster. My advice is to avoid both situations completely by having two sets of brushes in your work. You can even mark them in some way like dipping the ends of the handles in paint: for example, blue for water-based and orange for oil-based.

Storage

The hairs of your brushes can easily be damaged and lose their shape if they are not stored well. Allowing paint to dry in the hairs, especially inside the ferrule, will also ruin them. The simplest storage method is a flat tin. Make sure that the brush hairs are kept away from the end of the tin and that shaking and other movements are minimized. It is best if the brushes can be laid flat in the tin. Springs or rubber holders inside the tin will hold the brushes in place. Have a look at the storage products from A.S. Handover and Alpha 6.

If you are going to be traveling a lot with your brushes, as I do, I recommend using a wallet-like case that keeps the brushes strapped in with elasticated fabric. The cases sold by Better Letters and A.S. Handover are perfect, and are available in small and large sizes. Make sure you have separate cases for your oil- and water-based brushes.

Sign-painting brushes stored safely in a wallet-type case.

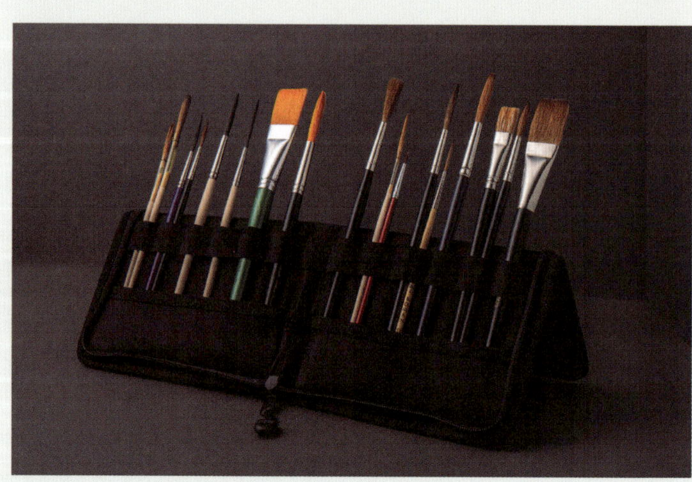

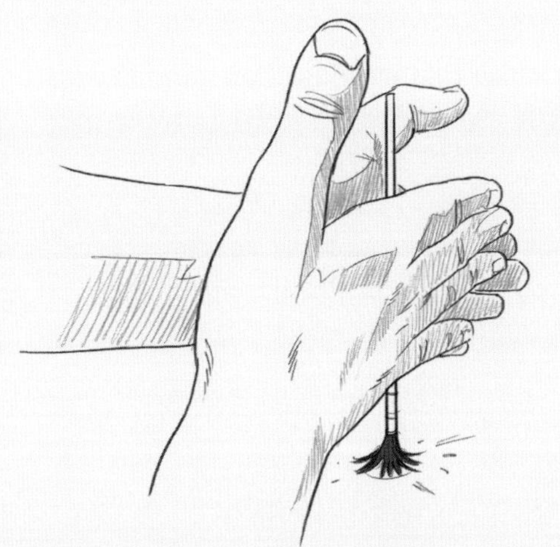

Clean out gum arabic using tap water and a little soap.

Dry the brush using the "ring spin" technique.

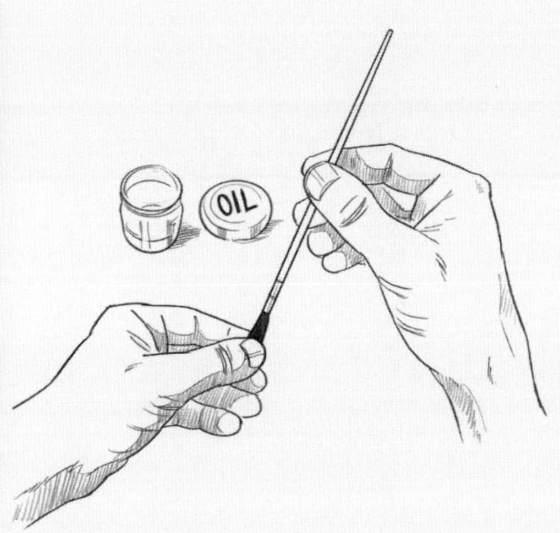

Oil the brush.

Brushes for Oil-Based Paints

Starting Out

Usually when you buy a new brush its hairs will be held in place with a little gum arabic. This preserves the hairs and prevents them from getting damaged while they are transported from the manufacturer and stored by the retailer. After buying a new brush, take the following steps to ready it for working with oil-based paints.

1. Clean the gum arabic out of the hairs. Hold the brush, hairs down, under some running warm water, using a little hand soap to massage the gum out of the hairs.

2. Dry the brush. This can be done by gently wiping with a clean cloth. If you wear a ring, like I do, another way of drying a brush is to use the "ring spin" technique. Hold the brush between the palms of your hands and spin it by rapidly rubbing your hands back and forth together. As the handle hits your ring, any liquid in the hairs will be expelled by the repeated impact with the ring. It also makes a satisfying sound!

3. Oil the brush. Dip the hairs of the brush in neatsfoot oil and gently massage this into hairs, while also pushing oil down into the ferrule or quill. For chisels, you can also work the hairs into the chisel shape at this point. If you do not have access to neatsfoot oil, engine oil (e.g. 30 weight) is a readily available alternative.

4. Your brush is technically ready to store now, but I recommend allowing it to stand upright (hairs at the top) overnight, if possible, to allow gravity to pull some of the oil down into the ferrule or quill.

Oiling the brush before you first use it serves three functions. First, it protects the hairs and prevents them from drying out and becoming brittle. It also ensures that any paint that might eventually end up in the hairs, ferrule, or quill cannot dry and affect the shape of the hairs. It is important to get oil down into the ferrule or quill, because this is where paint is hardest to reach when cleaning, and where the most damaging effects will be felt if that paint dries. Lastly, the oil can be used to shape the hairs into a chisel or a point, so that over time this becomes their "natural" position.

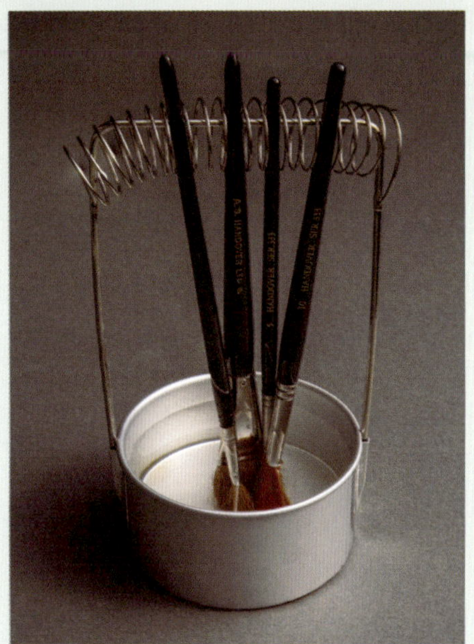

Mike's Tip

You'll often need to stop working for a short while. This is a risky time for your brush: while you're not keeping it wet with paint it will be drying out and possibly getting damaged.

If you stop for any length of time, it's best to clean and oil your brush. An alternative is to have a little bucket of mineral spirits in which the brush can be suspended from a spring arch above. You can also use a clothes peg to clip the brush and balance it on the rim of a smaller jar or tin. This technique saves you having to oil the brush, and allows you to return to work more quickly after your break.

Some painters also suspend their brushes in this way for a while when cleaning them in preparation for storage, to allow paint to be drawn downward out of the ferrule or quill before drying and oiling.

Whatever you do, never—and I mean *never*—leave your brush hairs crushed down in a cup or tin of cleaner. This is extremely cruel to the brush and those guilty of this crime will be severely punished.

Get Painting

When you are working with oil-based paints there is a simple routine to keep your brushes in good condition as you move them from storage, to painting, and back to storage again.

Before you begin any painting work, select a brush from your collection and prepare it.

1. Wipe the oil off the brush hairs using a rag or tissue. Do this by gently squeezing the hairs between the rag and pulling it from the heel to the tip.

2. Give the hairs a good rinse in some mineral spirits to remove any remaining oil. If you are sensitive to the fumes from mineral spirits, there are alternatives, such as products from Zest-it, that you can try instead.

3. Dry the hairs off with a clean rag or tissue. You can also use the "ring spin" technique (see page 33) to do this.

4. Get the brush into some paint and start working.

Once you have finished working with a brush, you will need to clean it before storing it again or switching to another color.

1. Wipe out as much paint as you can using a rag or tissue. Just like when you removed the oil, work from heel to tip applying gentle pressure to squeeze the paint out.

2. Rinse the hairs in mineral spirits. I use a series of three jars of spirits to (1) get out the bulk of the paint, (2) clean out the dirty spirits, and (3) finish off with a clean rinse. Using

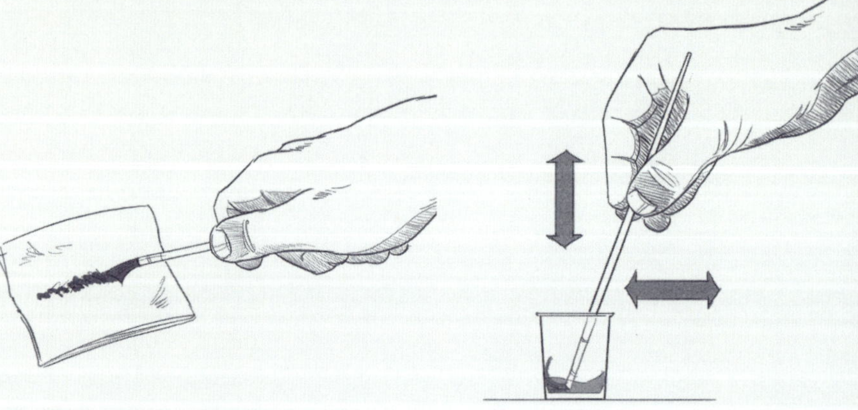

Wipe excess oil/paint from the hairs using a rag.

Rinse the brush in mineral spirits.

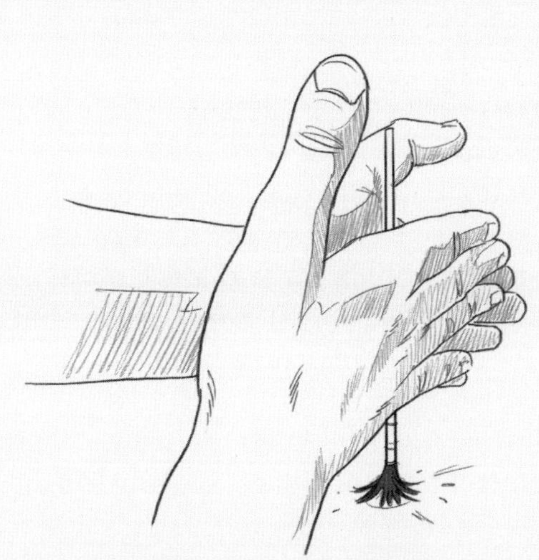

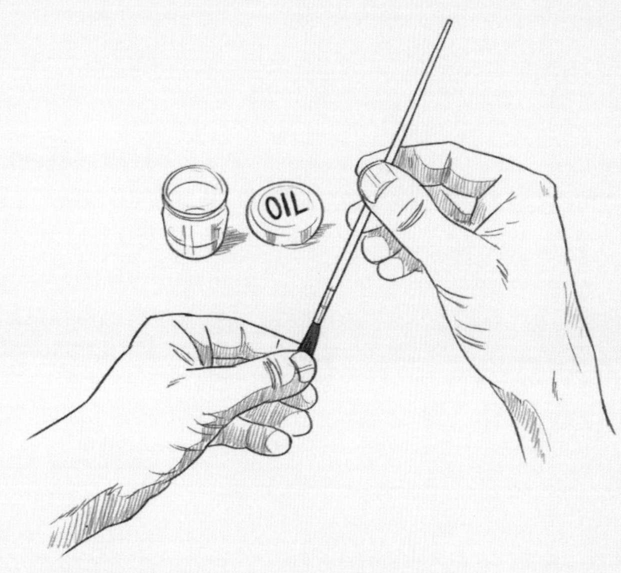

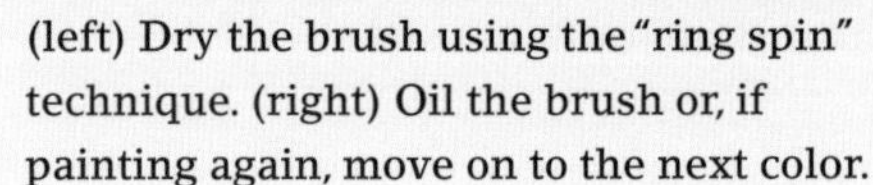

(left) Dry the brush using the "ring spin" technique. (right) Oil the brush or, if painting again, move on to the next color.

this 1-2-3 method, the mineral spirits in jar 3 should remain clear if you have properly cleaned the brush in jars 1 and 2.

3. Dry the hairs off with a rag or tissue or use the "ring spin" technique (see page 33).

4. If the brush is going back into storage, work oil or grease into the hairs and the ferrule or quill. Gently massage the hairs into shape before placing the brush back into your box or case. If you are going to carry on painting, do not use the oil; just move straight into the next color.

5. If you have not used a brush, or set of brushes, for a long time, it is worth getting them all out, wiping the oil off, and giving them a clean and a fresh oiling every few months. This will help stop the oil from drying out and keep the brushes fresh and ready for their next outing.

The simplest way to approach oil-based paint brush care is to remember that your brush is either in storage (oiled) or working (covered in paint). In between these two states, the old liquid (oil or paint) needs to be wiped off and rinsed or cleaned out using mineral spirits, before you dry the brush and cover it in the new liquid (paint or oil). Following the steps above when transitioning between storage and working will ensure long and productive lives for your brushes.

Brushes for Water-Based Paints

Although I have said this already, I will say it again because it is so important: never try to use brushes that have been oiled or used with oil-based paints for water-based paints.

Caring for water-based paint brushes is much more straightforward than caring for oil-based paint brushes, but it is just as important for giving them long working lives.

Starting Out

Clean any gum arabic out of the hairs by holding the brush, hairs down, under some running warm water, using a little hand soap to massage the gum out of the hairs. Then dry the brush. This can be done by gently wiping with a clean cloth or using the "ring spin" technique (see page 33).

Get Painting

Nothing needs to be done before you start working with the brush. Get it straight into the paint. When you finish with a color, and you are ready to change colors or return the brush to storage, follow these simple steps to clean the brush.

1. Give the brush a good wipe on a rag to get the majority of the paint out.

2. Clean it in slightly soapy water, or run it under a hot tap or hose. Next I recommend using a series of three buckets filled with clean water (warm if available) to progressively clean your brushes. Wipe your brush with a rag between dunking it in each bucket. If you have cleaned your brush properly, the last bucket should remain clean.

3. An alternative is to place some mild soap or brush cleaner (e.g. "The Masters" Brush Cleaner and Preserver) in the palm of your hand and push and twirl the hairs into this, pressing down so that you are reaching the ferrule. Rinse and repeat until no paint is coming off the brush into your hand.

4. Rinse in fresh, non-soapy water before drying with a rag or using the "ring spin" technique (see page 33). Shape the brush and place it back into your box.

5. If you are not using the brushes regularly, get them out occasionally and give them a little bath in some clean water to help stop any remaining paint from drying out.

"The Masters" Brush Cleaner and Preserver can be used to clean brushes used with both oil- and water-based paints.

Tools & Their Uses

Apart from brushes, paints, and additives, there is plenty of other equipment that you will need to have on hand for painting signs.

Mike's Tip

I highly recommend decorating your box with your name and services offered. It'll always be with you on site and provides a perfect miniature billboard to sell yourself. Be wise, advertise!

Some of this you probably have already, but there are quite a lot of specialist items that you will need to stock up on. The list below will provide you with a comprehensive kit, but I have also suggested a Basic Starter Kit to begin with, which you may also use when carrying a heavy box is not practical.

Sign Kit

Most sign painters have their essentials in a box, or kit, that is easy to carry around. I use a wooden kit, roughly 18 x 14 x 8in (46 x 36 x 20cm) which, as well as holding my gear, doubles as a stool (with three different working heights) to sit or stand on. Always test the strength of your kit before using it as a stool!

Alternatives are general DIY boxes, which are sold in hardware stores. These are usually plastic or metal boxes with handles, but they also come in backpack styles that can be practical if you need to carry your kit for long periods of time.

Brush Boxes

See page 32 for more detailed notes on keeping your brushes in good condition when not in use and when traveling with them. I use reinforced fabric brush cases because of how much I travel, but most painters I know use a metal or wooden box for general day-to-day storage. Many specialist kit boxes will come with a brush box or tray at the top, which helps keep everything organized.

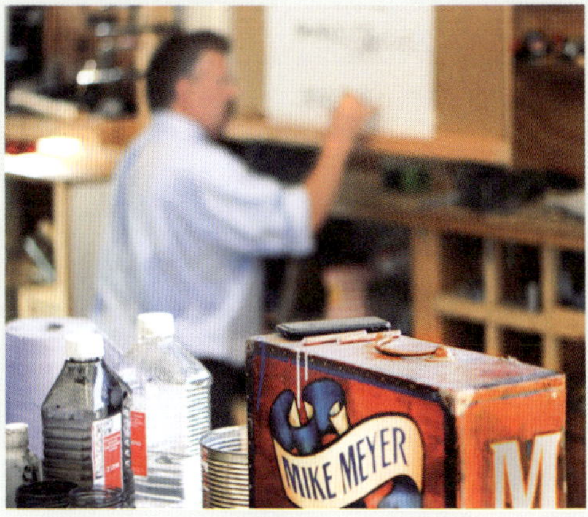

Mike's trusty sign-painting kit, a.k.a. "Pony."

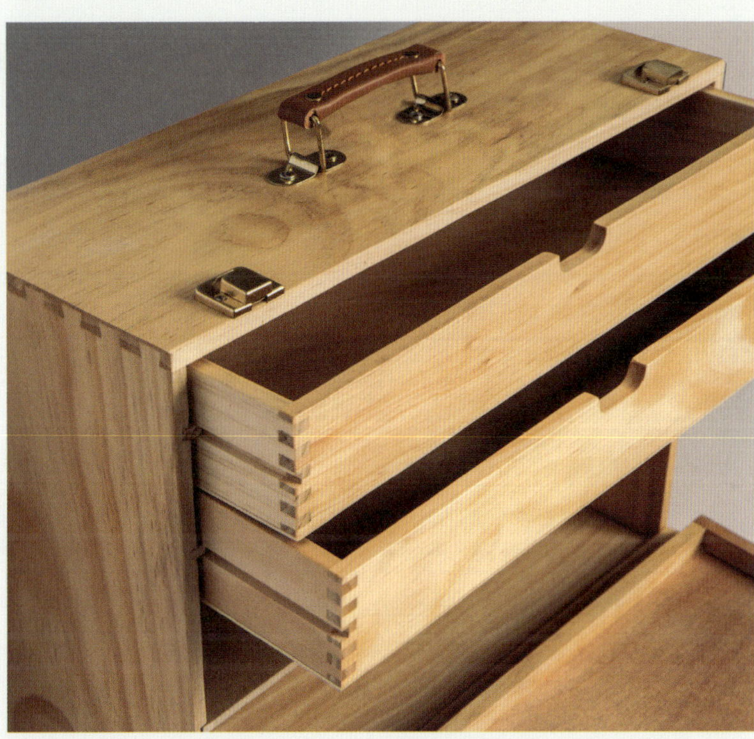

Simple wooden kit box with main compartment, open shelf, and two drawers.

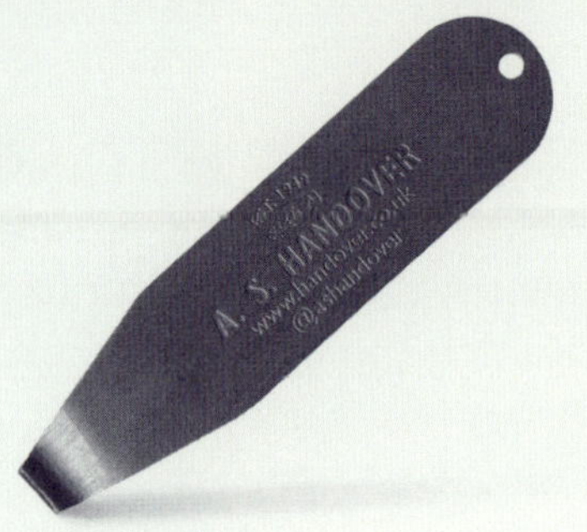

| Key-ring style tin opener.

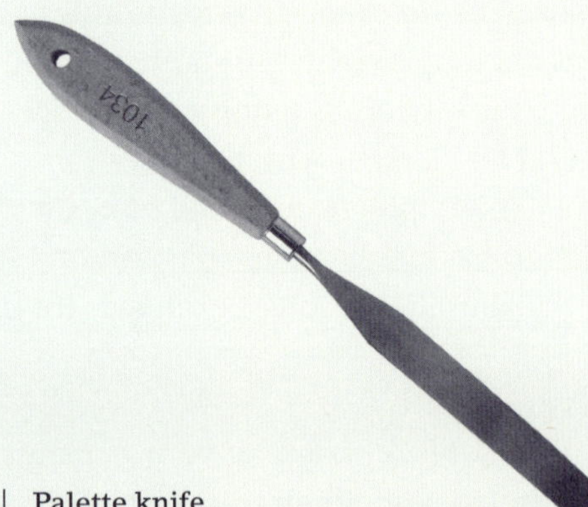

| Palette knife.

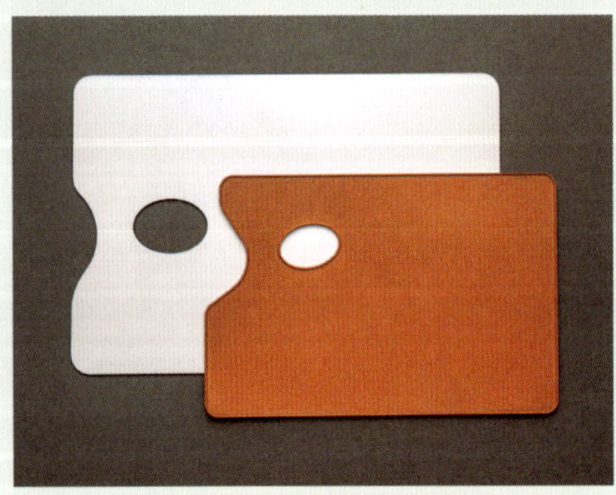

| Rattlers.

Paint Handling

Tin Opener

It is useful to have a firm piece of flat metal for opening tins. You can buy something just for the job, but a regular screwdriver or large flat coin works just as well. Whatever you use, keep it in your kit, and close to your paints in the shop, so you do not waste hours looking for it every time you need to open a tin.

Palette Knife/Stirrers

A palette knife with a rounded tip is useful for mixing paints and for getting paint out of a tin. Alternatives include wooden coffee stirrers and tongue depressors, which are usually sold inexpensively in bulk.

Rattlers

Pieces of metal inside a tin of paint can help to agitate pigment that has settled at the bottom when shaking. You can use large nuts and bolts, or bespoke products like those from Alpha 6 (pictured). Make sure that whatever you use is clean and free from rust.

Palettes & Dippers

Palette

A palette is a piece of timber, metal, or plastic that is used to work a brush into the required (chisel) shape, a technique called paletting (see page 79). Palettes usually come with a hole for the thumb on your weakest hand to hold it, while you work with the brush in your stronger hand. You can make your own out of a piece of plywood, although they are inexpensive to buy.

The decision to work with a palette or not is a very personal one, and I recommend trying both methods before making up your mind. Even sign painters who do not work with a solid palette will often use lighter-weight surfaces to shape their brushes. These can include glossy postcards and magazine or catalog pages, either held in the hand or fixed to a surface within easy reach of the working area.

Dipper

Dippers are small metal cuplike containers that clip onto the palette. They are used in different ways by different sign painters. A single dipper can hold paint that has already been thinned for working with. A double dipper can be used

| Plastic palettes with thumb holes.

Mike's Tip

Rather than cleaning your palette
after each color, use a bulldog
clip to fix a trimmed-down glossy
magazine or catalog to it, and
simply tear off the top sheet when
you've finished and need a clean
sheet to palette on.

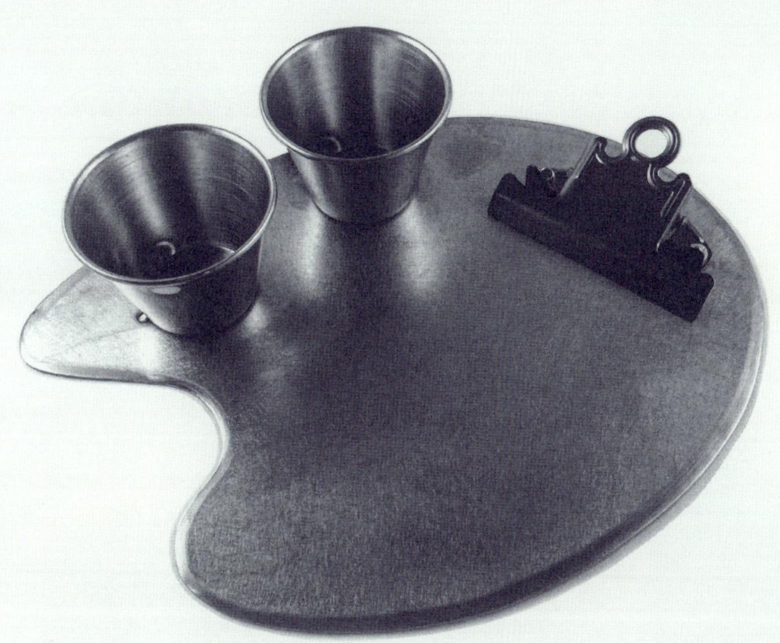

All-in-one stainless-steel palette,
dippers, and clip from Alpha 6
(right-handed).

to hold paint in one section and thinner in the other, so the
thinner can be worked into the paint during the paletting
process. This is very much the traditional British approach.

Paint Cup

For paint cups, I use 3–4oz (c.90–120ml) paper cups. There
are many options available, including those used for serving
takeaway espresso. Make sure that the inside of the cup
doesn't have a wax, or other, coating, as this can be dissolved
by solvents and lead to the contamination of your paint.
Paint cups can be used alone, as I do, or placed inside
dippers (see tip below).

Mike's Tip

If you decide to work with dippers,
I recommend placing paint cups
inside them. This will reduce the
time taken to clean the dippers; it
also allows for easy changing of paint
without having to empty the thinners,
and vice versa. If you are working
with two dippers, but not cups, it's
best to use two single dippers, rather
than a double, as this also allows the
emptying/changing of one without
having to remove the other.

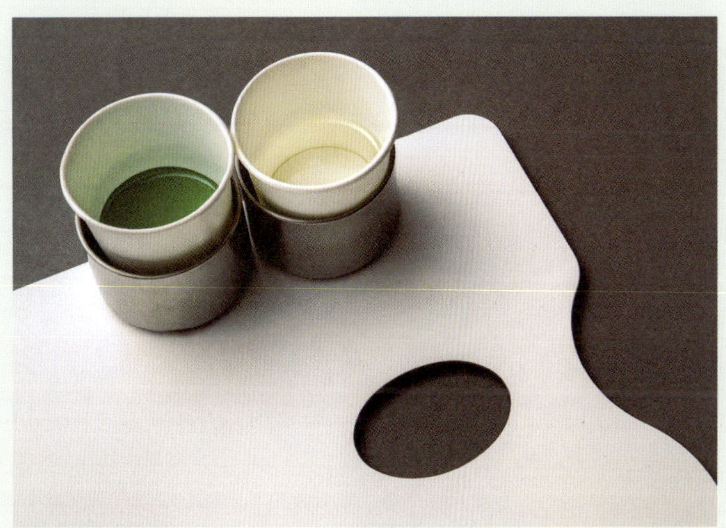

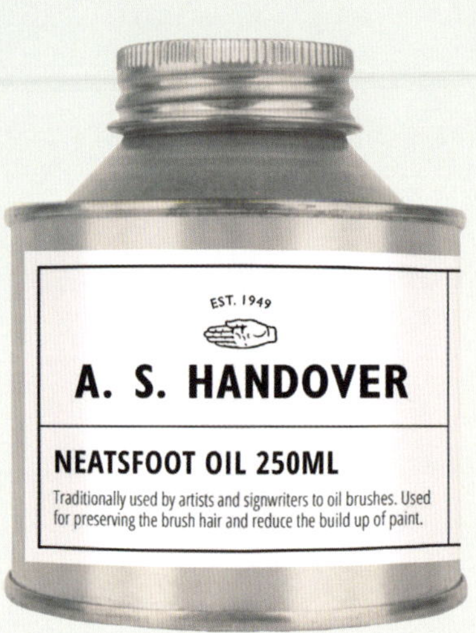

Neatsfoot oil for storing brushes used with oil-based paint.

| Stabilo grease pencils.

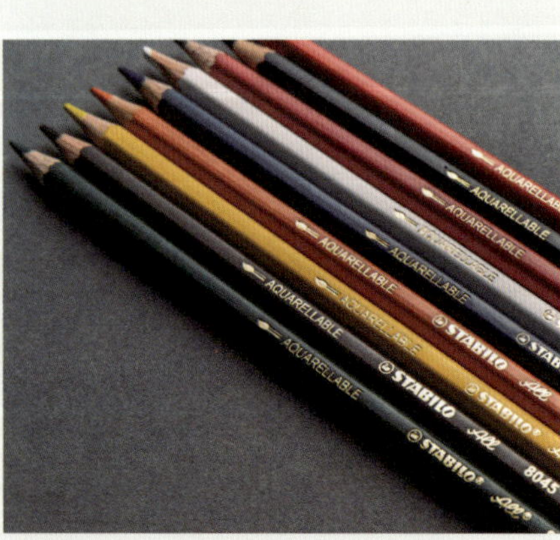

Brush Care

Neatsfoot Oil/Engine Oil
Either of these oils can be used to store oil-based paint brushes.

Brush Cleaner
For oil-based paint brushes, I use mineral spirits for cleaning. If you do not like the fumes or just want something less toxic, try products from Zest-it. For water-based paint brushes, or as another alternative to mineral spirits for oil-based brushes, try specialist brush cleaner products like "The Masters" Brush Cleaner and Preserver.

Clothes Pegs
If you are working with a number of different brushes on a job, use clothes pegs to clip them to the edge of something in your immediate working area, such as a small tin or jar containing thinners or brush cleaner. This allows you to switch between brushes without having to fully clean and oil them, although you should do that as usual at the end of the day or session.

Comb
Use a fine comb to remove any solid matter from the hairs of a brush. You can also use it to fix your own hair when working in windy conditions!

Marking-Out Tools

Graphite Pencil
Use standard (well sharpened), retractable, or clutch pencils, according to your personal preference, for sketching ideas and for creating finished designs on paper ahead of pouncing or scanning.

Grease Pencil
Regular graphite pencils do not work on many glossy surfaces, such as sign boards topcoated with enamel, glass, and aluminum panels. For these you will need grease pencils, which are made from wax; they are also called chinagraph pencils or china markers. A widely available brand that I use is Stabilo.

Chalk & Charcoal
Both chalk and charcoal are useful for setting out (marking the outlines of) signs and can be sharpened to a point with a razor for greater accuracy. They can also be used to dust the back of a pattern for the pressure transfer method (see page 66), and

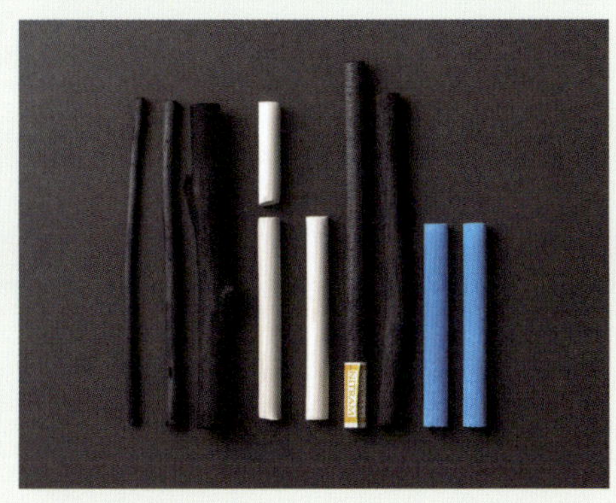

Chalk and charcoal suitable for setting out signs.

Mike's Tip

To avoid wastage due to chalk and charcoal sticks breaking, take some Scotch tape and wind it around the stick diagonally, like the tape on a tennis racket, leaving only the tip exposed for working with. When required, the tape can be peeled off bit by bit while keeping the rest of the stick intact.

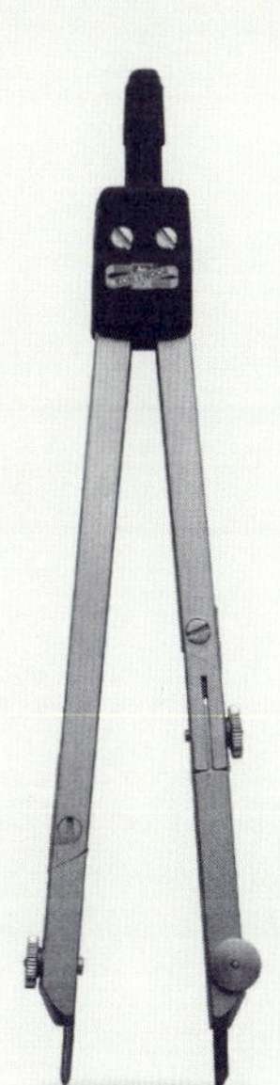

Regular (above) and large (right) compasses.

to coat a chalk line to snap markup lines (see page 71) onto substrates.

Marker Pen

These can be used as an alternative to chalk or charcoal when setting out signs using the projector method (see page 67), for inking artwork before removing pencil lines (not essential, in my opinion), sketching, and labeling materials that regular pens will not work on. I use Sharpies and keep a stash of different colors, but mainly black, on hand.

Compass

In addition to regular compasses used for drawing circles, you will also need a bigger pair for working at larger sizes. The important thing with these is to ensure that the stationary end does not have a point, but instead has a soft end such as a rubber sucker. This will prevent the compass from scratching or poking holes into your substrate, especially boards that you have primed and topcoated.

Rulers & Measures

A yardstick is used for marking up lines when setting out a sign, either directly or through the ruler pull method (see page 74). A folding rule is useful for traveling with

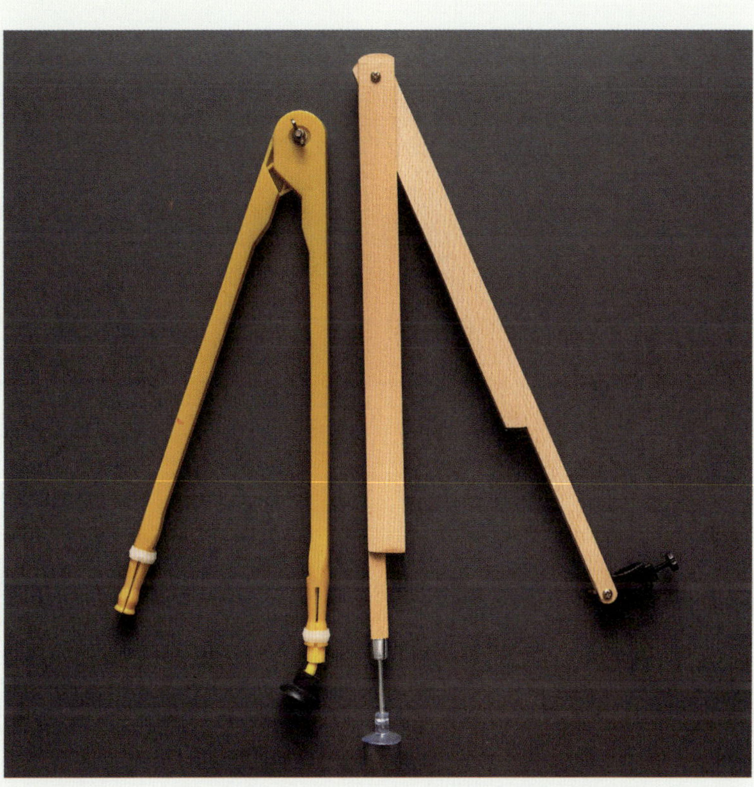

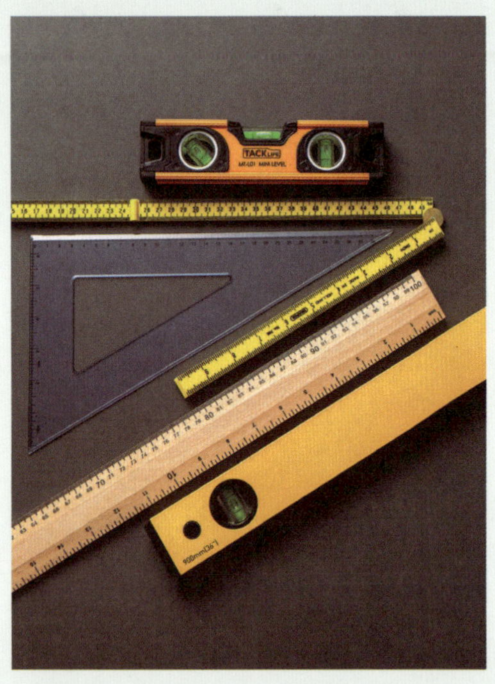

| Key measuring tools for marking out.

when a long yardstick is not practical. A regular tape measure is also handy, especially when taking measurements on a site visit.

Clear Angle

I do the majority of my marking up using a simple clear angle (set square or triangle). It is small, lightweight, and perfect for the majority of work that I do day to day.

Spirit Level

It can be useful to have a couple of these: a large one for the workshop and a smaller one that can travel easily with you to jobs outside. Use a spirit level to make sure that markup lines, patterns, and lettering are set out perfectly horizontally before you start painting.

Chalk Line

Chalk lines can be purchased as off-the-shelf products (as pictured) or you can use a piece of thick thread or nylon coated with chalk. Use them to "snap" a straight line between two previously marked points (see page 71).

Mike's Tip

To make your own chalk line, avoid threads that are already coated with a waxy finish. Thread will hold chalk better if you first cover it with some latex or acrylic paint: get a good quantity of paint on your thumb and forefinger and pull the thread through so that the paint evenly coats the whole length required. Let the paint dry before applying the chalk.

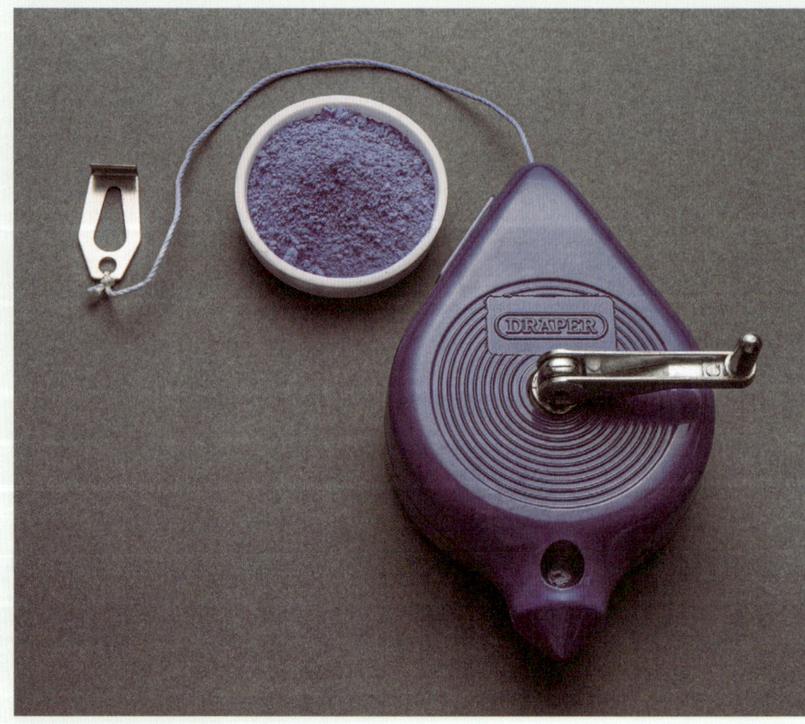

| Off-the-shelf chalk line with blue chalk for refilling.

Pounce Wheel Sizes			
Size	Diameter (inches)	Diameter (mm)	Hole per inch (25mm)
12	$7/16$	11	15
11	$5/16$	8	15–18
10	$1/4$	6	15
9	$1/4$	6	21–24

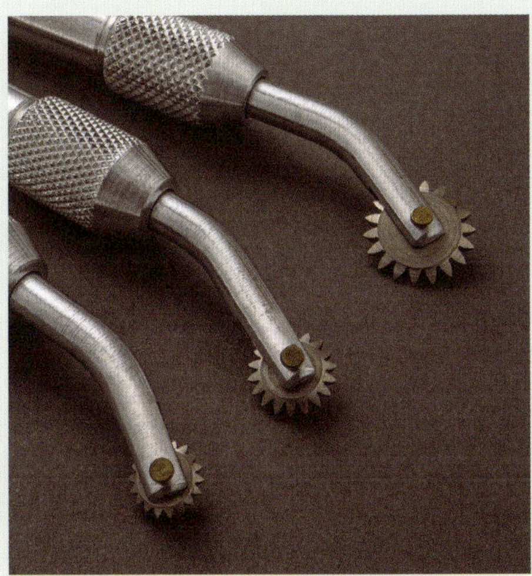

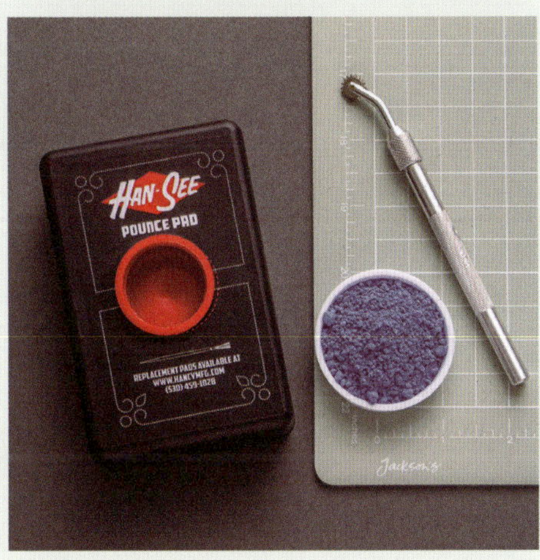

Pounce wheels (top) and set of pouncing tools (bottom).

Pouncing Materials

Pouncing is a technique in which powder is forced through holes pricked in a paper pattern to transfer a design from the paper onto a substrate. There are some basic materials required to do this type of work.

Pounce Wheel

Pounce wheels are like mini pizza cutters with spikes running around the rotating circular end. They are used to perforate holes in a pattern (paper with a design drawn or printed on it). Wheels come in different sizes according to the diameter of the wheel and the number of holes per inch that they produce.

For day-to-day work I use a size 10, but depending on the level of detail in your design you may prefer a smaller (more detail) or larger (less detail) wheel. For very large work, including patterns being produced on fabric, you can try a quilter's tracing wheel. Some sign painters also prefer a pin or bodkin for accuracy in very detailed work.

Pounce Pin/Bodkin

There are many different varieties of pin that can be used for perforating patterns, including the bodkin, which usually has a wooden handle. A simple do-it-yourself pounce pin can be made by inserting the eye end of a sewing needle into a cork from a wine or champagne bottle.

Pounce Surface

For the pounce wheel or pin to work effectively, there needs to be a slightly soft surface underneath the pattern being pounced. This allows the points on the wheel or pin to pass through the paper or fabric as desired. The surface should not be *too* soft, however, as that can easily lead to the paper tearing.

A cutting mat/memory board works well, as does lino board or flat PVC. Alternatives are medium-weight card, a newspaper, felt, or a thin blanket, but make sure you are working on a surface that is protected against damage from the wheel, which may pass through to the table or bench underneath.

Electro-Pounce

If you are doing a lot of work with patterns, then an electro-pounce will be a shrewd investment, saving you time and making your work more profitable. It also eliminates the need to sand the back of pounce patterns as it burns the

Mike's Tip

Pounce wheels are made of metal, with moving parts, so it is good to apply a drop or two of oil to them from time to time to keep the motion smooth.

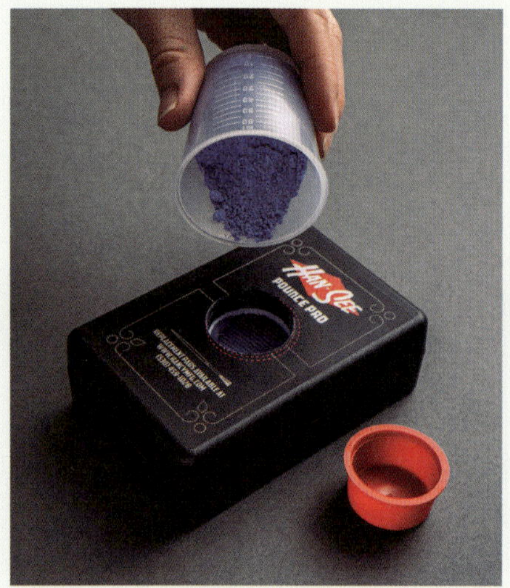

Refilling a pounce pad with blue pounce powder.

Different colors of pounce powder for pouncing onto different tones of substrate.

holes, rather than just pushing paper away. In addition to the electro-pounce itself, you will need a sheet of earthed steel set upright to fix the paper to. You can fix the paper with tape or magnets. The main supplier of electro-pounces in North America is McLogan.

Pounce Pad/Bag

A pounce pad contains either dark or light powder and is hit and rubbed over a pattern to transfer the design to a substrate through the perforated holes. A widely available brand of pounce pad is Han-See, which has a small cap that can be taken out to fill and refill the pad with powder. Avoid putting light powder into a pad you have previously used for dark powder. It is best to have two pads, one for light and one for dark powder, otherwise you will end up with gray.

Before manufactured pads were widely available, most people used pounce bags. These are made from thin fabric (e.g. cheesecloth) tied into a ball, which holds the powder, but then lets some out when the bag is hit and rubbed against the pattern. An old sock can also work well.

Pounce Powder

Pounce powder is made from finely ground chalk, pastel, or charcoal, which will transfer through the soft pad material or pounce bag. The tone of the powder is selected based on the shade of the substrate it is being used on: dark powder for a light background, and vice versa.

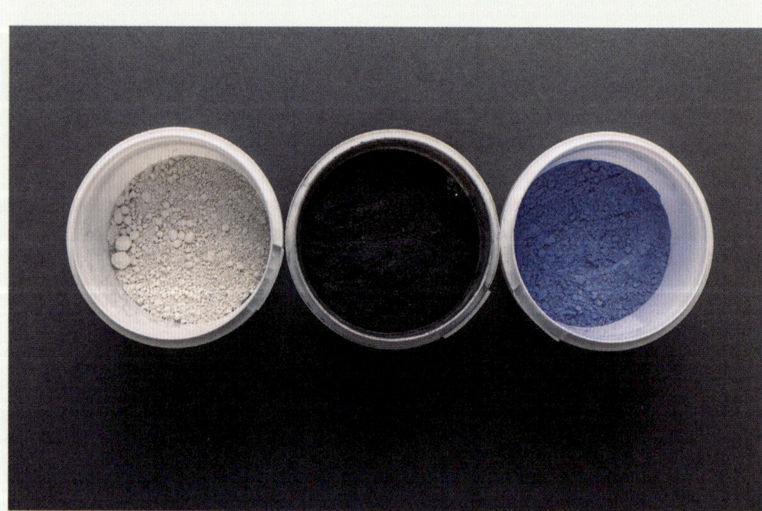

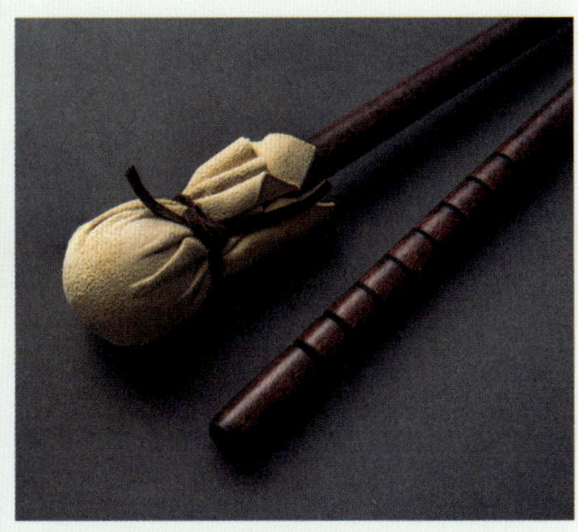

Two-part mahl stick with chamois-leather end covering.

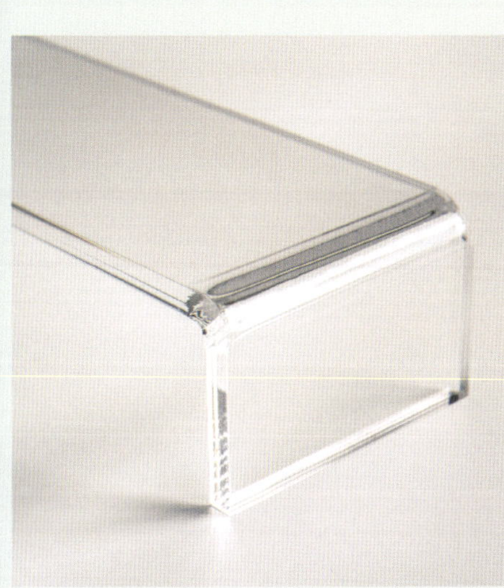

Simple perspex bridge.

Rests

Mahl Stick

The mahl (paint) stick is mainly used as a rest for your hand when painting (see page 78). However, it can also be used to mark horizontal guidelines (page 74), as a straight edge for lining work, and as a pivot for curves (page 80). There are various types, ranging from single lengths of wood to collapsible multipart wooden and aluminum sticks. Light-weight carbon fiber and telescopic sticks are also available.

Important things to consider when selecting a stick are:

– **Weight: you will be holding it with one hand for extended periods of time.**
– **Conductivity: metal sticks can be very cold on the hand in winter, whereas those made from wood or carbon fiber will not take the warmth away from your skin.**
– **Size: multipart and telescopic sticks are easier to transport.**

You can also make your own mahl stick using a piece of ¼–½in (c.6–12mm) dowel, around a yard (c.90cm) in length— or less, as you prefer. A cut-down pool cue or the thicker parts of a fishing rod are other options. You can even adapt a selfie stick to create your own lightweight telescopic stick. The important thing is that the stick does not bend under the pressure that your hand will be applying.

At the end of the stick, you will need something bulky, usually wrapped in chamois leather to prevent slipping. Various types of balls work (e.g. Styrofoam, rubber, wooden), as can a champagne cork: drill a little hole in it to fit the end of the stick and then glue it in place.

For the handle, you will need a grip. This can be as simple as the tape used for tennis rackets, or you can dip the top of your stick in Plasti Dip, a specialized rubber coating that works well for tool handles.

Bridge

Also called a hand rest, a bridge is a flat length of timber, metal, or plastic that is elevated by supports at either end. It can be used to keep your hands off your work when working flat and without a mahl stick.

45

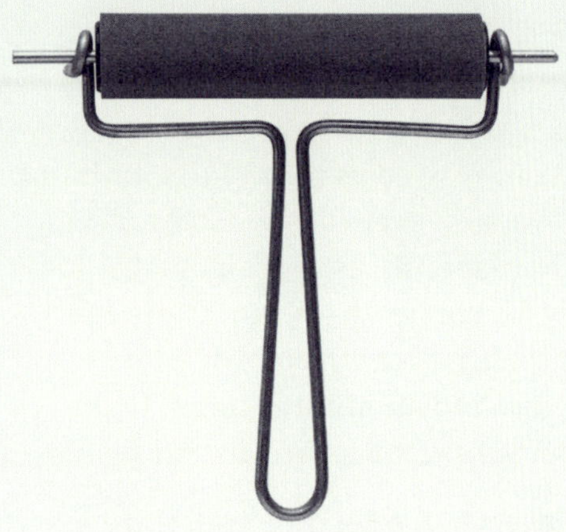

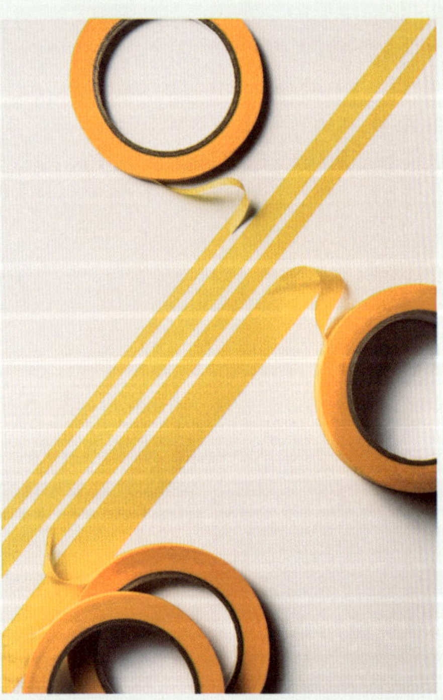

Application Tools

Brayer (Ink Roller)

A brayer is a rubber cylinder fixed to a handle so that it can be rolled, just like a paint roller. Brayers are useful for rolling out anything that you might be gluing down to ensure a smooth finish with no bubbles. The roller makes it more efficient than a squeegee for larger surfaces.

Squeegee

A squeegee is a simple firm rubber edge with a handle. Pull a squeegee over vinyl decals to ensure correct adhesion and avoid bubbles and other defects.

Tapes

Masking Tape

Used for masking off areas that are to be kept clear of paint while working: for example, window frames when working on windows. It can also be used to tape paper to an easel for practice.

Fine Line & Low-Tack Tape

These tapes can be used to mark out the edges of lettering work, giving a clean finish to the tops and bottoms of letters, especially slanted block letters or when working at smaller sizes (see page 70). Another use for fine line tape is to lay down two strips in parallel and paint in between to create a perfectly straight single line. While tape can help to speed and neaten up your work early on, I recommend getting your speed on the brush through practice and avoiding the use of tape unless absolutely necessary.

Scotch Tape

This has slightly more adhesive than masking tape and can be used to wind around the base of chalk or charcoal to prevent breakage.

Gaffer Tape

This is a strong adhesive tape made with cotton and is good for fixing patterns to walls outside in windy conditions. It is also very useful for emergency repairs to all sorts of tools and materials.

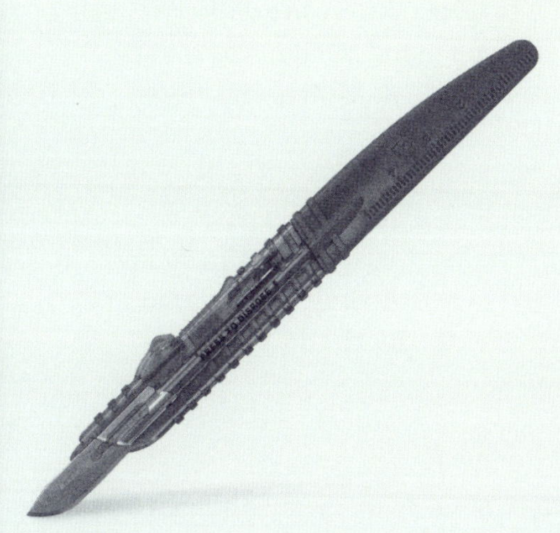

(above) Retractable scalpel. (below) Box cutter. (bottom) Scraper.

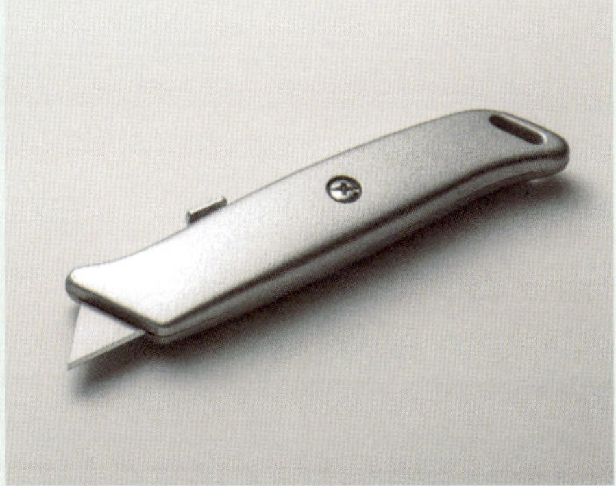

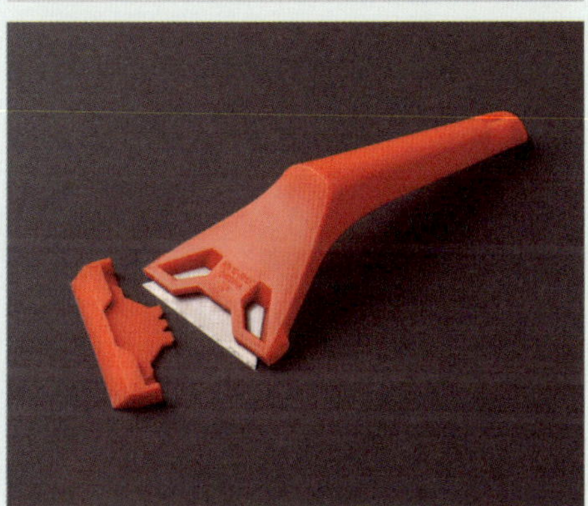

Clips & Fixers

Bulldog Clips

These can clip patterns onto signboards, and hold temporary material, such as a trimmed glossy magazine, on a palette.

Thumbtacks (Drawing Pins)

These come in handy for pinning designs and other paper-based reference materials. You can also use thumbtacks to improvise a pair of compasses. Set a thumbtack just off the surface of your substrate and tie a piece of string to it. Fix the other end of the string to a pencil or piece of chalk. Make sure the string can move freely around the thumbtack to avoid ending up with a soft spiral instead of a circle.

Magnets

Magnets are perfect for fixing a pounce pattern to a truck or other vehicle door. They can also be used for fixing paper in place if working with an electro-pounce.

Elastic Bands

These are useful for securing rolled-up patterns.

Door Stop

If you are working on a door, a rubber door stop will keep it open—handy if the doorway is in use while you letter.

Blades

Scalpel

A scalpel sharpens grease pencils and trims paper, chalk, charcoal, and other materials to size. When working on aluminum composite panels, use a scalpel to cut sections of the protective coating away for use as an improvised mask. Use on regular vinyl to cut a standard mask.

Box Cutter (Stanley Knife)

A heavy blade like a box cutter is useful for cutting through packaging and heavier materials that would break a scalpel. You can also use a box cutter (along with a metal ruler or other straight edge) to score aluminum composite panels before bending them back and forth to snap along the line.

Scraper

A razor scraper, found in most hardware stores, is useful for removing old paint from windows.

Abrasives

Sandpaper
Sandpaper (glass paper) is essential for preparing boards for lettering and for opening holes on the back of pounce patterns. Its coarseness is identified by a "grit" number, running from low (coarse) to high (very fine). Stock your kit with 40, 50, 60, and 100 grit. In the USA grit standards are known as CAMI, while in Europe they are called FEPA. For the sandpaper that you'll be using in sign work, these standards overlap, so you can just ask for the numbers given in this book.

Steel (Wire) Wool
This can be used as an alternative to sandpaper to scuff substrates before priming. It is also useful when cleaning glass ahead of painting. Grades 0 (finer) and 1 (coarser) are sufficient for most sign work.

Scuff Pads/Scourers
These are less abrasive than steel (wire) wool and can be used to clean glass ahead of painting. Switch to steel wool if something stronger is required.

Wire Brush
A firm wire brush can be used to remove loose material from walls ahead of priming and painting.

Glass Cleaners
Bon Ami and whiting are mild abrasive cleaners for glass. Both come in powder form and are used with a little water and clean lint-free cloths or towels. Though Bon Ami is most readily available in powder form, every now and then the old bars can be found secondhand—I highly recommend buying these if you see them.

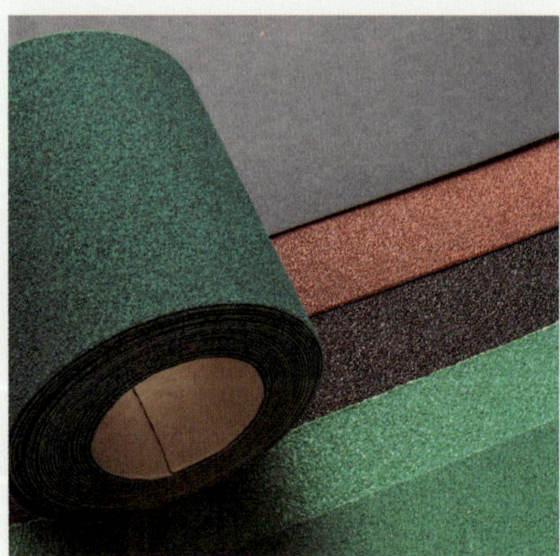

Different grit sandpapers (top) and grades of steel wool (bottom).

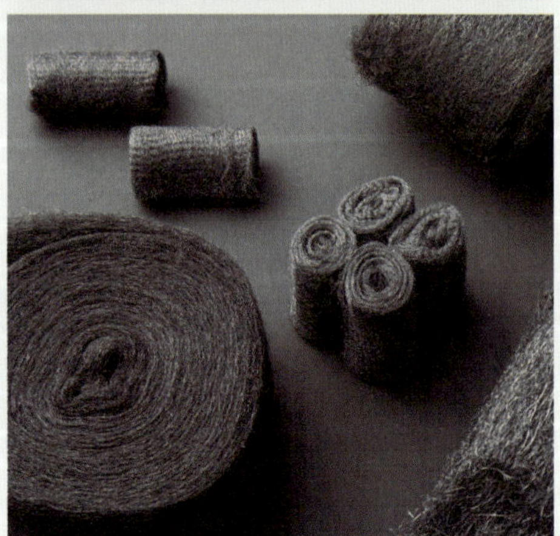

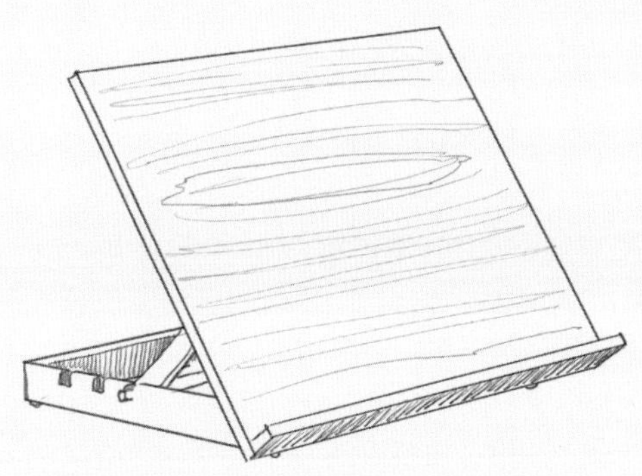

Adjustable table-top easel/ drawing board.

Mike's Tip

If you've made the bottom ledge of your easel from timber, cover the base of it with some gaffer tape to avoid splinters when using the ruler pull method (see page 74) for setting out horizontal lines.

Hardware

Easel

For general practice on paper, an adjustable desktop drawing board that can almost stand upright will work just fine. You may need to fix some pieces of rubber to the bottom of the board, brace it against a wall, or set it on a rubber mat to prevent it from slipping when pressure is applied by your chosen rest.

As you begin to work on larger pieces, you will want a bigger set up. An 8 x 4ft (244 x 122cm) sheet of ¼in (c.6mm) plywood, either in full or cut in half lengthwise, makes a good starting point. Screw an 8ft (244cm) length of 2 x 4in (5 x 10cm) timber, or angle iron, to the bottom of the plywood sheet to form a bottom ledge. Attach two more lengths of timber to the back of the sheet to create a simple lean-to support. Two easel boards can be set up back to back on an A-frame, which is useful if you are working on more than one piece at the same time.

If you would rather sit than stand to work, create a simple frame that can be set on a regular trestle table and then attach one or two easel boards with ledges to the frame. This is the way I prefer to work: it helps to keep me in a relaxed position when painting.

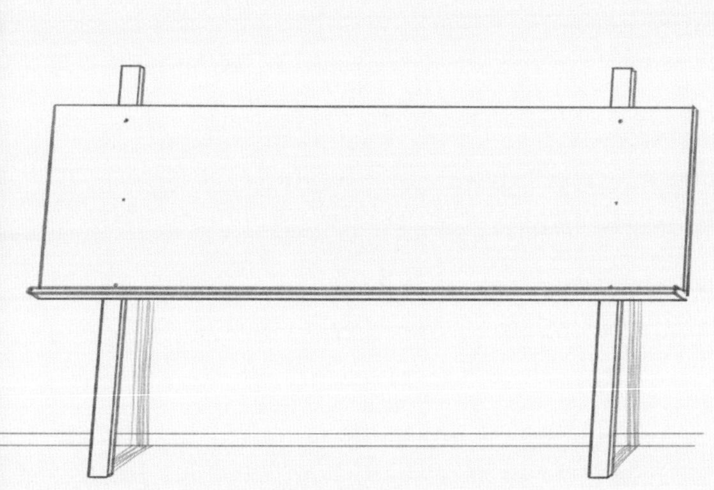
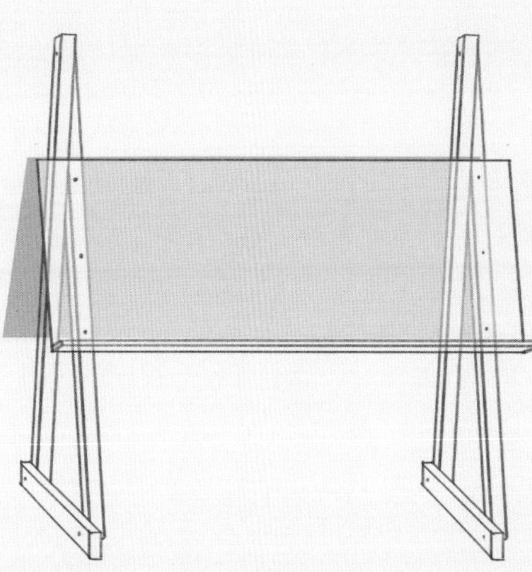

(left) Lean-to easel. (right) A-frame easel.

Mike's Tip

Fit wheels (casters or dolly rollers) onto the bottom of your workbench, A-frame easels, and/or skids so that this heavy equipment can easily be moved around the workshop, and out of the way, as required.

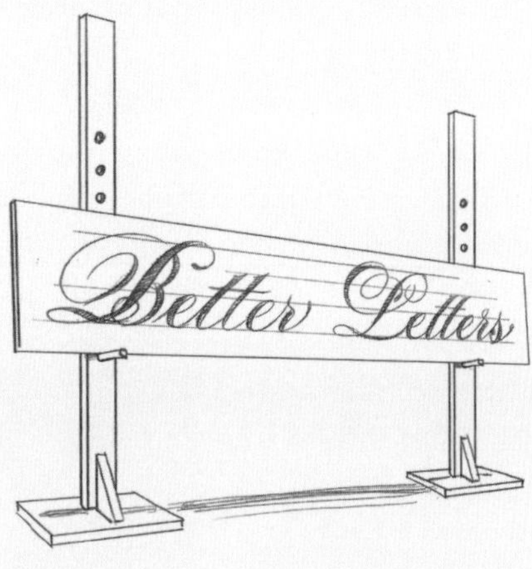

Simple skids for supporting sign boards.

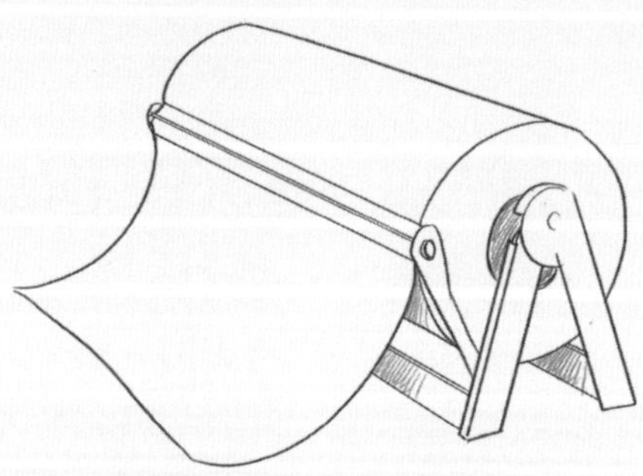

Paper dispenser and cutter.

Skids

For working directly on wide signs, a set of skids is a simple and portable option. You can make these from a pair of wooden beams and some pieces of dowel or large bolts.

1. Take two 2 x 4 x 72in (5 x 10 x 183cm) beams and drill holes around 1in (2.5cm) in diameter at regular points along the middle of the widest side.

2. If you are using pieces of dowel, do not drill all the way through the beam: stop drilling just short of the back of the beam so that the short pieces of dowel sit snugly in the hole, supported at the back.

3. If you are using bolts, drill all the way through the beam and secure the bolt with a nut on the other side.

4. Lean the beams against a wall and place short pieces of dowel or large bolts into the holes at the height you want your sign board to sit.

5. Rest the board on the dowels or bolts.

As with easels, it is possible to construct a simple A-frame with skids either side so that you can work on more than one piece at a time. For smaller signs, skids made in the same way from 1 x 3 x 48in (2.5 x 7.5 x 122cm) beams work well.

Paper Dispenser

A simple roller-based paper dispenser is useful for pulling lengths of kraft and other paper when required. The dispenser can be wall-mounted or stand on a tabletop, and many come with a serrated blade that can cut the paper once pulled out. I usually work with 18in (45cm) paper rolls.

Paint Trolley

A simple catering trolley on wheels with two or three shelves is perfect for holding paints and other materials while you work. The wheels mean you can move it easily around the workshop as you paint. It can also be used for raising the height of a projector (see page 67) when setting out using this method.

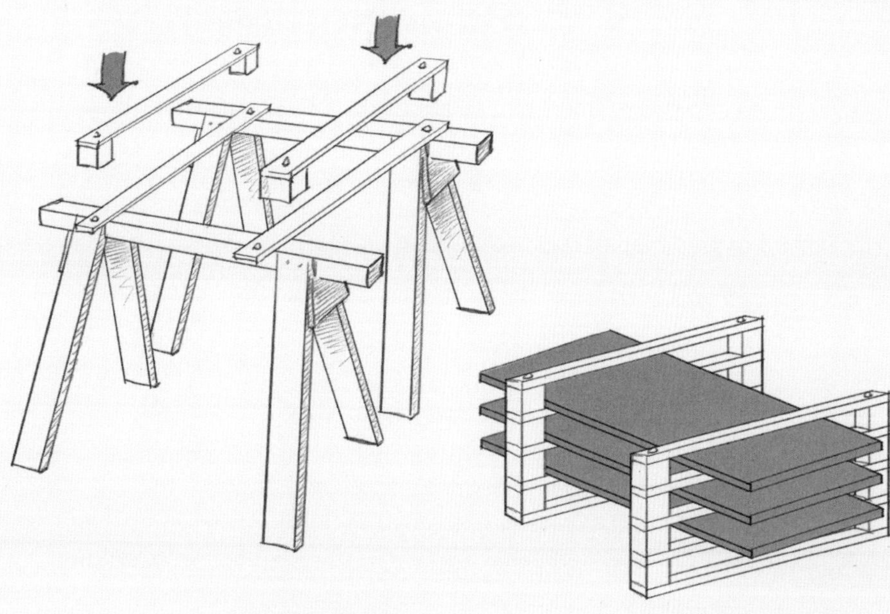

Drying planks to stack boards
as they cure.

Drying Planks

To save space in the workshop, it is useful to have a
number of simple planks with blocks on the ends to stack
boards while they are drying. The blocks should be large
enough to stack one on top of the other while giving
enough clearance for the drying sign underneath.

Box Stool

A simple box stool is useful for having around the workshop and can be constructed to provide a range of different
working heights.

Low-Down Chair

For working on vehicles and anything else that cannot
be raised up to a comfortable working height, a low-down
chair is useful. It can be made simply with four pieces
of timber as shown.

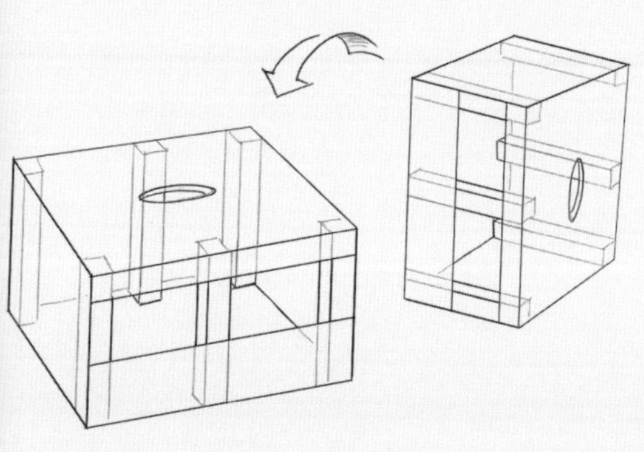

Box stool showing two of three
possible working heights.

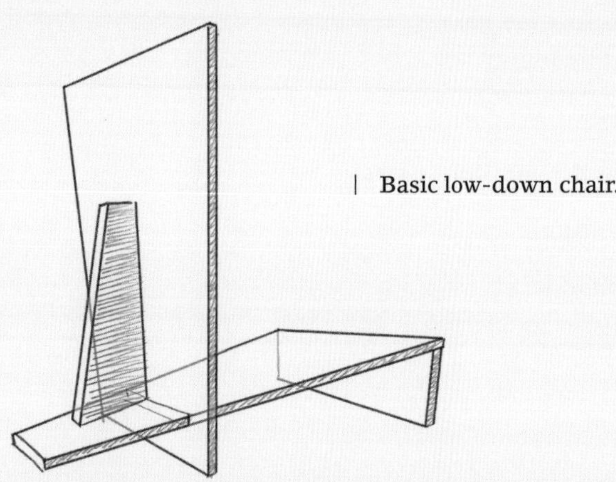

Basic low-down chair.

51

Basic Starter Kit

Here are my recommendations for someone just starting out in the trade. This is assuming that you are mainly working at home or in a small studio/workshop. If you are regularly heading out for jobs on-site, add a kit box for ease of transportation to this list.

- **Lettering paints**
In black, white, red, blue, and yellow. These will be enough to get you started, and you can practice mixing colors from scratch using the primaries. For general practice, use oil-based poster colors or acrylics. If you are already working on signs, you will probably want enamels as well as, or instead of, these.

- **Brushes**
» 2 x pure sable chisel-edge writers, sizes #4 and #6 (go with synthetic if working with water-based paints).
» 1 x synthetic chisel-edge writer, either size #5 or #6 (not required if you are working with water-based paints, as you will have the two sizes listed above).
» 1 x sable or synthetic pointer, in a small size such as #2 or #3.

- **Mahl stick**

- **Paint cups**

- **Containers for holding brush cleaner**

- **Turpentine** (water or acrylic floor wax if you are working with water-based paints)

- **Mineral spirits** (water or brush cleaner if you are working with water-based paints)

- **Boiled linseed oil***

- **Hardener***

- **Driers***

- **Neatsfoot Oil***

- **Rags**

- **Yardstick and folding rule**

- **Clear angle**

- **Spirit level**

- **Grease pencils** (one light, one dark)

* Not required for working with water-based paints.

- **Graphite pencil**

- **Pencil sharpener**

- **Chalk**

- **Charcoal**

- **Pounce wheel**

- **Pounce pads/bags** (one for light and one for dark pounce)

- **Pounce powder** (light and dark)

- **Scalpel**

- **Tin opener**

- **Screwdriver**

- **Masking tape**

- **String**

It is also useful to carry some basic administrative items such as a notebook (for jotting down customer copy), blank invoices, and business cards. You will be amazed at how many jobs come from people seeing you working outside.

In addition to your basic kit, there are some things that will be useful to have at home or in the studio/workshop.

- **Easel or skids**

- **Workbench**

- **Kraft paper**

- **Paper dispenser**

- **Trolley**

- **Pounce surface (e.g. cutting mat)**

You have now got your kit together and, over time, you will refine and adapt it based on the particular ways that you work. Whenever you meet other sign painters, take a look in their kits for inspiration. We are an innovative and creative bunch, and I am always amazed by the custom tools that other painters develop for different purposes.

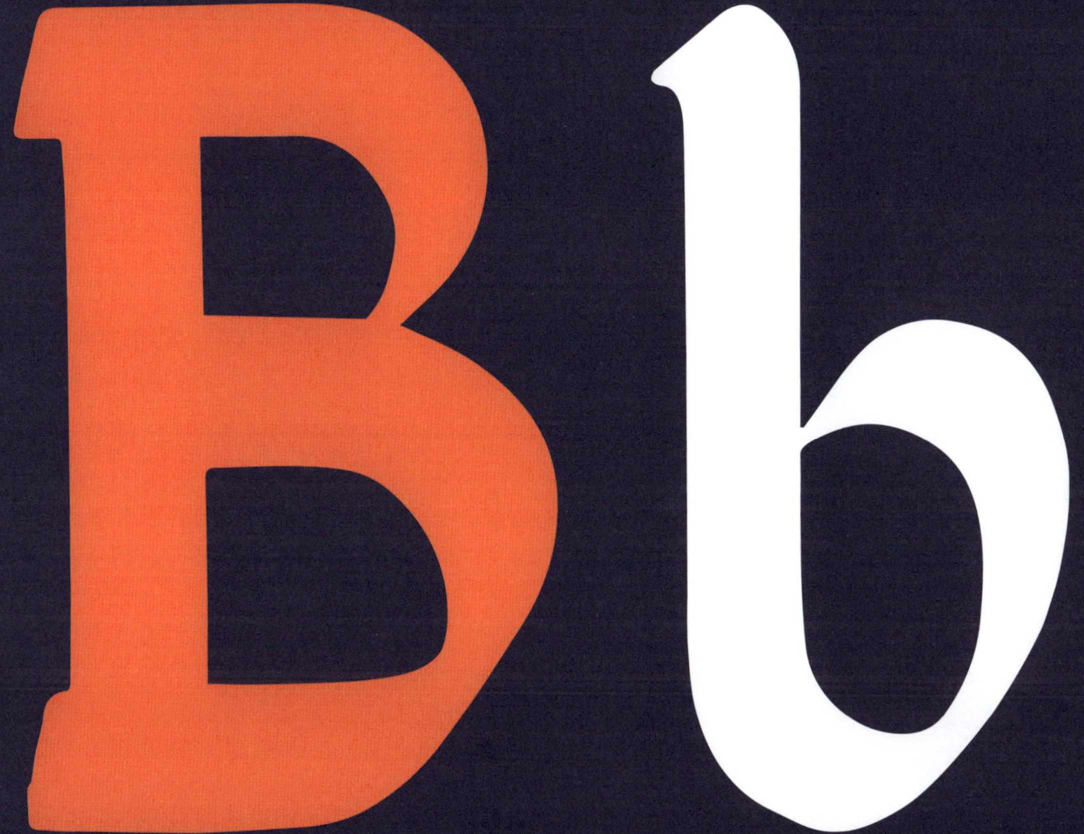

Core Techniques

Lettering by Dave Correll, Dave's Casual, see page 108

Preparing & Finishing Substrates

As a sign painter, you will be asked to paint on a whole range of substrates (surfaces).

Lettering on ice at Mazeppa Mardi Gras Letterheads meet, 2014.

Mike's Tip

It's very easy to underestimate the time needed for preparatory work when quoting for jobs. Make sure you include all the stages required, and allow for travel to and from the job site, curing time, and materials.

Some of the more unusual things I have painted on are ice, grass, cows, human bodies, basketballs, bananas, and watermelons. However, day to day, there are a few main types of substrate that you will find yourself asked to work on.

Before you start laying out and lettering, it is important to prepare the substrate. This will provide a strong foundation for your work, and contribute to the longevity of the sign. Often the deterioration of a sign—cracking, peeling, poor adhesion of paint, rapid fading—is due not to the lettering work but to the way the substrate has been prepared.

There are four main stages in preparing a substrate, although not all substrates require all of these.

1. Scuffing. This involves the use of (usually fine) sandpaper or steel wool to take the smoothness out of wood or aluminum, allowing the primer to "bite" or grip when applied. If the substrate is too smooth, paint can easily come loose. A rough surface gives more texture to which the paint can adhere.

2. Cleaning. This is important to ensure the substrate is free from dirt, grease, and any excess matter before applying paint.

3. Priming (undercoating). This is a layer of paint to seal the substrate and ensure optimum adhesion and curing of the topcoat.

4. Topcoating. This is the final stage and provides the background color and finish required ahead of laying out and lettering.

Once you have laid out and painted the sign on the prepared substrate, there is sometimes a need to finish things off, usually with a varnish, or "clear coat." However, in the majority of cases, if the correct materials and processes have been used to prepare and paint the sign, a clear coat is not required.

Timber

As a general rule, if you can source the materials yourself, use medium density overlay (MDO) plywood. Avoid regular timber, which is prone to warping, and also anything that comes "pre-primed," as you cannot be sure of the quality of materials used. I would use ½in (12mm) thickness MDO for a shopfront, and ¾in (18mm) for a sign to be installed outside between posts. If you are having MDO cut to size, make sure

Mike's Tip

You can save yourself time, and your clients money, by working with a variety of board dimensions that can be cut cleanly from a single sheet of MDO.

For example, a 4 x 8ft (48 x 96in or 122 x 244cm) sheet can, with just four cuts, be turned into five pieces: two sized 48 x 32in (122 x 81cm), one sized 32 x 24in (81 x 61cm), and two sized 24 x 16in (61 x 41cm). Or you can cut six boards sized 32 x 24in (81 x 61cm).

These boards can be primed in advance, so that they only require topcoats before lettering. This has the added benefit of allowing plenty of curing time for the primer, which will improve the durability of the final signs.

Five boards

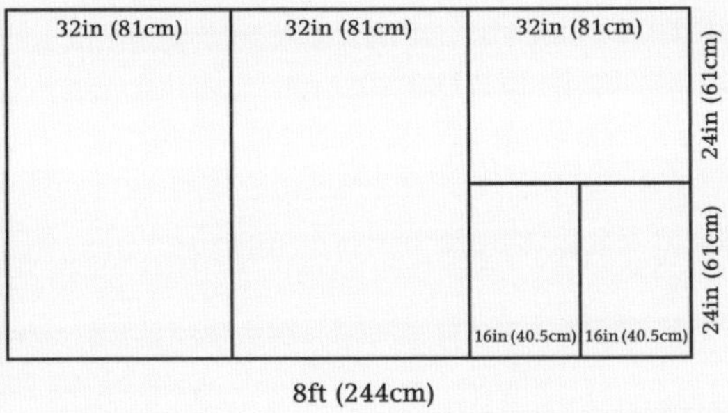

| 32in (81cm) | 32in (81cm) | 32in (81cm) | 24in (61cm) |
| | | 16in (40.5cm) | 16in (40.5cm) | 24in (61cm) |

8ft (244cm)

Six boards

| 32in (81cm) | 32in (81cm) | 32in (81cm) | 24in (61cm) |
| 32in (81cm) | 32in (81cm) | 32in (81cm) | 24in (61cm) |

8ft (244cm)

you allow for any fittings, such as a frame; make sure that your eventual layout accounts for these too.

Often you will be asked to work on an existing shop-front or board. In these situations, assess whether you can work with what is there, or whether it would be better to replace or cover that with a board of your own. Finding out what paints were used for the initial work, and estimating the time involved to prepare the existing board for new work, will help you make a decision based on the client's needs and budget.

If you have to work on a board that has already been painted, the first thing you will need to do is remove any loose paint, varnish, and dirt using a coarse sandpaper (e.g. 40 grit). Sand the board back to the previous topcoat, then follow the steps below, as you would with a new board.

1. Take some medium-grit sandpaper (e.g. 60 grit) and rub the whole surface, front and back if possible, until the smooth finish has been roughed up slightly. You are aiming to just skim the surface, avoiding digging into the board with the sandpaper. Once you have finished, remove any sanding dust by brushing off the board and wiping it with a damp cloth.

2. Prime the whole board—front, back, and edges—with a good-quality exterior latex (emulsion) paint. The color of the paint should be white, or white tinted with a little of the ultimate topcoat color (in latex), to reduce show-through when topcoating. Apply the paint using a roller (for bigger boards) or a decorator's brush (for smaller pieces). A decorator's brush can also be used to prime the edges of the board. When using a roller, work the paint both horizontally and vertically across the board, while gradually decreasing the pressure on the roller. Make sure your final passes over the board are vertical, as any streaks or lines in this direction will be less visible on the final sign.

For a really flat, even finish, let the primer dry a little before "tipping off" (going back over it) with the roller using virtually no pressure at all. This will smooth out any tiny bubbles that may be present. It is important to time this stage perfectly: the paint should have dried enough to not be picked up by the roller. Ideally, work the roller perpendicular to the last direction used when applying the primer.

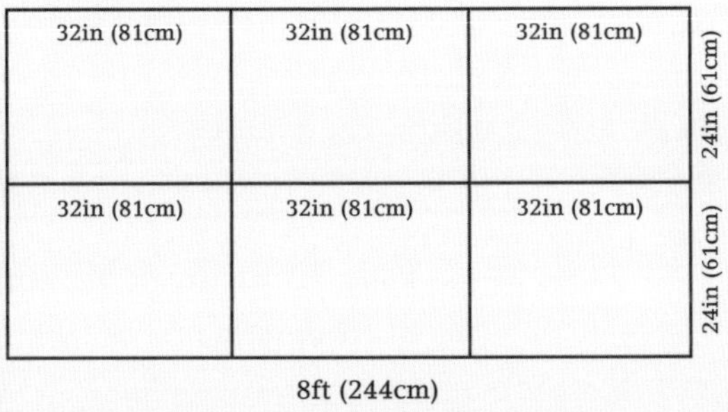

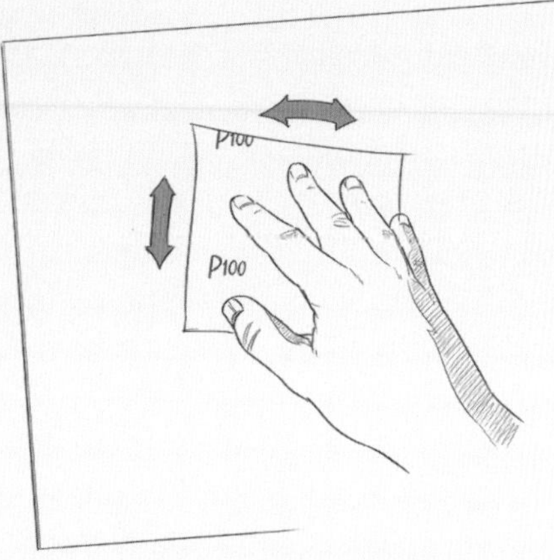

Sand gently before starting, and after each of the primer and topcoats have been applied and cured.

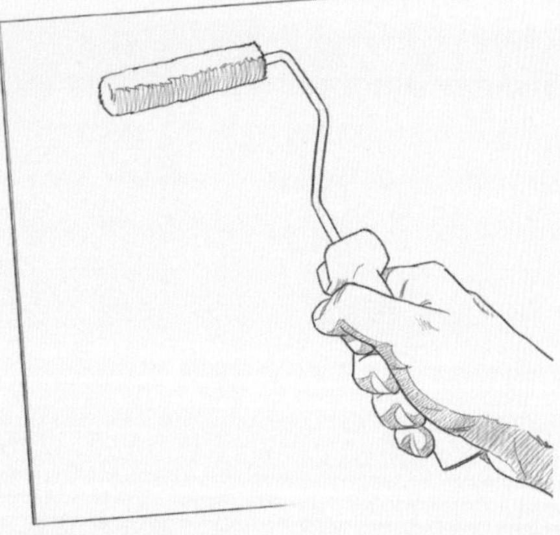

Use a roller to prime and topcoat timber boards.

Mike's Tip

When prepping boards of any sort with primers and topcoats, always work and leave the boards to dry in a dust-free environment. This will lower the chances of unwanted dust adhering to the curing surface, which will affect the quality of your finish.

3. Lay the board flat to cure in a dust-free environment. It is important to let the paint cure fully—ideally overnight or longer, depending on the external temperature and humidity. If necessary, you can speed the drying process with fans and sunlight, but never use direct heat sources.

4. Take some finer sandpaper (e.g. 100 grit) and gently sand the primed board until you have a smooth surface. Remove any resulting dust with a brush and damp cloth.

5. Paint the whole board—front, back, and edges—with your topcoat, using a roller and/or decorator's brush, ensuring a smooth, flat finish, including "tipping off," as you did with the primer. (Spraying is also an option if you have access to the necessary equipment.) You should use an (oil-based) enamel paint for this coat if the final lettering work is also going to be done in enamel, but for larger boards it is expensive to use sign and lettering enamels, so go for something like a coach paint or other lower-cost enamel. Poster paint (oil-based) is an option for interior signs, providing that a matte finish is desired. You can use water-based paint for topcoating if the final lettering is also going to be done in water-based paint.

6. Allow the topcoat to fully cure—again, overnight or longer if possible, depending on external conditions.

7. Gently sand the board again with the finer sandpaper (100 grit) and remove dust with a brush and damp cloth, so that you are left with a finished board that is nice and flat, ready for lettering on. You can also give the board a final wipe over with a clean rag dampened with mineral spirits to remove any grease that may be present from handling.

For signs that need to endure a lot of wear and tear—such as A-boards (sandwich boards) or signs that are south/southwest facing (north/northwest facing in the southern hemisphere)—or where there is show-through of the primer after the first topcoat, it can be necessary to add additional topcoats. If this is required, repeat the last few steps: allow the current coat to cure fully, gently sand it for a smooth finish, and apply the new coat.

Finishing

Once you have painted the sign, nothing more needs to be done to finish it, apart from allowing plenty of time for the paint to cure. If you do add a varnish or clear coat for protection, or to create a high gloss, use one that is consistent (i.e. oil- or water-based) with the paint used for the topcoat and lettering.

Aluminum

Aluminum composite panels (ACP) are an excellent modern alternative to timber for signs. A lightweight core of either polyethylene or polyurethane is sandwiched between two thin aluminum sheets, which gives the panel good structural rigidity while keeping the overall weight down. I tend to work with ¼in (c.6mm) ACP for signs, as thicker panels often have a corrugated core that is at greater risk of water damage and delaminating (coming apart). Find a supplier who can cut panels to size. As with timber, working in standard sizes that can be cut from a single sheet makes efficient use of the material. If you are working frequently with aluminum panels, it is worth investing in a scroll saw so you can cut them down yourself.

Preparing an ACP panel is less time-consuming than timber because the aluminum usually comes with a coating of paint and so does not require priming. However, if you are working with untreated aluminum, then you will need to apply a metal primer after the initial sanding.

1. Slightly rough up the surface. This can be done by gently rubbing with fine sandpaper (e.g. 100 grit) or using fine or medium steel (wire) wool (e.g. grade 0 or 1). It is important not to sand through the paint that is already in place to the bare aluminum underneath.

2. Wipe the surface with a clean cloth dampened with lacquer thinner. This will remove dust from the sanding and any grease that might be present.

3. Apply your topcoat of (oil-based) enamel using a roller, working the paint vertically and horizontally, gradually decreasing the pressure on the roller. You can then smooth over with a decorator's brush, or come back over it with the roller 5–10 minutes later to ensure a smooth finish. As with timber, you can use a water-based topcoat if you are going to do the lettering in water-based paints.

4. Once the topcoat has fully cured—overnight, and ideally for 24 hours if possible—gently sand the panel with fine sandpaper to leave a smooth finish ready for lettering.

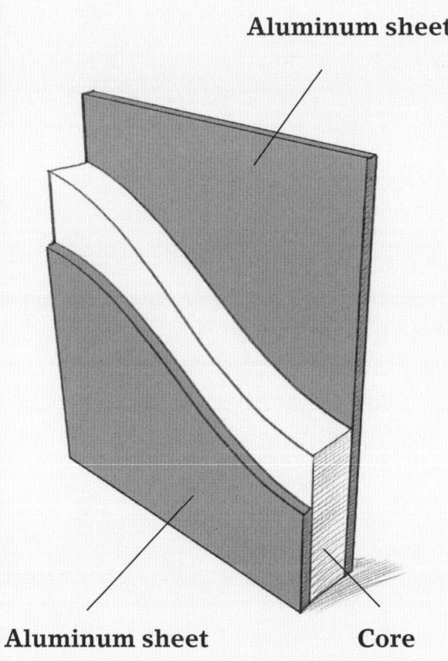

An aluminum composite panel.

As with timber, additional coats may be applied if the panel is likely to be exposed to a lot of wear and tear and/or sunshine. If required, repeat the process of gently sanding, wiping, and painting above, ensuring that each coat has fully cured before applying additional coats.

Finishing
As for timber (see page 56).

Walls: Brick, Concrete, & Plaster

Wall/mural signs are popular again, and companies like Colossal Media have perfected the process of recreating photo-realistic artwork at scale on walls across the United States. There are a variety of health and safety considerations when doing this type of work: consult with your local authorities to find out what permits, plant (access equipment), and training you need to have before working at height and on walls, especially in public places.

Walls might be made of bricks and mortar, concrete breeze (cinder) blocks, or plaster. Not all walls are suitable for painting on, and it is important to carry out an assessment of the surface before committing to a job. Look out for cracks, loose mortar, cracking paint, and other damage that will affect the integrity of the wall and the sign that you are painting on it. If you find any of these defects on a site visit, you should recommend that repairs are made to the wall ahead of painting.

For a plaster wall, very little preparation is needed, as the surface should be relatively flat with no need to clean or prime it; you can start work straight away with your chosen paint. For brick and concrete walls, follow these steps:

1. Scrape the whole wall with a wire brush to remove any loose matter. Some sign painters use a vacuum cleaner to then go over the wall and suck up any remaining dust, although I have never felt the need to do this myself. A good alternative to brushing the wall is to pressure-wash it with hot water, but this requires access to additional equipment that you may not have, so stick with the wire brush when you are starting out.

2. Prime the whole wall with a good-quality exterior latex (emulsion) paint. This can be done with a nap roller. Use a regular household brush to tidy up and push paint into any recesses, such as mortar lines, that may get missed by the roller.

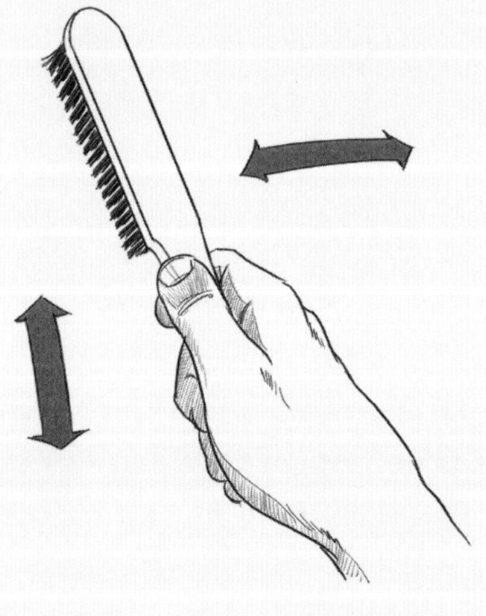

Preparing a wall for painting: removing loose material with a wire brush.

Mike's Tip

An effective alternative to fixing the wall that I have used in the past is to propose painting the mural on large aluminum composite panels, which are then fitted to the wall. This method has the additional benefit of allowing the work to be completed offsite in a more controlled environment.

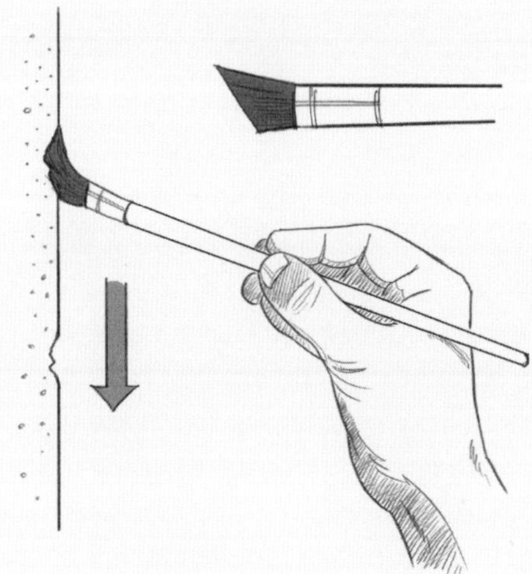

Angle of a lining fitch for painting signs on walls.

3. Allow the primer to cure, ideally overnight, but for at least four hours, depending on external conditions. Apply a second coat of primer in the same way as the first, allowing this to cure before you start setting out and painting.

4. If you are going to have a flat background in a color other than white on the final sign, apply three coats before starting to work. The first should be white, the second white tinted with a bit of the final color (e.g. blue), and then the third in the color itself. Make sure that all of these are latex paints of the same kind for exterior use.

5. Work on the wall using exterior latex paints and lining fitches.

When working on walls, be aware that mortar lines are not always horizontal. They can provide a false sense of security when setting out (see page 63). Always check them with a spirit level before using them as guides. If they are horizontal, use this to your advantage by creating a design that makes use of these naturally occurring grid lines: for example, set your letter heights as whole numbers (2, 3, 4, etc.) of bricks, and do the same for spaces between lines.

Finishing

Usually it is not necessary to do anything more to the wall once it has been painted, but some sign painters like to apply a water-based varnish or clear coat. This is optional, but always make sure that the clear you are using has an equal or longer life than the paint: it is no use putting a

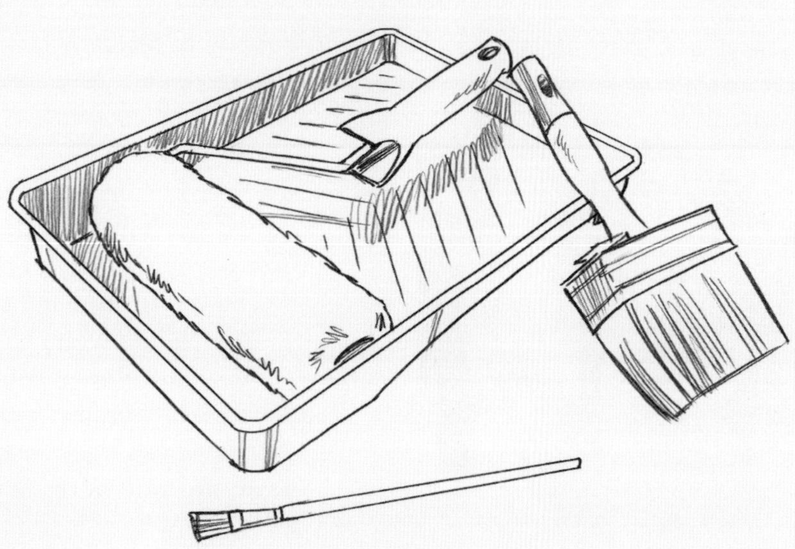

Basic kit for preparing and painting wall signs.

10-year clear over 20-year paint, as it will deteriorate before the paint underneath does.

Glass

One of the most common types of glasswork is gilding, which involves applying gold leaf to the reverse of a glass surface. The basics of that craft are a whole book in themselves, so I am not going to cover it here. However, there are many types of sign-painting work on glass that can be done without gold, from temporary window splashes to more permanent pieces such as names and opening hours, house numbers, etc. This sort of lettering is often done on the front of the glass, especially when working on tinted glass where the colors will be dulled if painted on the reverse.

The most important thing when working on glass is to clean it before you start painting. This can be as simple as using a spray glass cleaner and a clean cloth to remove grease and other dirt on the surface. Even better is using Bon Ami, whiting, or a similar powder cleanser: apply these with some water and a clean, lint-free cloth or paper towel, then wipe the glass clean once the cleanser has dried. The benefit of powder over spray cleaners is that, because they dry white, you can easily see when you have covered the full surface of the window without missing any places.

For anything tougher that might be stuck to the glass, use a scuff pad/scourer or steel (wire) wool with the glass cleaner. If you need to remove earlier paint work, use a razor scraper with some solvent to soften the paint: water for water-based paint, or mineral spirits for oil-based paint. Finish off with glass cleaner or Bon Ami, as above.

If you are working with oil-based enamels, you can start working on the glass straight away. I usually mix a small amount of a second color into the paint to increase the final opacity: I add a little silver to most colors, and a little magenta or light blue to white.

When working with water-based paints, I put down a white layer first to improve color reproduction and opacity. I often add a little alcohol to water-based paints to increase flow when working on window pieces. This layer needs to be allowed to cure before starting the lettering.

A layer of white is also essential if you are using fluorescent colors (oil-based or water-based), as they will not have any impact if painted directly onto the glass.

Discuss larger window pieces with your client before beginning any work. Covering large areas of their windows will reduce the natural light entering their premises: it is

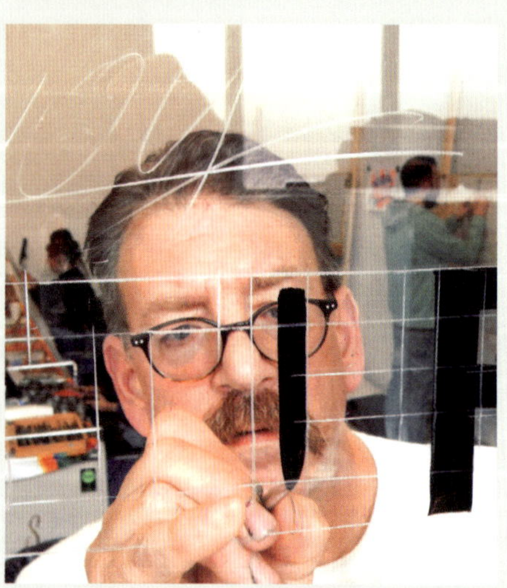

Lettering in reverse on glass.

Mike's Tip

If you're working on the inside of the glass, with a light-colored (e.g. white) background that spans more than one window, there can be a noticeable difference in the tone of the background color due to slight variations of tone in the glass itself. To avoid questions from your client after the job is done, do a few samples on adjoining windows to test and highlight any variation that might affect the final piece.

Lettering on a vehicle in Antwerp, Belgium, 2016.

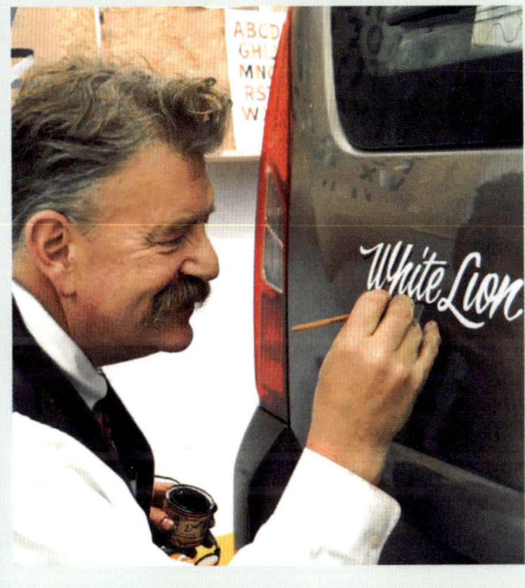

better to warn them of this before you design and paint something, rather than have them unpleasantly surprised when the job is finished.

Think about the colors that you use on windows. Never use dark colors for lettering, unless they are set on a lighter contrasting background, as they will not be easily visible against the darkness of the transparent glass. Also, where possible, avoid using red in more permanent window signage, as this color will fade most quickly in the sun.

For work done on the inside of windows, be conscious of the weather, especially if it is cold outside and there is a risk of condensation on the glass. In these conditions, it is useful to have a fan or hair dryer blowing at the window before you start work to completely dry it out. Once you have finished, leave a fan blowing on the window overnight to avoid condensation building up as the paint cures.

Finishing

If you are working in just paint on glass, you do not need to do anything more to finish it. If you have been gilding, backing up and applying a pencil line of varnish is important to protect the work from condensation damage; consult a specialist source for more information on these techniques.

Vehicles

As with glass, it is essential to make sure any vehicle surfaces that you are painting on are clean. Even if your client says they will get the surface cleaned, do it yourself as well, so that you are confident that all the dirt, wax, and grease that builds up in the day-to-day use, cleaning, and maintenance of vehicles has been removed.

I use Prepsol Wax & Grease Remover to thoroughly clean all the vehicle areas that I am going to be working on. Firmly wipe over the area to be painted with a clean rag dampened with Prepsol, and then go over it again with a clean dry rag.

Lettering work should be done with sign enamels with a few large drops of hardener added.

Finishing

The hardener added to the paint is fine for finishing most types of vehicle work, but where repeated cleaning is expected (e.g. fire trucks or stock cars), apply a clear coat of varnish to the lettering for additional protection.

Mike's Tip

The preparation process is often the cause of problems later in the life of signs. For this reason, preparation is an important step, and time should be taken to do each stage properly. It is tempting to rush through this part of the job and get onto the fun of lettering. But that lettering needs a good foundation, and the preparation of the substrate is what provides this.

Paper & Card

Little preparation is required for work on paper or card stock, besides trimming sheets to the required size. It is better to select the paper/card stock in a suitable color rather than have to paint a flat background. To avoid wrinkling in lighter-weight papers, use stock that has a slight coating. I usually work with oil-based poster colors, but acrylics are also popular for showcard work.

Finishing

Nothing is required to finish off paper and card signs, except anything your client might be doing to present them: for example, laminating or mounting.

Fabric & Vinyl Banners

The most important consideration when working on fabric and vinyl banners is their flexible nature. This requires the use of paints that have greater elasticity, so that they can flex as the substrate does, rather than being rigid and cracking with movement.

For fabrics, prepare the surface by wiping it over with alcohol or lacquer thinner, which helps to open up the material to receive the paint. Use a good-quality acrylic or specialist fabric paint for the work.

For vinyl banners, prepare the surface by wiping it over with lacquer or acetone thinner to open it up to the paint. Use good-quality acrylic paint for the work, to give the flexibility required as the banner moves, and if it is rolled for storage.

Finishing

Nothing is required once the lettering is complete.

Setting Out

Once the substrate has been prepared, you are ready to start setting out the sign that you want to paint. There are two main ways to do this: marking up directly onto the substrate, or transferring onto the substrate a pre-prepared design using one of a variety of methods.

Mike's Tip

Use rainy days at the workshop to create a set of stock patterns. These can include frequent motifs (e.g. pointing hands, arrows, etc.), decorative sign borders and corners, and common truck layout lines. Having these on hand, in a variety of sizes, can greatly speed up your work. You can do the same with transparencies and digital files for projecting.

Direct markup is often done on-site in front of clients and members of the public, and so requires confidence. You can build up this confidence by setting out patterns in the workshop, before taking the plunge and doing it in situ later on.

Transferring Designs

Many jobs will require the transfer of a design to the substrate before painting. The most common way to do this is through the creation of a full-size drawing that can then be transferred using the pouncing technique or with carbon paper and equivalents. Alternative methods include the use of projectors or vinyl masks.

Full-size drawings help ensure accuracy when setting out, especially where specific artwork has been approved by your client. Drawings will also save time on repetitive jobs where the same artwork will be used at the same size over and over again, such as for truck fleets or chain stores. Larger pieces such as murals may require multiple drawings that combine to form the whole design.

The drawing itself can be created on paper (or fabric) by hand, or printed when working from digital files. It is also possible to use a projector to set out the design on paper if it is not possible to do so on-site. It is important to check measurements on the drawing, especially when printing, to ensure that the design will fit correctly onto the sign. When printing, it is best to work with a high-resolution 1:1 scale PDF, or a vector file with the width of the sign specified, to avoid having to adjust the scale of your drawing.

Place a straight horizontal line on the drawing, and a vertical center line. These will be useful when positioning the drawing for the final transfer process. These lines can be added with a colored marker pen or pencil to differentiate them from the main lines of your drawing.

Your choice of paper will help with both pouncing and chalking techniques. The best types are kraft papers with a relatively high weight (e.g. 80–100gsm), such as brown packing paper. Other types of paper can be used, provided they are thin enough to perforate easily but thick enough to resist tearing and damage from repeated use. Tracing paper has the advantage of transparency where there is a need to see through the paper when transferring the design.

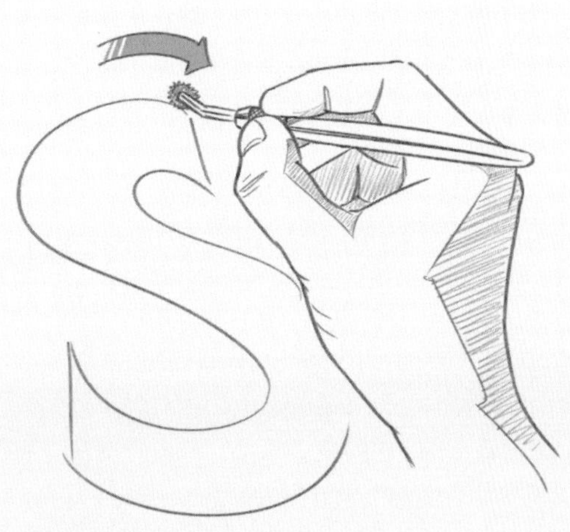

Perforate the key lines on your drawing using a pounce wheel.

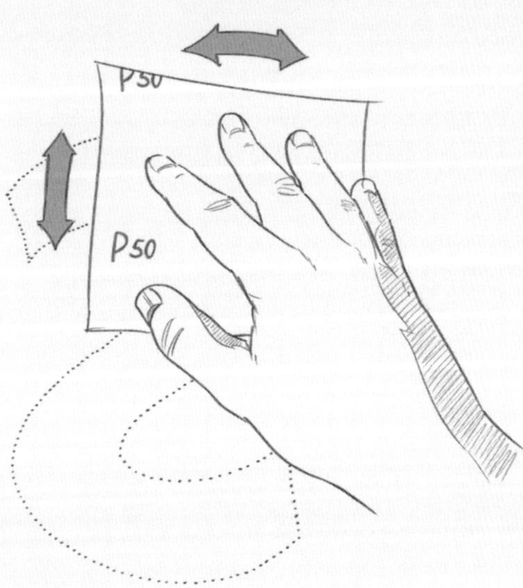

Sand the back of the perforations, both horizontally and vertically, to open up the holes.

Pouncing

Pouncing involves creating a series of perforations along the main lines of a design, placing this over the substrate, and pushing pounce powder through the holes to transfer the design onto the substrate.

Perforating a Design

The perforations required for pouncing can be created using a number of tools, but the most common are pounce wheels, sometimes called tracing wheels. You can also use a pounce pin or compass point to make perforations one by one, which is much slower but useful for smaller detailing. To get started, lay your design drawing over a surface that is firm, but which has some give. This allows the points on the wheel or pin to pass through the paper, while providing some resistance to prevent tearing.

If you are using a pounce pin, simply prick holes along the lines of the design. The distance between these should be close enough to give a true impression of the design when you are only able to see the holes, but far enough apart to avoid tearing the drawing and make the process as efficient as possible: in general, make as few holes as you can get away with.

If you are using a pounce wheel, position it with the short length parallel to your drawing while you hold the handle. Pull the wheel toward you while applying enough downward pressure to rotate the wheel and for the points to perforate the drawing. Too much pressure will cause the drawing to tear, so test the wheel on scrap paper or a blank part of the drawing before beginning. Check that you are perforating the paper correctly by holding your test paper up to the light to ensure you can see through the holes.

Once you have finished, hold it up to the light to make sure that you have done every line that you need. It is easy to miss part of the design, and a simple check at this stage is much better than trying to rectify problems later when you are on the job. Then lightly sand the back of the drawing with a medium to coarse sandpaper (e.g. 50 grit), both vertically and horizontally, to open up the holes. Test the sandpaper on a piece of scrap first to avoid tearing while ensuring the holes are correctly opened up.

Electro-Pounces & Plotters

In larger sign shops, or when pouncing is undertaken regularly, it is worth investing in either an electro-pounce or an electronic plotter. The cost of these will be paid back

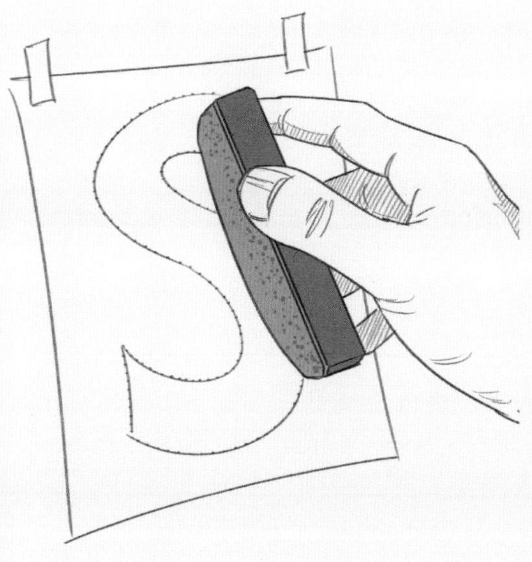

Fix your pattern in place with tape.

relatively quickly in time saved hand-pouncing drawings. An electro-pounce can be used on both hand-drawn and printed designs. A plotter requires artwork to be digital as it works much like a printer, fed by a computer.

Pouncing a Design

Your pounce pattern is now complete and ready for use. First position the design drawing on the substrate. Assuming that it is to be positioned centrally, mark a vertical center line on the substrate that can be aligned with the center line on your drawing. At the relevant height, mark a horizontal line on the substrate and double-check it with a spirit level. Align the horizontal line on the substrate with the corresponding horizontal line on your drawing.

Once your drawing is correctly aligned, fix the pattern to the substrate with tape. Masking tape is generally fine for this, although for rougher walls you may need gaffer tape. Stand back and check if it looks correct, especially the left-right alignment.

With the pattern in place, you can now pounce it with light-colored powder for a dark substrate, dark for a light-colored substrate. Hit the pattern with the pounce pad to release the powder, then rub the pad left and right, up and down, to push the powder through the holes. On a smooth substrate very little pressure is required, but on a rougher surface like a wall you will need to apply more.

65

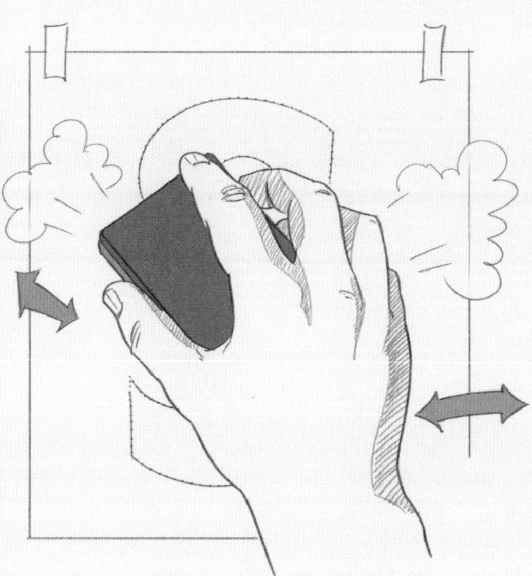

Pat and rub the pattern with a pounce pad/bag.

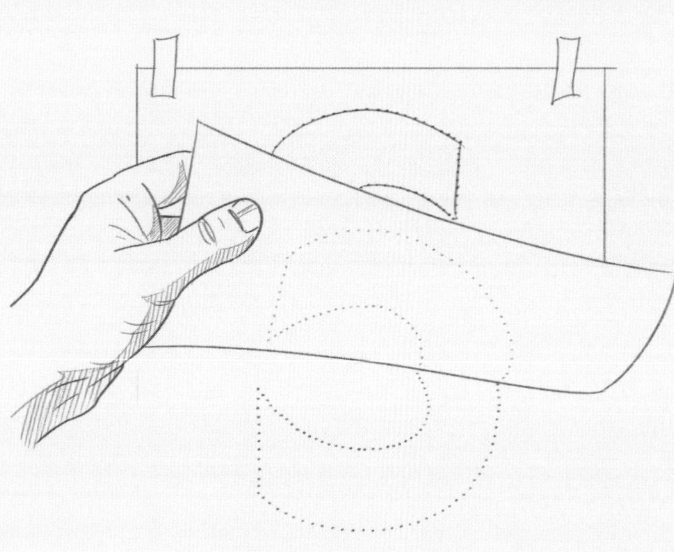

Check the transfer for any missing parts while the pattern is still taped up.

Before removing the pattern from the substrate, check that the design has been properly transferred: remove some tape from the bottom of the pattern and lift it up while keeping it in place with the tape at the top. Tidy up any missed portions before removing the tape at the top.

Use a spirit level one more time to confirm the alignment of the transferred design, then trust your eye to do the final check by standing back and taking a look. Now is the time to make any necessary corrections—do not wait until the sign is all painted!

If you are working on a larger piece, you may need to spread the design over multiple paper patterns. In this case, you will need to include registration marks on each sheet that allow them to be accurately lined up with each other. The sheets should overlap by 2–3in (5–7cm). When aligning the patterns on a substrate, start with the one in the middle of the design, then work outwards from there.

Pressure Transfer

Pressure transfer can be used on relatively smooth substrates when only one transfer of a design is required. Powdered material can be added to the back of an existing design drawing on paper, or transfer paper (e.g. carbon or graphite paper) can be inserted between the drawing and the substrate. Applying pressure to the lines of the design transfers the material on the back of the drawing, or in the transfer paper, to the substrate.

Carbon or graphite paper, or a product such as Saral Transfer Paper, can be used for pressure transfer. You can also create your own transfer paper by chalking the back of a piece of kraft or tracing paper, or coating it with pounce powder, shaking or blowing off any excess. You can also use other materials to coat the back of the paper: pastels, or even grease pencils or regular soft graphite pencils for smaller pieces. When working on lighter substrates, use a dark pounce powder or charcoal as the transfer material.

Your choice of transfer material (pounce powder, chalk, charcoal, etc.) can also be applied to the back of an existing drawing for direct transfer. Creating a bespoke transfer paper instead of using a direct transfer will keep your original drawings relatively clean and free of dust for storage and future use.

Pressure transfer is a good method when you only need to transfer a design once. When multiple copies of a design need to be painted, however, it is worth investing the time to create a pounce pattern from your drawing.

Pressure-Transferring a Design

Position and tape the drawing as required on the substrate. If you are working directly from the drawing, you can also tape the bottom of the drawing at this stage. If you are working with transfer paper, position the paper between the drawing and the substrate and tape it in place, then tape the drawing over the top.

With everything in place, trace over all the key lines of the design with a ballpoint pen, hard pencil, or similarly firm pointed tool (e.g. the handle of a paint brush). The pressure will transfer the design onto the substrate.

Sometimes your drawing will be larger than your transfer paper. You have a number of options: chalking the back of the drawing directly, moving one piece of transfer paper from section to section, or taping a number of pieces of transfer paper together to make one big piece.

As with pouncing, it is important to check that all parts of the design have been successfully transferred to the substrate by removing some tape from the bottom of the drawing and lifting it while leaving the tape along the top in place. If you are using pounce powder, chalk, or charcoal, blow or dust off any excess using a soft brush before doing any final alignment checks and then painting.

Projecting

For the majority of my larger signs, and especially murals, I use a projector for the initial setting out. Success depends on there not being any other bright light sources nearby, so it is best done after sunset, or indoors with the lights off. (It is possible to cover or shield problematic light sources with aluminum foil, but never use anything flammable.)

Mike's Tip

When you prepare the design, either as a transparency or a digital file, it's useful to mark it with some evenly spaced (e.g. 1–4ft or 30–120cm) horizontal lines to scale. I then mark lines with the corresponding spacing on the wall to help with lining up and scaling the design while projecting.

Mike's Tip

Always carry spare bulbs for your projector, as the bulb will always fail when you have the least time available. They aren't sold in general stores, so it's best to maintain a small stash of this specialist item.

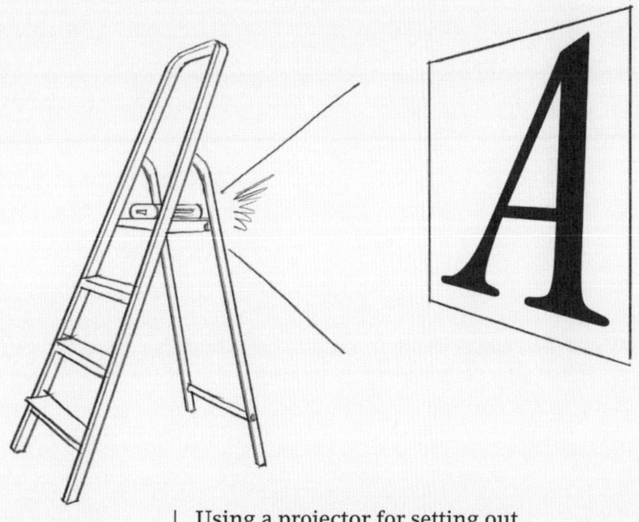

| Using a projector for setting out.

I normally use a traditional overhead projector with printed transparencies, but it is now easy to get good-quality portable electronic projectors for use with digital files. Make sure you can obtain a suitable stable position at the right distance from the wall or substrate you will be working on, and that you have access to a power source.

Once you have aligned the projected design correctly on the wall or substrate, mark up the key outlines directly on the substrate with a piece of chalk or charcoal. A marker pen is an alternative, but some colors can bleed through your eventual paintwork. If you are working indoors, mark out a little bit of the design then turn the lights on to double-check that you can see the transferred design clearly.

Vinyl Mask

Another common technique for transferring designs is to use a vinyl mask. This involves masking the substrate, leaving the areas to be painted exposed, as opposed to the usual use of decals to adhere the lettering itself. I use vinyl masks when a client requires a very precise reproduction of a logo, for repetitive work, or where there is a requirement that no brush strokes are visible. It is also one way of creating nice even color blends or chrome effects on your lettering.

If you are going to work with a vinyl mask, it is easiest to do so using a plotter. If you do not have a plotter, you can get a mask cut at a shop, or you can transfer the design to vinyl yourself using one of the previous transfer techniques. (Do not forget to create the design in reverse if it is for the inside of a window.) You can then use a scalpel to carefully cut through the vinyl, but not the wax backing paper. It can take a few test cuts to determine the correct pressure for the scalpel, so practice on a piece of scrap vinyl before starting. Use medium-tack vinyl, which won't allow paint to bleed underneath, but will be easier to remove than high-tack (high-tack is best for long-term applications).

Once the design is cut into the vinyl, manually or using a plotter, follow these steps to complete the masking process:

1. Weed out (remove) the letters and other areas (e.g. decorative elements, lines, etc.) from the vinyl. Usually when making a decal you weed out everything *except* the letters, but for masking you are working in the negative.

2. Cover the (letter-free) mask with application tape and use a squeegee to ensure good adhesion of the tape to the vinyl.

Cut through the vinyl, stopping before the wax backing paper.

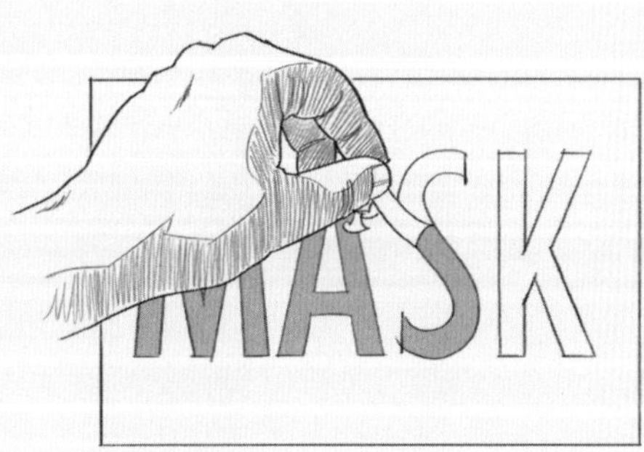

Weed the letters from the vinyl.

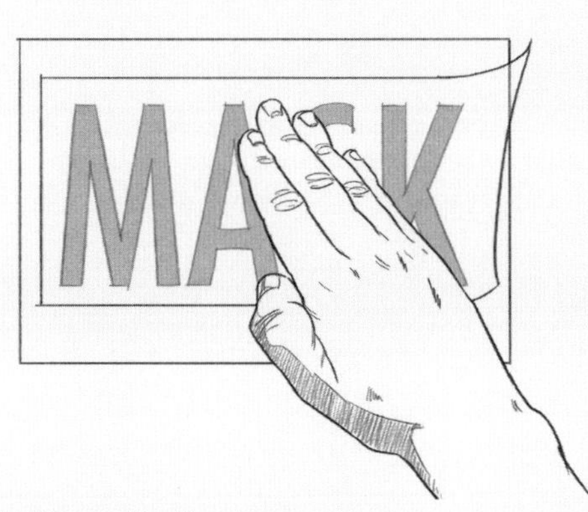

| Apply the application tape.

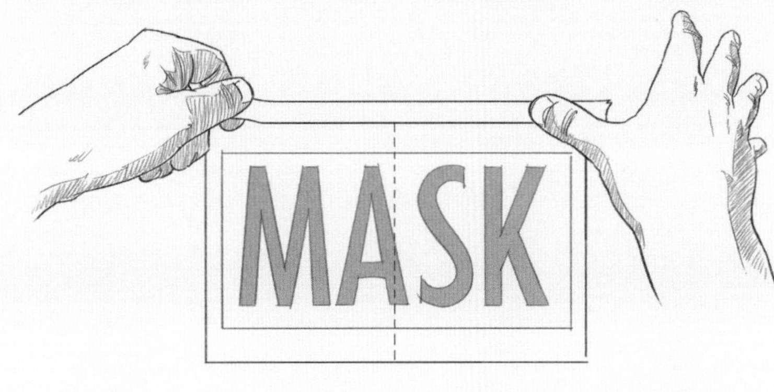

| Position the mask on the substrate.

3. Clean any dust and grease from the substrate to ensure proper adhesion of the mask.

4. Mark your horizontal baseline and a vertical center line on the application tape, and mark corresponding lines with a grease pencil on the substrate to be masked.

5. Use masking tape to fix the top edge of the mask in position.

6. Carefully peel off the wax backing paper in a downward direction, allowing the mask to stick to the substrate. (An alternative is to peel off the backing paper on a flat surface and then position and stick at the same time, but it is safer to position first.)

7. Pull a squeegee down hard on the mask, from the center out, to stick it to the substrate, then remove the application tape using the same technique used to remove the backing paper. If any of the mask starts coming up as you are removing the application tape, place it back down and use the squeegee again to make sure it is properly adhered before continuing to peel back the tape.

With your mask in place, you are ready to paint the lettering. This can be done with a brush or roller, or you can spray with a flat, blended, or other finish as required by your client. While the paint is still wet, carefully peel off the vinyl mask, ensuring that it does not fall back into the paint. Use a scalpel to remove any lone pieces, such as the counters inside letters such as O.

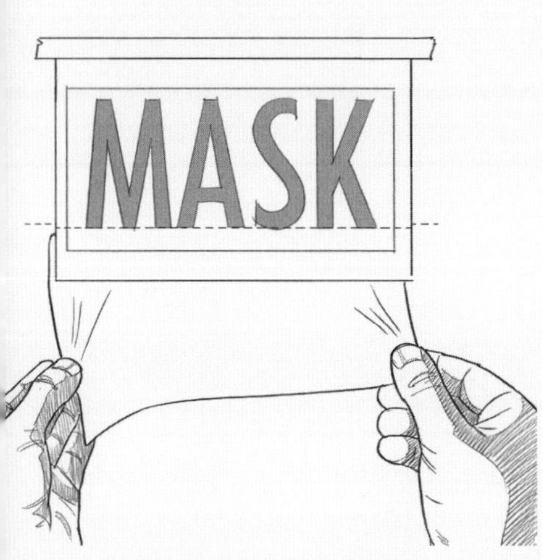

| Remove the wax backing paper.

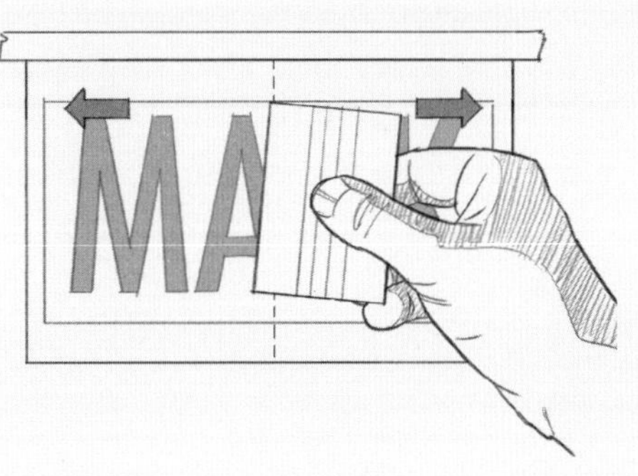

| Stick the mask down firmly with a squeegee.

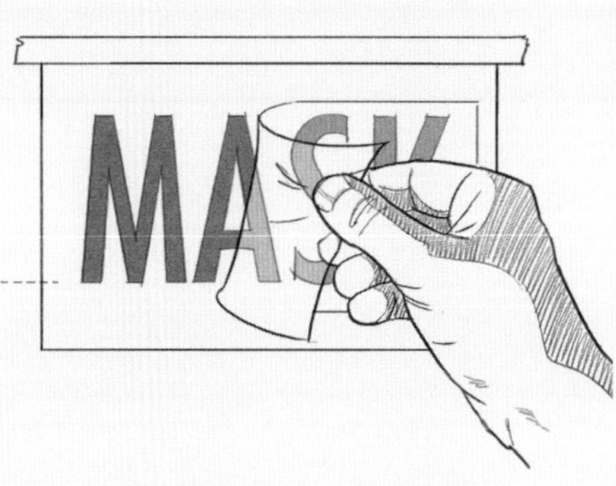

| Remove the application tape to leave the vinyl masking everything but the letters.

69

Mike's Tip

If you are peeling off long lengths of tape (e.g. when using it for lining), roll it around an old drink can or tin as you go to prevent mess and reduce the risk of anything falling back onto the sign.

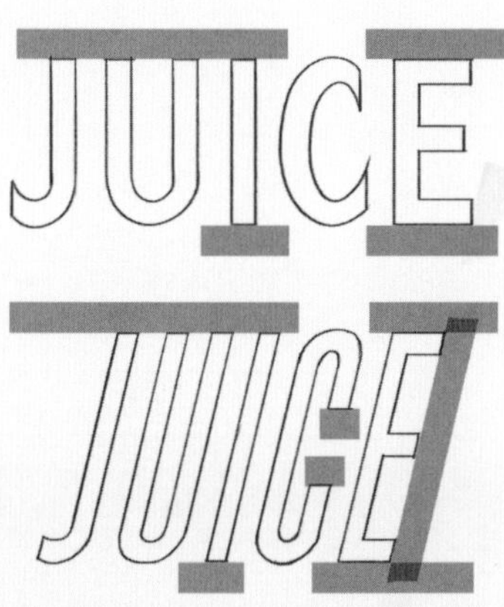

Use tape to ensure sharp edges and corners on block and slanted block lettering.

Using Tape

My personal approach to sign painting is to get good brush control and speed through practice and complete all my lettering without the help of tape. However, tape can be useful to speed up your work as it reduces the need for care when turning into corners in block lettering, or easing the brush out into a sharp pointed serif in Roman.

I do use tape when working on slanting block letters (especially at smaller sizes), where it helps with the sharper corners, and for thin lines and borders (using parallel lines of tape). To use tape, follow these steps:

1. Place low-tack vinyl lining tape, cut to a suitable size, along the top and bottom of your lines of lettering, leaving spaces at the tops and bottoms of curved letters (C, G, J, O, Q, S, and U in most alphabets), which will extend slightly above and below the markup lines. (Some sign painters will also tape off straight vertical lines such as the ends of the E, but if you do this, I recommend using a vinyl mask for your lettering instead, given the time it takes to apply this much tape.)

2. Paint the letters, taking care to start and finish your strokes *on* the tape to get the sharp edge required.

3. Gently peel the tape off, pulling it toward the lettering as you go. This is best done before the paint has completely cured to avoid pulling paint/letters off with the tape.

Copying

If you are asked to make a copy of an existing sign, or to redo work that already exists at the size required, then making a tracing and using this as the basis for a pounce pattern is the best way to go. Regular (e.g. 60–90gsm) tracing paper and a soft, well-sharpened graphite pencil works just fine. If you do not have tracing paper to hand, tape a piece of regular copier paper to the existing sign and wipe it over with a rag made damp with mineral spirits, turpentine, or kerosene. Once the solvent has evaporated, you will be left with a piece of improvised tracing paper ready for copying the design.

Direct Markup

Direct markup of a substrate involves setting out a sign without any reference, or scaling up a smaller drawn or printed reference. It is important to develop both these skills: they are especially useful when a client asks you to do extra, unplanned work while on-site, or when time does not allow for careful preparation of drawings and patterns.

Snapping a Chalk Line

At various stages in the process of marking up, you will need to "snap" a chalk line. This is an effective way of marking perfectly straight lines, especially those longer than a yardstick. The technique below is just one way of doing it, but there are other grips that can be used, so do experiment to find one that's comfortable for you.

1. Clearly mark the two points to be joined by the snapped line.

2. Pull out the length of chalk line required from the unit holding it, ensuring that it is filled with appropriately colored chalk powder that transfers onto the line as you pull. (An alternative is coating a length of nylon thread with chalk.) You will be using both hands: one to hold the line taut and the other to snap it. Which hand you use for which task is up to you; try it both ways to find your own preference.

3. With one hand, wind the line around your pinkie (little finger) and, with palm open (facing you), line it up with the first of two marks that you are joining with the final line. Turn your hand away from you, into the line, and then pinch the line nearby with thumb and index finger. Now take your other hand and pull the line tight while lining up this end with the other mark to be joined.

4. Finally, pull the line off the surface with your first hand, keeping the tension with the second hand, then release the tension to snap the line as it moves quickly onto the substrate, transferring the chalk as it does so.

If you need to mark out lines that are longer than your arm span, fix one end of the chalk line to a screw or other strong anchor. Otherwise, find a helper to hold the line while you pull and snap.

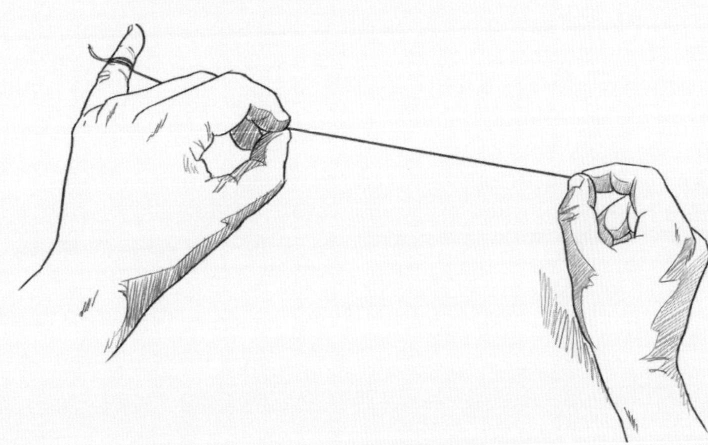

Chalk line positioned and ready to be snapped by releasing a line from the grip of left thumb and forefinger.

71

Mike's Tip

If you don't have a grease pencil to hand, the eraser on the end of a regular graphite pencil makes a workable substitute for marking up high-gloss substrates such as vehicles.

Marking Materials

Different marking-up materials are better suited to different substrates. This table summarizes these, and what you can use to correct mistakes and then remove markup lines once the sign is complete and all the paint has fully cured.

Substrate	Marking-Up Tool	Removal
Timber	Grease Pencil	Rag with warm water and mild detergent or soap
Aluminum		
Glass		
Vehicles		
Vinyl Banner		
Walls	Chalk or Charcoal	Rag and water
Paper/Card	Graphite Pencil	Eraser
Fabric	Chalk or Grease Pencil	Rag and cleanser*

* A cleanser such as Bon Ami can be used (see page 48).

Getting Started

An important first step in direct markup is to find the horizontal center of the sign and mark a vertical line from top to bottom. This is done by measuring from left to right along a horizontal determined by using a spirit level. Mark the halfway point and then draw the vertical line using a spirit level or a plumb line and yardstick. For larger signs, mark two points using the spirit level and then snap a chalk line to connect them (see page 71).

Next, mark a horizontal baseline at the bottom of the sign. Again, this can be done using a spirit level or, for larger signs, marking two points to position a chalk line for snapping. For wall signs, laser levels can be used effectively for marking out horizontal baselines and vertical center lines. They are not very expensive and can be a useful addition to your kit if you are doing lots of this type of work.

Mike's Tip

If you are setting out with a piece of chalk or charcoal, use the edge and gently turn the stick as you draw so that it is gradually being sharpened while you work. This will avoid wastage, and save you the time needed to frequently sharpen the stick with a blade.

72

Scaling Up

One of the most common forms of working directly is scaling up a smaller sketch or drawing. If the size of the sign is known, a sketch or drawing can be prepared with a simple scale. For measurements in the imperial system, a scale of 1:8 works well: this means 1½in on the drawing corresponds to 1ft on the sign, and ⅛in corresponds to 1in. If you are working in the metric system, a scale of 1:10 or 1:5 is perfect.

The drawing can then be "gridded up." Mark a vertical line (or fold in half) at the horizontal center of the drawing, and mark a horizontal line at the bottom. Continue marking vertical and horizontal lines until the drawing is sitting under a grid of squares. These squares should be sized according to your scale (e.g. 1½ x 1½in or 4 x 4cm) to simplify the transfer to the larger size. (If you are not working to a defined scale, then grid up using an even number of squares that can be matched easily on the larger sign: for example, a 4 x 8 grid of any size only involves bisecting lines without taking direct measurements.)

Mark a corresponding grid on the sign at the scaled-up size (e.g. squares of 1 x 1ft or 40 x 40cm). Sketch out the drawing square by square, using a ruler and your scale to check any key points as you go along. Step back occasionally to check the sign by eye, so that you can make any corrections sooner rather than later.

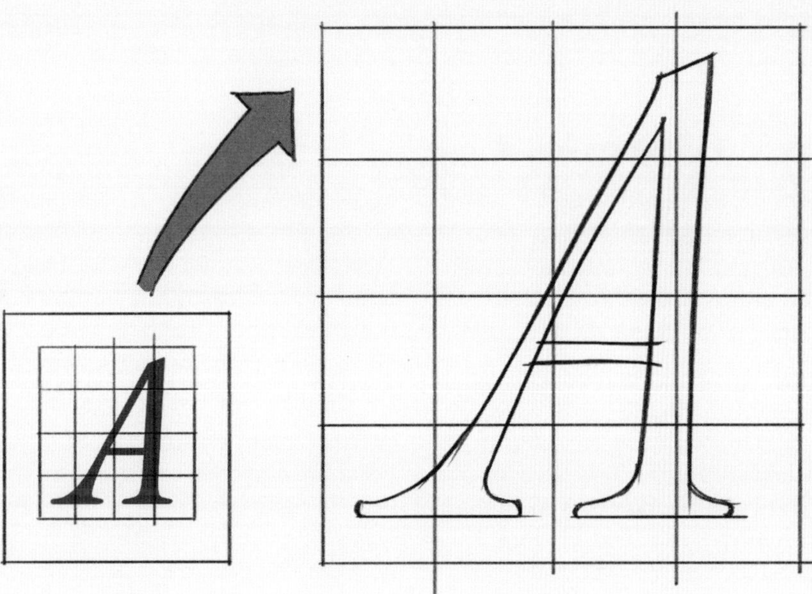

| Scaling up using a grid.

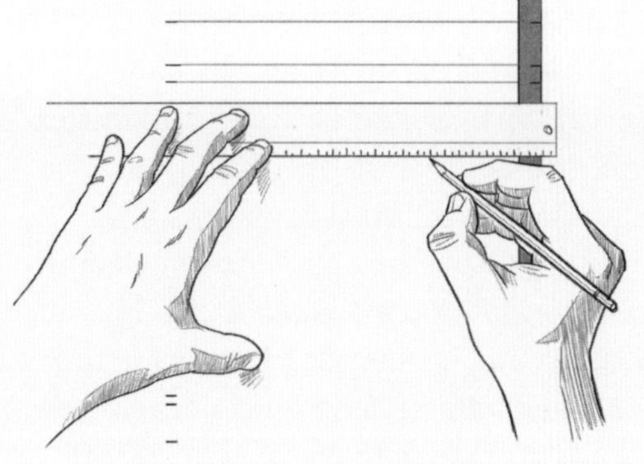

Mark positions of horizontal lines on the left side of the substrate while copying to the legend tape.

Legend positioned on the right side of the substrate for marking final horizontal lines.

Horizontal Lines

Using a thumbnail sketch, you can set out lines of lettering and how they will be spaced, allowing for some margin around the whole sign. Depending on the lettering style, you will have two or more horizontal lines per line of text. For lettering styles with shadows, include a "shadow line" underneath the baseline to show how far down the shadows will come.

If I am sketching out a job, I usually work from the center out, starting with a very rough positioning of the letters. Once I am satisfied that they will fit on the line as I want them, I will begin to thicken them up. Another way to work is to set out the letters aligned to the left and then determine the center point for each line. Use these points to help you set out the lines from the center on the final sign.

Once you have decided on the heights and positioning of the lines, mark them up on your substrate. Fix a vertical length of low-tack vinyl or masking tape to the left of the sign, checking it with a spirit level, and mark the point where it intersects with the baseline (bottom) of the sign. Then, using your scale, draw a series of marks for the tops and bottoms of lines of lettering, ensuring that they are also marked on the substrate as you go. This tape is now your master "legend" or guide, sometimes called a "tell-all tape."

The tape can then be removed and stuck to the right side of the sign, aligning it with the baseline of the sign and using a spirit level to check that it is straight. You can then join the marks on the left side with the corresponding

Ruler Pull Method

If you're working at an easel, or anywhere with a solid ledge under the sign, you can get away with just marking the position of the lines on the left side and using the ruler pull method.

Use one hand to set a pencil or other marking tool firmly on the top of a mahl stick or yardstick. With the other hand, grip the bottom of the stick so that it is held vertically and the marking tool is aligned with one of your marks. Hook the index finger of your lower hand under the ledge and, with one firm

and swift movement of your whole body, pull the stick and marking tool across the substrate to create a horizontal line. Right-handers will likely find it easiest to pull from left to right, and vice versa for left-handers.

When I attended sign school, we spent the whole first week practicing this method. No paint, no lettering, just pulling lines. I hated it at the time, but it's a skill that I use every day in my sign work.

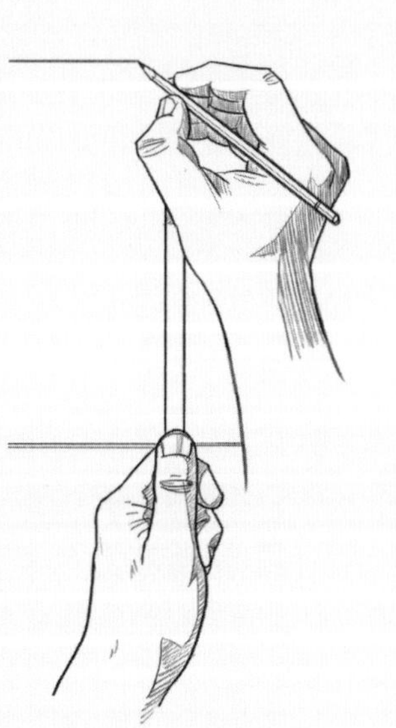

Mike's Tip

If you want to use thumbtacks to hold a guide string without damaging the substrate, build up a stack of small pieces of masking tape. The tape stack will hold the pin, and can be removed without damage afterwards.

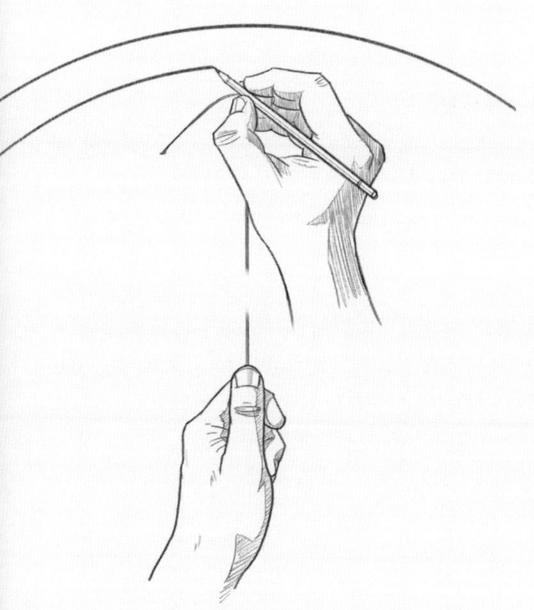

Drawing the baseline for lettering on an arc.

marks on the legend (right side), to create a set of perfectly horizontal lines. Use these lines to sketch out the lines of lettering with reference to your thumbnail sketch.

Arcs

Lettering on an arc will usually have its highest point horizontally centered. To mark this, tie your marking-up tool to one end of a piece of string, then fix the other end at a point much lower down on the horizontal center line. This can be done with tape or a thumbtack (drawing pin), or by holding the string with your thumb. Pull the string taut and mark the top of the arc by moving your tool from one side to the other. Next, keeping the fixed point of the string in place, shorten the length to draw the bottom line of the arc. This can also be done with a large pair of compasses, keeping the point or sucker fixed and shortening the span for the lower line.

Another way of marking out an arc is to use a bendy ruler, fixing one end in place and flexing it until you have the shape of curve that you want. Mark this up and then repeat lower down with more bend for your bottom line.

I usually draw my letters so that they follow the arc, which leads to the overall shapes of the letters being slightly wedged (i.e. thinner at the bottom than they are at the top). Other sign painters will have their letters standing upright on the lower line of the arc. Neither of these styles is right or wrong—it is a matter of personal preference.

However you have marked up your sign—by transfer or by direct markup—you are now ready to paint, working with your brushes to produce the lettering and other designs that you have created.

Mike's Tip

If you're going to be painting any shadows on your lettering, it's important to allow for this in your layout, which should have enough space between letters for the shadows. The lines of letters should also be aligned slightly left or right to allow for the shadow that will appear on one side and not the other, depending on which side of your letters you choose to shadow.

Painting

Painting lettering, for me, is the most fun you can have with your clothes on. It might even be the most fun you can have, period.

The process of learning to paint lettering is time-consuming, but progress can be made quickly with regular practice and the right attitude. Do not be deterred if everything is not perfect straight away. Dedication and discipline will win in the end.

Most of the instructions that follow are for working with a chisel-edge writer, as this is the main type of brush that you will use for most lettering work. The principles are more or less the same for working with flats, and notes on other brushes are included where relevant.

Posture & Positioning

Are You Sitting Comfortably?

As a sign painter you will often have to find ways to letter in all sorts of awkward positions but, where possible, you should be sitting or standing comfortably. Your work will be improved greatly if it is done from a position of comfort and relaxation. My personal preference is to set things out while standing and then to paint sitting down. In general, you want to be working at eye level, with space to move your arms freely.

With any job, you have two choices to help you find a more comfortable position: move the object being painted or move yourself. Easels and skids can be adjusted for many types of shop work. Vehicles can be jacked up or hoisted for easier access, and a low-down chair can be used when lettering the lower portions. A standard sign-painting kit box can be used as a stool; they offer three different working heights when placed flat or on either side. For shopfronts, murals, and other exterior work, use ladders, towers, and scaffolds to provide the best working height(s) across the piece.

In general, you want to maintain a relaxed composure as you go about your work, avoiding tension building up in the hands, arms, neck, and shoulders. Try to be conscious of these parts of your body in particular, and whenever you feel tension building, focus on relaxing before continuing to paint. Regular rests and stretching will also help to keep your body supple and in the best shape for the job.

Brush Grip & Angle

Hold the brush in your preferred hand using the same grip that you would for a pen, between thumb, index, and middle finger. The brush should, however, be held much further back than a pen: 1–1½in (25–40mm) from the join of the ferrule to the heel of the hairs usually works well, but experiment to find where you feel most comfortable and have most control.

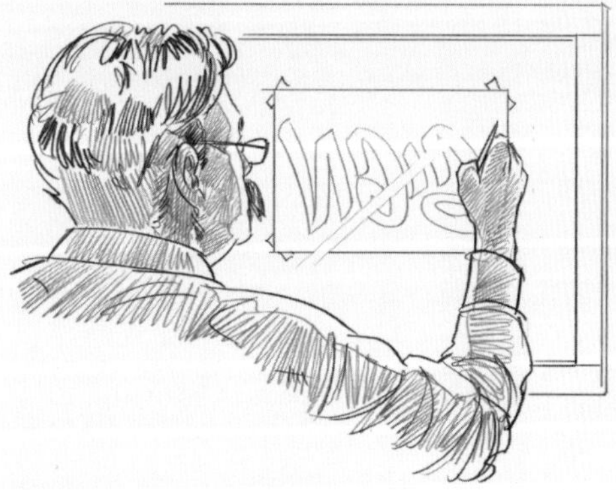

Mike's Tip

It's especially important to be working at eye level when using a pattern for painting on the reverse of glass. This ensures that your eye, the glass, and the pattern are aligned, reducing distortions created when viewing the pattern through the thickness of the glass.

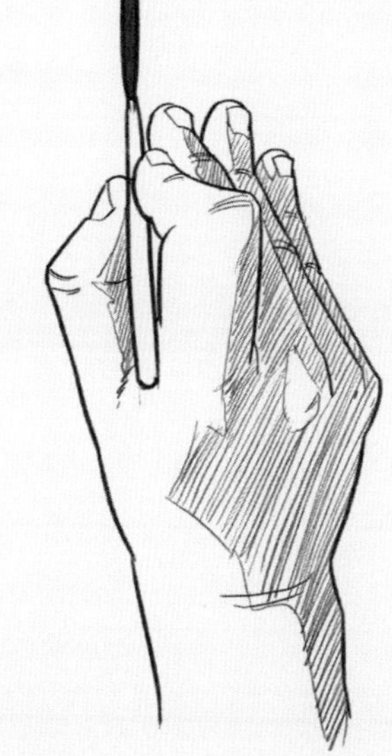

Grips for lettering and
lining brushes.

When you are starting out, it can be useful to place a piece of tape at this point on the handle to stop you moving your grip down closer to the hairs.

For the majority of lettering work, you should be holding the brush close to perpendicular (at a 90-degree angle) to the substrate. This will give you the best position to control the brush as you form your strokes, moving between different levels of pressure, angle, and rotation. It may not feel natural at first, mainly due to past experience working with pens and pencils, so observe and correct yourself as you practice. It is also a good idea to have someone experienced observe you, as they may be able to suggest small adjustments that can result in big improvements to your work.

Lining brushes are usually held between thumb and index finger only, close to the join of the ferrule and filling. The middle finger can then be used to guide the direction of the brush by following the line of a fixed object (e.g. a mahl stick) or the edge of the sign for a border.

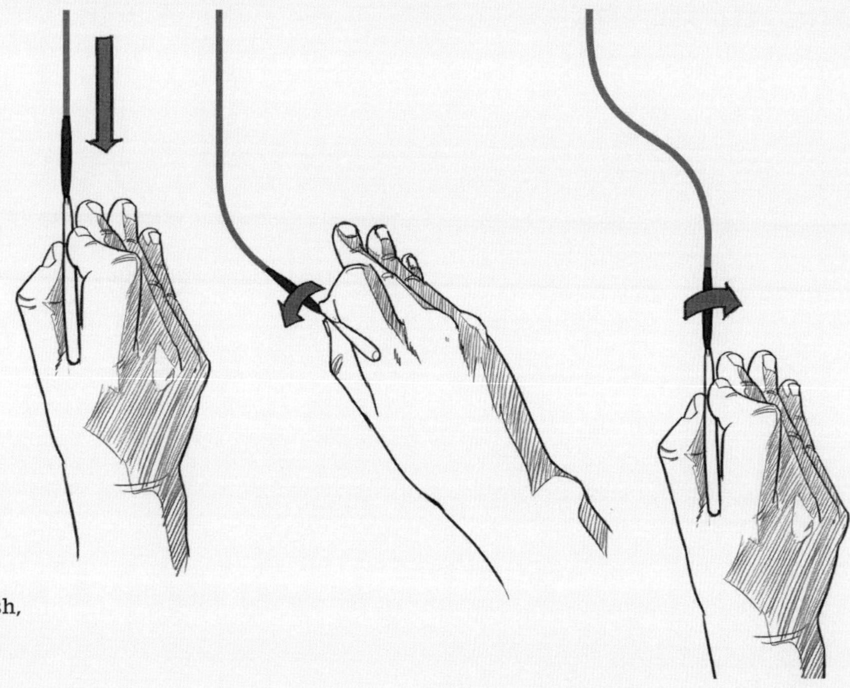

Pulling a line with a lining brush,
using subtle rotations to move
through curves.

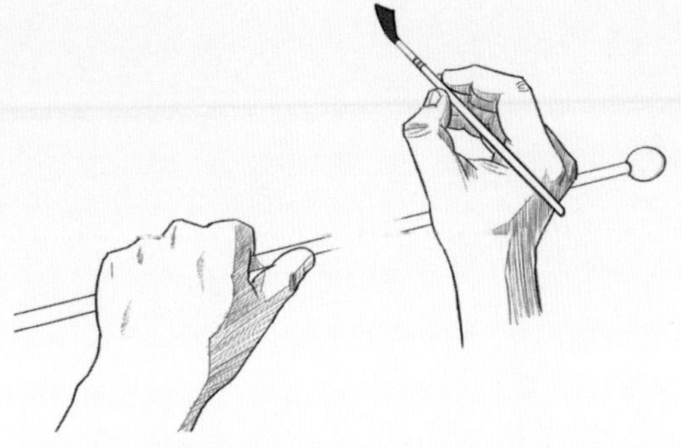

Two hands positioned for lettering work using a mahl stick.

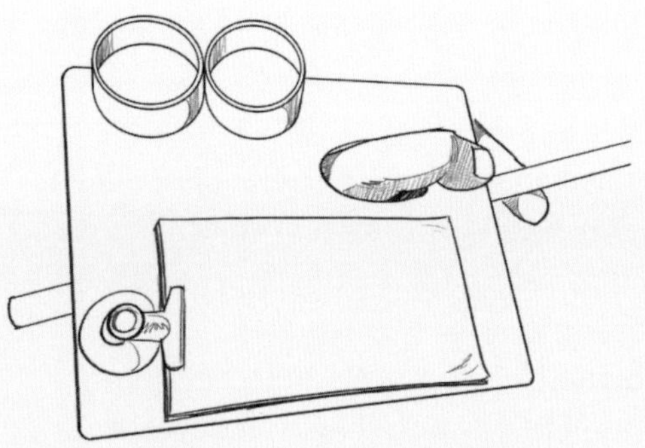

Working with mahl stick, palette, and dippers.

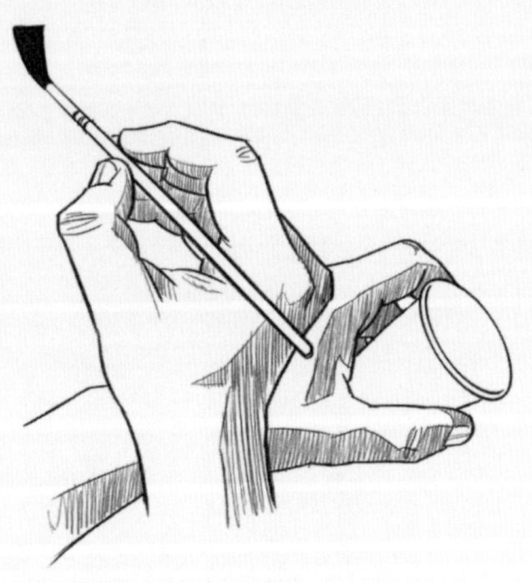

Working hand over hand while holding a paint cup.

Rests

There are three main ways to steady your hand as you paint, and to avoid smudging paint that you have already laid down: using a mahl stick, working hand over hand, or with pinkie down (my personal preference). Practice with all of these methods until you are comfortable with each to find which one works best for you.

Mahl Stick

The mahl stick should be held in your weaker hand at a point that provides a comfortable distance between this hand and your other, which will have the lower part of the palm resting near the top of the stick while painting. The ball of the stick is fixed in position while working; only move it when required to adjust the working position of your brush hand. Take care to avoid picking up paint on the ball of the stick and accidentally transferring it to other parts of the sign.

While it will feel very odd to begin with, your weaker hand also needs to hold your paint cup and/or palette. It is a lot to manage, but over time you will gain the control required to keep the mahl stick stable, while holding the palette at one end and working with the brush at the other.

Hand Over Hand

A common alternative to the mahl stick is working hand over hand, which simply involves resting your brush hand on top of your weaker hand. The weaker hand remains in contact with the substrate as you work, helping to keep a good distance between your brush hand and the substrate. It is important to keep the supporting hand clean and free from paint, especially given that it is holding your paint cup, and postcard palette if you are using one.

Mike's Tip

When you're getting started, I recommend thinning the paint slightly more than you might usually do, especially if you're practicing on paper, which is slightly absorbent. Thinning the paint almost to the point where it runs when laid down on a vertical surface will help you develop your brush control and technique.

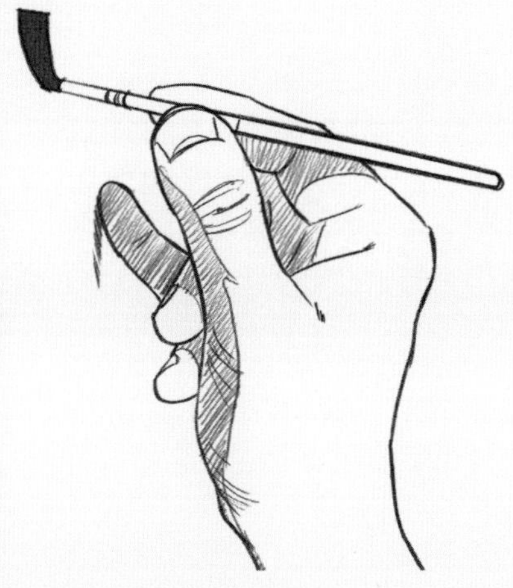

Working pinkie down.

Mike's Tip

Once you're in the process of lettering, you can use (wet) strokes that have already been laid down to palette your brush. This is especially useful when you're completing finishing strokes (e.g. top and bottom of the block letter I), where you want less paint on the brush and an extremely sharp chisel.

(left) Paletting a chisel-edge writer on a piece of glossy card. (right) Paletting a chisel-edge writer on the rim of a paint cup.

Pinkie Down

This technique involves placing the little finger (pinkie) tip down on the substrate to provide the necessary elevation for the brush as it works on the lettering. You can then hold the paint cup and/or palette in your weaker hand.

Paletting

Before applying paint to the substrate, you need to prepare the brush, loading it with paint and shaping the hairs, a process called paletting. With a chisel-edge writer, you want to have a very sharp, flat edge at the tip of the filling: I call this the "whale tail" because of the shape formed by paletting the brush.

First you need to load the brush with paint. If the paint is already thinned in the cup, dip the brush in until the paint reaches the ferrule and covers all of the filling. If you are working with dippers, get some thinner on your brush before dipping it into the paint.

When using a palette or glossy postcard, press the filling against the flat surface so that the hairs are bent at the heel, at close to a 90-degree angle to the ferrule. Pull the brush toward you so that the hairs flatten as you move the brush. Turn the brush over (180 degrees) to even out the chisel, and maybe wiggle it a little as you move it across the palette.

If you are working directly out of the cup, as I do, then the technique is slightly different. To achieve the whale tail, press the heel of the brush against the rim of the cup, forcing the hairs in the filling to splay. Pull the filling down a little, about halfway along the length of the hairs, and then repeat after turning the brush over (180 degrees) to flatten out the chisel. Try to avoid wiping all the paint back into the cup, so that your brush is well loaded for painting.

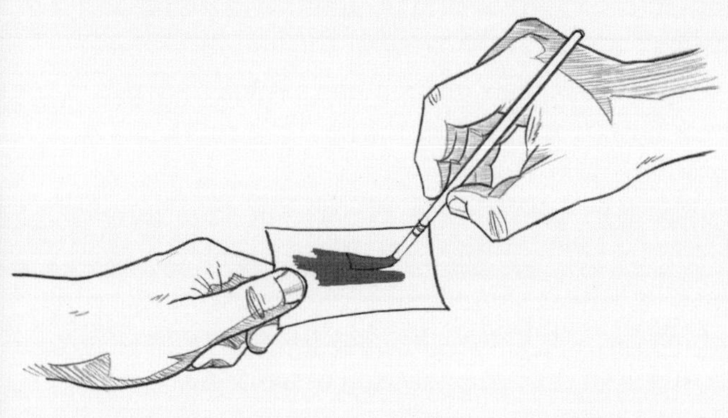

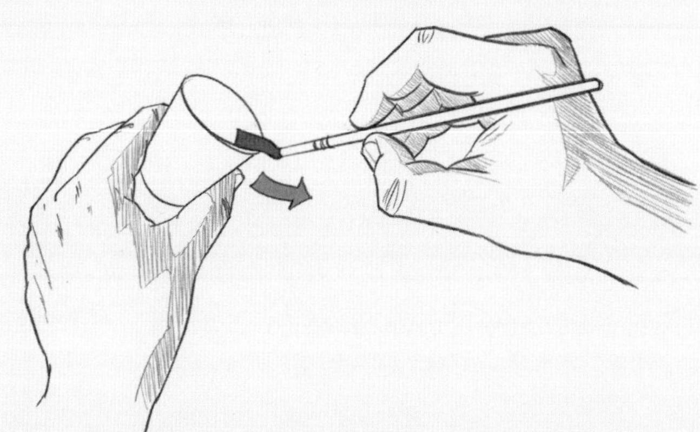

Mike's Tip

It's important to give yourself enough space to move through the entire length of a brush stroke while keeping your hand and brush position comfortable and consistent. For shorter strokes the motion can come from the wrist, but for longer strokes you will need to move your rest (mahl stick, supporting hand, or pinkie) in line with the brush stroke. Maintain awareness of both the location of the brush and the rest to avoid smudging layout lines or going into wet paint.

For larger curves, you can pivot the mahl stick around the fixed end.

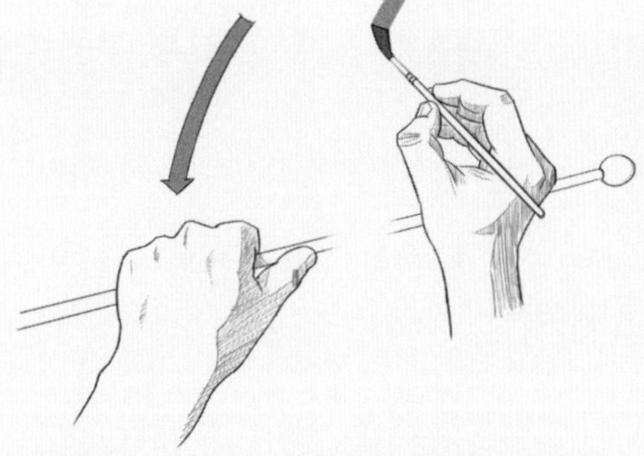

For very long strokes, you can use a mahl stick to guide your hand as you pull through the full-length stroke.

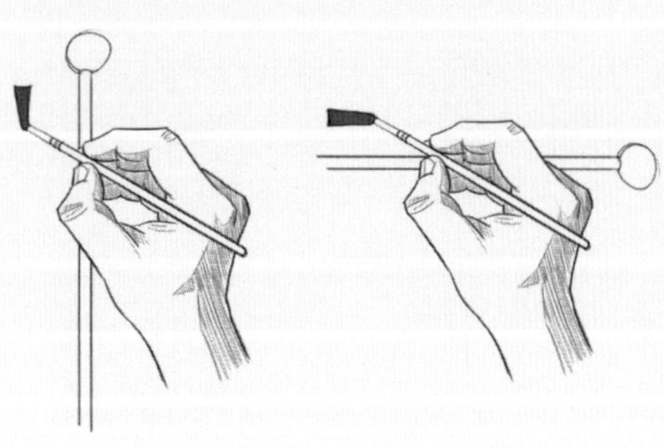

(opposite) Stroke order for Block and Thick 'n' Thin, from light (first) to dark (last).

Brush Strokes

Most of the letter shapes you need to create in sign lettering can be formed from a small number of basic strokes. These vary for different styles of lettering, and I recommend studying alphabets to extract the key strokes used to create them, including many of those at the back of this book. For this section I am going to focus on the core alphabets that I teach in my workshops, which will give you a good starting point and enough variety for most sign work. These are block, thick 'n' thin, casual, and script.

When starting out in sign lettering, it is vital to dedicate time to practicing the families of strokes for different alphabets. This is repetitive work, but it helps to build the muscle memory that will then give you the confidence and control you need for lettering. Put on the radio, or your favorite playlist, and lose yourself in the focus of practice. Like me, lots of fellow sign painters and students I have taught find this a relaxing and meditative experience, which then translates to relaxed strokes for lettering signs in the future.

Block & Thick 'n' Thin

Block (sometimes called gothic, sans serif, and Egyptian) is the bedrock of sign painting, and can be found on everything from plain NO PARKING signs, all the way up to highly decorated shopfronts. I tend to work with uppercase block lettering where the letter heights are roughly five times the stroke width, but there is lots of variation possible within the basic structure of the block alphabet. Using upper case only has the benefit of keeping line heights even, and avoiding possible layout pitfalls that can come with overlapping ascenders and descenders in lower case.

Thick 'n' thin alphabets are a variant of block in which the stroke widths have contrast between them. As a rule of thumb, vertical and downward diagonal strokes (sloping downward from left to right) are thick, while horizontal and upward diagonal strokes (sloping upward from left to right) are thin. The exception is the Z, which has a thick upward diagonal. Curves shift from thick to thin as they rotate from vertical to horizontal, and vice versa.

When working on thick 'n' thin, you will need to select a brush based on the width of the thin strokes, which means you will be working with a smaller size than you would use for a comparable block alphabet. Practice the strokes in both thick and thin forms so that you get used to working with different-sized brushes.

BLOCK

ADEFGHIJ
MNPQRST
UVWXY&Z

THICK&THIN

ABCDEFGH
IJKLMNOP
QRSTUVW
XY&&&Z!?

Mike's Tip

When working with marked-out lettering or a transferred design, try to keep your strokes just inside the markup lines. This helps avoid accidentally fattening up the letters by going outside of these lines, and gives you space to deliberately thicken any strokes as required when looking at the whole sign.

Six basic strokes are used to make up the letters in these alphabets: vertical; horizontal; two diagonals, sloping upward and downward; and two curves, left and right. These can be formed as single strokes or built up with multiple strokes. I suggest starting with the built-up method, which is easier for beginners, before attempting single strokes.

When building up the strokes, you want to be working with a brush that is just over half the stroke width of your planned letters when formed into a chisel. A #6 brush works for letters that are ½–¾in (12–20mm) wide, although you can go larger than this too. For single-stroke work, the width of the chisel should be the same as the stroke width, so a #6 would work for letters a little under ½in (10mm) wide.

Vertical Stroke

Start by placing the chisel of the brush almost square with the top of the stroke and aligned with the left side. Lay the hairs down until roughly half their length is in contact with the substrate and begin to pull the brush down, keeping the left of the chisel in line with the left side of the stroke.

As you reach the bottom, "tip out" the brush by simultaneously rotating it almost 90 degrees to the left (counterclockwise) between your thumb and fingers and pulling it away from the surface. This will cause the hairs to twist slightly, and the end of the stroke will take on a tapered appearance, with a sharp corner where the brush ultimately has just one hair in contact with the substrate.

I like to think of this whole motion as a broom (the brush) pushing dust (the paint) down and out of the inside of the stroke.

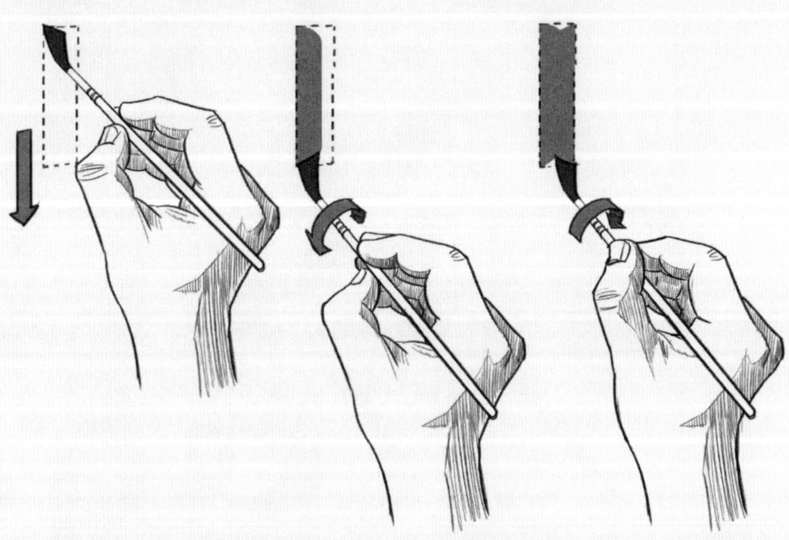

Building up a vertical stroke with a chisel-edge writer.

Mike's Tip

If you make a big mistake while painting, you can wipe off and paint again. If you've made a small mistake, you can push the paint back into the letter with a clean rag dampened with thinner.

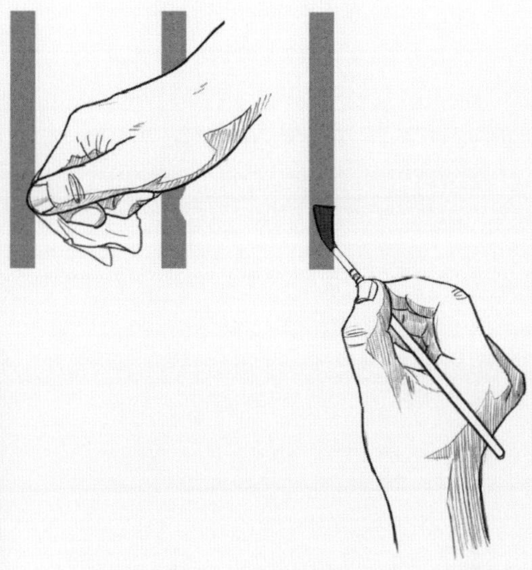

Palette your brush again and repeat the same motion, but this time aligning to the right of the stroke and overlapping in the middle as you come down. Tip out to the right, again tapering the stroke to a point in that corner.

Finish the stroke by filling in the small gaps at the top and bottom. Use half-moon shapes, working with less paint on the brush (you can palette inside the stroke to assist with this) and reducing the length of the hairs that come into contact with the substrate to about 25–30 percent from the tip.

To create the vertical as a single stroke, chisel the brush well and place it in line with the horizontal top of the stroke. Place the hairs down until half their length is in contact with the substrate and pull down in a smooth motion, keeping the chisel width consistent with the stroke width. As you reach the bottom of the stroke, pull the brush off the substrate until just the tips of the hairs forming the chisel are in contact at almost a 90-degree angle.

Once you have good control of the single-stroke technique, you may need to do nothing further. However, if greater precision is required, especially in the corners, then finishing strokes top and bottom can be used to square them off.

Horizontal Stroke

The technique for the horizontal stroke is exactly the same as for the vertical, just with everything rotated 90 degrees. Start with the chisel aligned almost vertically, and then tip out with it close to horizontal. The one-stroke horizontal is a single movement with the chisel held constantly at a vertical angle.

When practicing, make your horizontal strokes shorter than your vertical strokes. There are lots of letters with long vertical strokes, but none with long horizontal strokes.

Diagonal Strokes

Again, these are just variants on the vertical stroke, but take care at the start and end of the stroke to ensure that the smaller internal angle is as sharp as possible. The same applies to the finishing strokes, top and bottom, which consist of a slightly flattened half-moon shape to keep the corners sharp. When using a single stroke, the brush needs to be well chiselled and held at a constant horizontal angle as the stroke is pulled diagonally down, whether moving from left to right or from right to left.

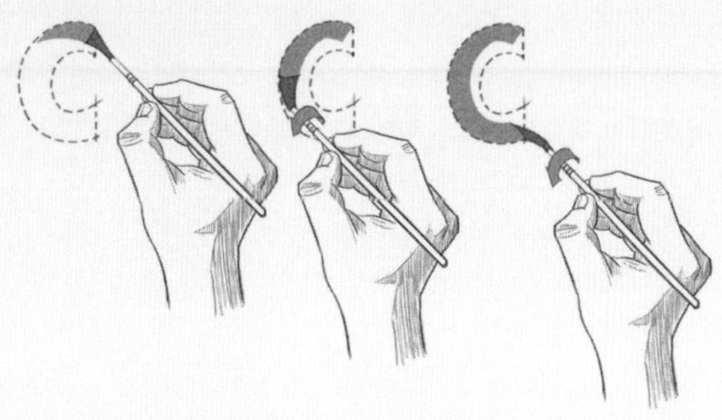

| Strokes for building up a block C.

Mike's Tip

As a general rule, you are aiming for efficiency in your lettering. This means painting each letter with the minimum number of strokes required, which will help to make your sign-painting work commercially viable. However, don't forget that "if it looks right, it is right." The opposite is also true, and you should use additional strokes where required to build the letters up until they look right.

Curved Strokes

Curved strokes require a controlled, steady rotation of the brush while moving around the stroke. This is done by manipulating the handle with the grip of thumb, index finger, and middle finger. It is important to maintain a relaxed grip, not too firm, so that the brush moves easily when rotating.

For the left-hand curve (like a C), start with the chisel almost vertical, slightly sloping down from left to right along the line of the chisel so that the top left of the chisel is just inside the top right of the curve. Place the hairs down until about half their length is in contact with the substrate and begin to pull the brush anticlockwise around the curve, keeping in line with the outside (longer) edge. As you move around the curve, keep the angle between the chisel and the edge of the curve at a constant 90 degrees. This is where the rotation using your thumb and fingers comes in.

If you have enough paint, the brush can be pulled all the way around to the finishing point, where you tip out inside the curve. Generally, I only go to just after halfway round a curve before loading and paletting again to start another stroke just inside where I finished the first one, and continuing this round before tipping out.

If you're forming a letter O, for example, you would then make the opposite motion, starting inside the top of the first stroke and moving around the outside of the letter in a clockwise direction before joining with the bottom of the first stroke. You can then repeat both strokes to paint up to the inside edge of the letter.

For a letter C, I use two shorter strokes that go from left to right at the top and bottom in order to tip out neatly into the corners of the terminals. The top one can be painted before or after the longest stroke according to your preference, with the bottom one coming last. Repeat for the inside of the curve and then the terminals can be tidied up with two little half-moons at top and bottom. As with the straight strokes, these should be done with less paint and less pressure, using a well-paletted brush.

When producing curves with a single stroke it is important to maintain a constant stroke width as you rotate the brush. Chisel the brush well, lay it down, and pull around the full length of the curve. Rotate the brush between your thumb and fingers to keep the chisel at a consistent 90 degrees to the edges of the curve. If you are painting an O, tip out into the inside of the letter width before painting the opposite side. For a C, aim to end the stroke with all the hairs on their tips to give a clean, square terminal.

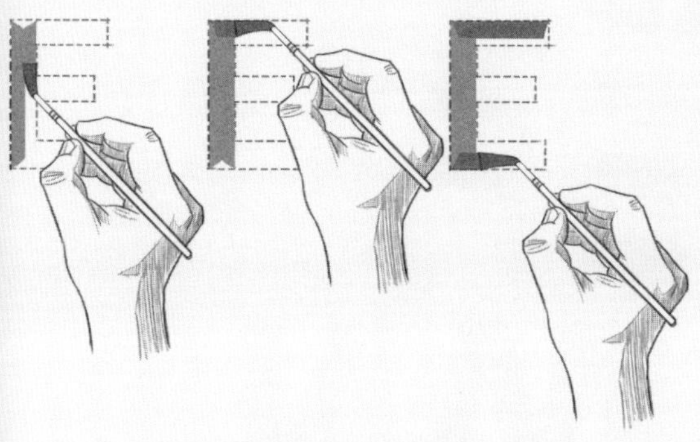

Using the top and bottom horizontal strokes to finish the vertical stroke of a block E.

Combining Strokes

When you are painting a letter E, for example, there is no need to finish the top and bottom of the vertical stroke. Instead, use the start of the top horizontal stroke to sharpen up the top left corner, and the bottom horizontal stroke to do the same at the bottom left. You then only need to use the half-moons to square off the terminals of the three horizontal strokes.

Casual

Casual (also known as flash, slash, and slapdash) is a family of one-stroke alphabets that are loose, informal, and quick to paint. Most sign painters will develop their own personal style by varying different elements of the letters. Do not be fooled by this alphabet's apparent simplicity: it takes a lot of practice to get a consistent-looking casual.

As with the block alphabet, there are a small number of basic strokes that you can build up into whole letters. These are executed with one movement of the brush in a quick (but not hasty) and confident way. It is very important to keep your paint well thinned, and your brush well loaded and paletted, when painting casual.

In the alphabet guides, I have included two forms: one upright and one on a slant. When painting these, I set out two horizontal lines to mark where the tops and bottoms of the letters will sit. For the slanted variant, I then set out every couple of inches (5cm) a faint diagonal line at the required angle, which is somewhere in the region of 30 degrees clockwise from the vertical (imagine a line joining 1 o'clock and 7 o'clock on a watch). These additional lines help to keep the slant consistent by providing a reference as I paint. Finally I do a "chicken scratch," which involves roughly marking out in lines where the letters will go. This helps with spacing and provides an approximate, but not rigid, guide for painting.

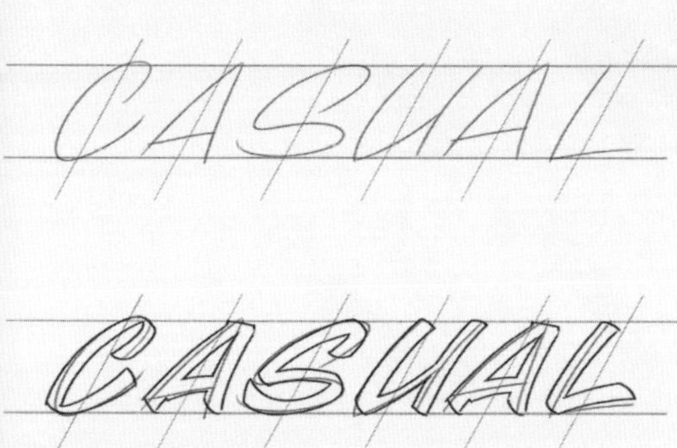

Basic chicken scratch (top) and more detailed guide (bottom) for setting out casual lettering.

Straights

The vertical, horizontal, and diagonal strokes of casual are all variations on a theme, created through changes to the angle and direction of the brush. The steps below are for a vertical stroke, and you can apply the same working method to horizontal and diagonal strokes.

Start with your brush well loaded and paletted to a sharp chisel. Hold the brush almost directly upright off the substrate, place the chisel just below your top horizontal markup line, and push up to the line while laying down the

CASUAL

A B C D E F
G H I J K L M N
O P Q R S T U
V W X Y & Z

SLANT CASUAL

A B C D E F G
H I J K L M N
O P Q R S T U
V W X Y & Z

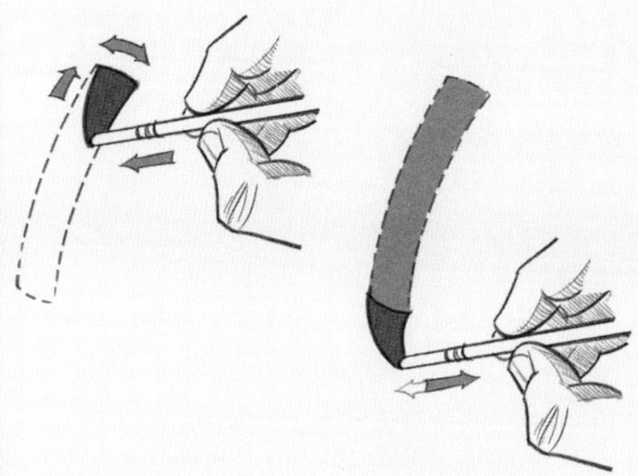

(left) Laying the brush down and first pushing up, with a little wiggle, to flatten out the hairs before pulling the stroke down. (right) Pushing the brush slightly into the substrate before pulling off with a spring of the brush away from the substrate.

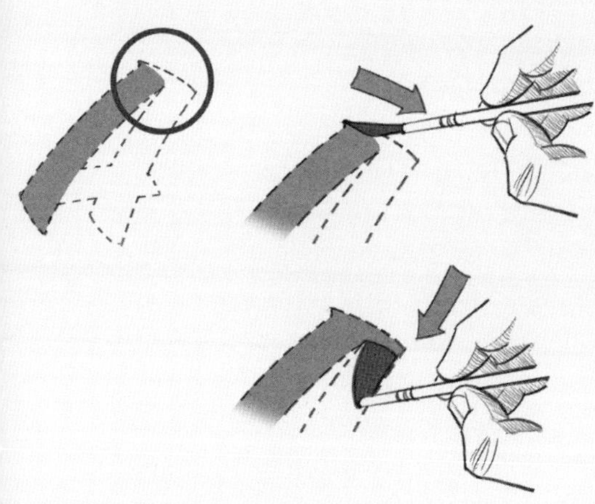

Pulling the brush across then down to give the width to the top of a casual letter A.

(opposite) Alphabet guides showing stroke order for each letter, from light (first) to dark (last).

hairs so that anything from 75 to 90 percent of their length is in contact with the substrate. (You can start with the chisel right on the line, but I find that pushing up helps to flatten out the chisel and sets you up for a more even final stroke.)

With the hairs laid down, pull your stroke downward, keeping the width constant as you move through the stroke by maintaining a firm and even pressure. As you reach the bottom of the stroke, slow down as you pull the brush up toward you. Finish the stroke on the baseline with a small controlled push of the hairs back toward the substrate before using the spring of the hairs to pull off completely— this should feel like when you bend your knees to jump, bringing your body closer to the floor before moving away and losing contact with it.

When you are building up a letter that has two connected straights (e.g. A, M, N, V, W, Z), remember that the width at the join is wider than a single stroke. This requires a slight variation on the joining stroke. For example, if you look at the M on my alphabet chart you can see that I start with the chisel roughly horizontal inside the top of the first stroke. I then pull the brush across a little to give the join its width, before laying the brush down and pulling the second stroke in the usual way. You can practice this by painting a series of connected but alternating diagonal strokes that zigzag up and down across the width of the substrate.

Once you have gained some confidence, experiment with tipping out slightly at the end instead of just pulling off. This will add more character and variation to your straights and give your terminals a little lip, but it is important to keep these features consistent, which will come with practice. You can see the subtle use of this technique in Dave Correll and Fernando Mello's alphabets at the back of this book, most easily on the uppercase I. They also start their strokes with a little horizontal movement of the brush, rather than laying it down flat straight away.

Curves

To paint curves in casual, you will need to learn to move the brush upward, as well as in the more usual downward direction.

For a left-hand curve (e.g. the left part of the letter O), start with the brush well chiselled and tilted slightly downward from the horizontal. Establish contact with the substrate slightly over on the right side by applying pressure until the hairs have 75–90 percent of their length in contact. Bring the brush up a little into the top of the curve, and then

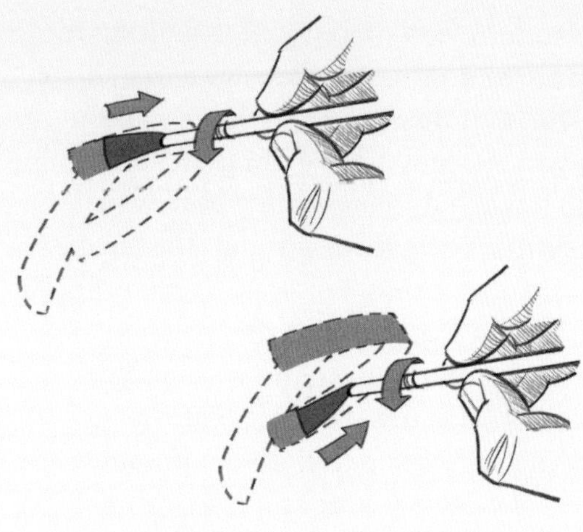

Two strokes used to form the "eyebrows" for use on casual letters B, D, P, and R.

down and around, maintaining the pressure and keeping the angle of the chisel almost constant. Finish the stroke by tipping out with a little upward flick as you reach the bottom of the curve.

The movement for the right-hand curve is the opposite of the description above. A good way to practice both of these curves is to paint the letter O repeatedly using just these two strokes. When finishing the second (right-hand) stroke, you can, instead of tipping out, rotate the brush as you move into the lower portion of the curve and "spring up" as you do at the end of the straight strokes. You can see how this looks in the O in my upright casual alphabet sample. As you practice, try experimenting with contrast in the stroke width, as you can see in the alphabets from Dave Correll and Fernando Mello.

For the C, G, and S in the upright casual alphabet, you will need to practice a slightly different curve for the top portion. Start with your chisel positioned almost vertically on the left side before laying down the brush and applying pressure as you move it up and to the right over the top of the curve. Finish with a little "spring up" to leave a flat end to the stroke. For an example, see the second stroke in the letter G in my upright casual reference.

The "Eyebrows"

There are two special strokes in the casual, which are used for the curves on the B, D, P, and R. These are pairs of strokes that I think of as eyebrows, which combine to form the upper and lower portions of the curve.

The upper stroke starts with the brush slightly less loaded than usual, and the chisel almost vertical. Apply pressure and, with a confident movement, push the brush to the right and upward, before pulling the brush back and tipping out with a slight pull downward.

The lower stroke starts with the chisel angled slightly downward (from left to right) before applying pressure and moving the brush up toward the upper stroke. For my upright variant, you finish the stroke with a little spring out to give a flat end, but for the slanted form you can do a slight tip out as you move into the upper stroke.

Customizing

Casual offers lots of scope for experimentation and for you to develop your own unique style. This book contains some different styles to inspire you, and I recommend looking at other sign painters' work to see what unique features they

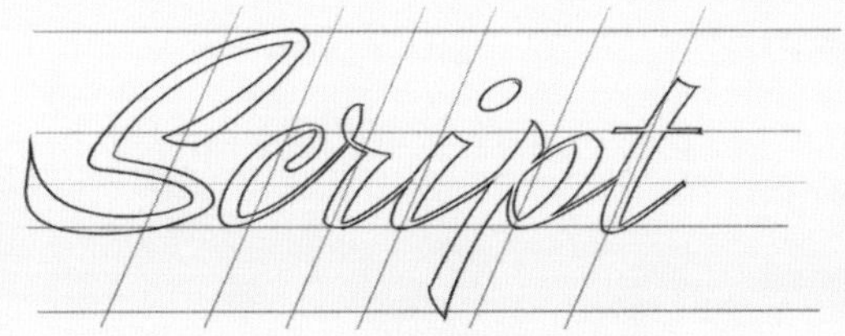

Horizontal and diagonal layout lines used for setting out script.

use. The key ingredient in successfully developing your own characteristic style is ensuring that you treat similar features of letters in a consistent way: for example, the top curves on B, P, and R, or the horizontal strokes on E, F, and L. Have a look at Gaston Castagnet's alphabet in this book for a good example of applying variations consistently.

Script

Like casual, script is a whole family of cursive alphabets, again produced with single strokes. It is one of the styles that really shows the personality of individual sign painters, and you can often recognize a painter's work by looking at the script.

A key feature that differentiates script from the previous alphabets is the variation, and transition, between thick and thin strokes. As with the slanted casual, the script I have shown in my sample alphabet is tilted forward at a 25–30-degree angle, but upright variants can also be painted (e.g. see Barbara Enright's alphabet) or it can be done with a much slighter angle (e.g. James Cooper's alphabet).

Another feature of script is that the letters are joined up, like handwriting, so that the end stroke of one letter is in contact with the first stroke of the next letter. The lowest point of contact between the letters is what I call the "paint-up-to line," and keeping the height of this consistent as you paint will give balance to your lettering. To help with this, I usually mark out five lines for script: the baseline, the x-height (height of lowercase letters), the cap height (height of uppercase letters), the descender line (where descenders terminate), and the "paint-up-to line." As with casual, I include a series of faint slants at the required angle for the lettering and then sketch out a rough chicken scratch to check spacing and guide my painting.

The Strokes

With script the emphasis is on painting consistent thicks and thins, and being able to move smoothly between these. For example, the left stroke of a lowercase a starts with the chisel angled upward (left to right), then pressure is applied to the brush and it is pulled down through the curve while being slightly rotated. This gives the stroke thickness. As you reach the bottom of the stroke, slightly twist and pull the brush up as you move to the right, so that you are finishing the stroke working only on the tip of the hairs. This gives the transition from thick to thin, ending with a thin line.

For the second stroke on the a, start with the chisel angled upward again before pulling it up and then down

Script

abcdefghij
klmnopqrs
tuvwxyzk

lower case

Basic Strokes

Each alphabet is constructed using a small number of basic strokes. These can form the basis of your practice early on.

Shown here:
1. One-stroke block
2. Built-up block
3. Slanted casual
4. Script

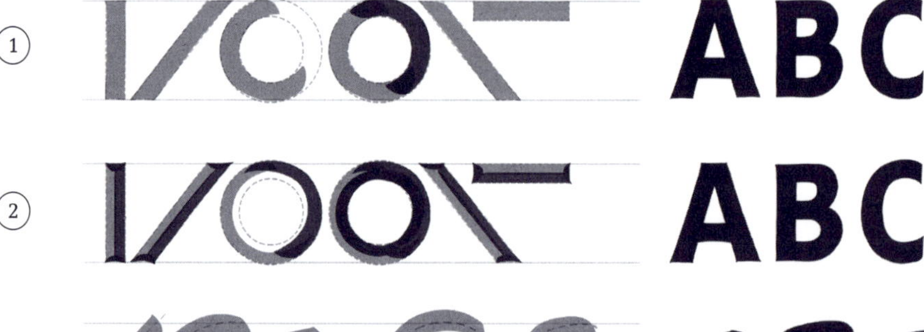

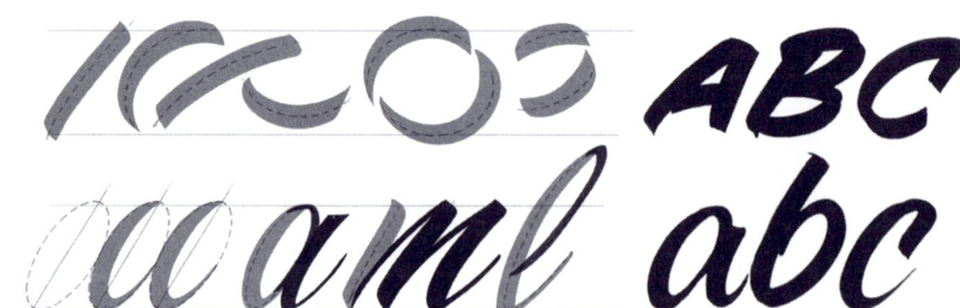

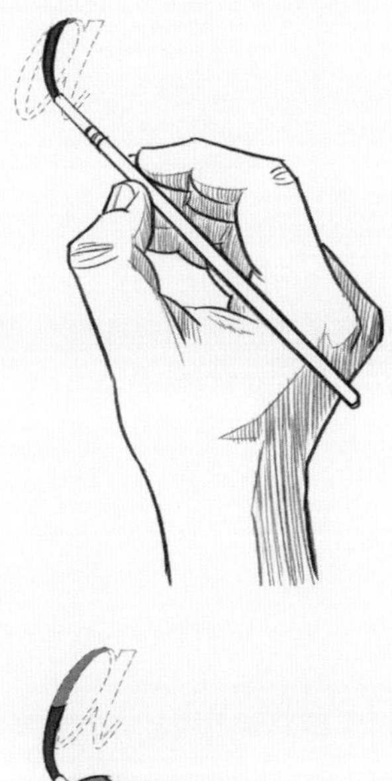

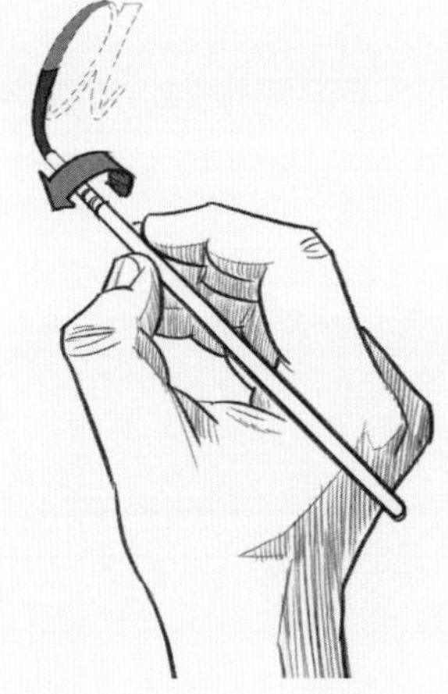

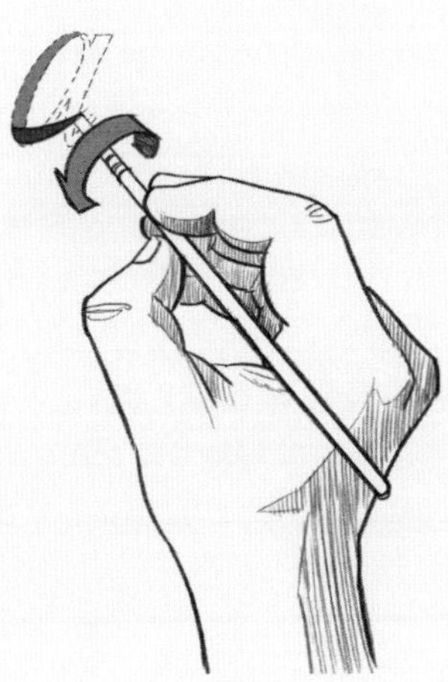

Manipulating the brush to paint
the first stroke of a lowercase a.

(opposite, above) Alphabet guide
showing stroke order for each letter,
from light (first) to dark (last).

with a little less pressure than before, so that you are working more on the tip of the hairs and producing a thinner stroke that joins with the first stroke near the bottom. Finish with a slightly shorter version of the first stroke, flicking up into the thin portion that will join with the next letter.

The vertical strokes (actually a slight diagonal if the script is slanting like mine) are very similar to the straights in casual. Sometimes you will use a little horizontal movement at the start to give a small lip to the top of the stroke (e.g. lowercase m and n), and sometimes you will tip out at the end of the stroke in a similar way to the left stroke on the lowercase a to end with a thin upward stroke (e.g. lowercase b, l, t).

The thin strokes in the lowercase m are painted by moving the brush with the chisel on its edge in an upward direction, from left to right.

When you gain confidence in the key strokes that make up a script alphabet, the process of painting with it should be similar to that of handwriting. It should flow and show your personality as you bring your own character to the letter forms. Keeping consistency between your thick and thin strokes, the slant of the script, and the position of the paint-up-to line where letters join is crucial to developing your own beautiful script.

Summary

These are just the basics of a small number of alphabets that can be used effectively for sign work. However, the strokes and techniques described here offer great scope for variety and adaptation, and can be applied to other alphabets that you feel inspired by and want to copy.

As a next step, I recommend looking at alphabets containing serifs, notably the sharp serifs of Roman, or alphabets with slab serifs. For Roman, the key is to balance your thicks and thins, and tip out at the end of strokes to form fine, tapered serifs. (David Kynaston says they should be so sharp that you'll need a bandage after painting them!)

As with all the skills in this book, seek out any opportunities available to observe others working with them, and get feedback on your own technique. These will help accelerate your learning, and identify areas where you can make quick and easy improvements.

Your Learning Journey

I believe that anyone can become a proficient sign painter, and it is not always the most "artistic" people who excel. All it takes is the desire, dedication, and discipline to pursue the trade for the long haul.

Mike teaching in New York (above). Our trade can be a solitary one, and Letterheads meets (below) offer an understanding and non-judgmental support network for everyone who loves sign painting and lettering.

Learning Opportunities

People enter sign painting from a wide range of related disciplines including graffiti, calligraphy, illustration, tattoos, pinstriping, and fine art. Many people who attend my workshops have studied graphic design or typography, or work in these areas. This sort of background is beneficial, but not essential. Extended study programs for sign painting are rare; exceptions include Los Angeles Trade Technical College and TEC in Copenhagen.

Workshops

The lack of formal learning opportunities means that most newcomers learn through their own efforts. At the time of writing, over 1,500 people have attended my own workshops, and there are many other excellent sign painters doing similar work around the world. I recommend attending as many of these as you can to expose yourself to different techniques and teaching methods. As well as improving your skills and knowledge, you will also make new friends.

Letterheads

In addition to workshops, attend Letterheads meets whenever you can. These not-for-profit events vary in size from a few people spending an evening discussing a particular technique or sharing a project, to larger international gatherings over multiple days. The bigger events usually feature a mixture of formal taught sessions, informal "panel jamming," and impromptu demonstrations. I attended my first Letterheads meet in 1988 and was so scared that I did not even get my brushes out. Please do not do this! The way to benefit from attending is to participate by getting stuck into a project, sharing something you know, and asking questions of everyone you meet. I can honestly say that my own learning accelerates at every event I attend, and I come away from each one with new friendships.

Apprenticeships

Apprenticeships (three–five years) are very rare, at least in their traditional form. However, many sign painters, including me, will take people under their wing for shorter periods, or on a less formal basis, when they see the right desire, dedication, and discipline. If you are going to approach someone to guide you, try thinking about what you can offer them in return. An exchange of skills for mutual benefit will always be an easier sell than a one-way passing on of knowledge. And, once you are working alongside someone,

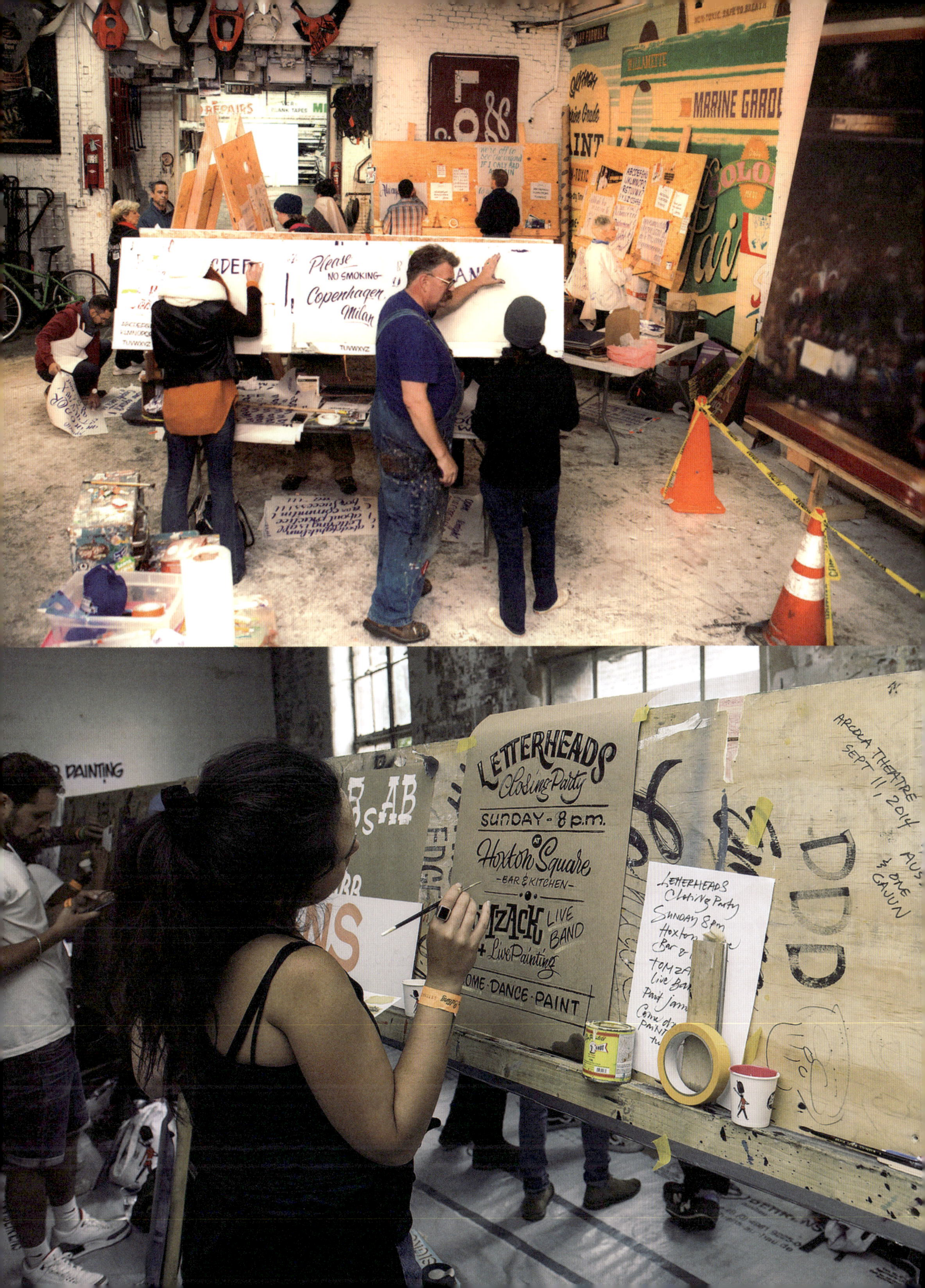
LETTERHEADS
Closing Party
SUNDAY · 8 p.m.
AT
Hoxton Square
- BAR & KITCHEN -
TOMZACK LIVE BAND
+ Live Painting
COME · DANCE · PAINT
AREOLA THEATRE
SEPT 11, 2014
AUS
IN ONE
GAUUN
LETTERHEADS
Closing Party
SUNDAY 8PM
Hoxton
Bar & K
TOM ZA
Live Ban
Paint Jam
Please
NO SMOKING
Copenhagen
Milan
MARINE GRADE
PAINT

Mike's Tip

It's important to think about how you want to come across online. Remember, most social media is public. Develop a positive, constructive persona that people want to have a relationship with. It's very easy to come across as an asshole, so don't be that person!

94

get the basics right. As they say at Colossal Media in New York, "Early is on time." The value of reliability, a positive attitude, and hard work cannot be underestimated.

Books & Videos

The fact that you are reading this book shows that you have a willingness to learn in this way. On page 188 there are recommendations for Further Reading, many of which are out of print but available secondhand or as PDFs. There are increasing numbers of sign-painting videos on YouTube and other sites, which are a great way to see the brush in motion, and to increase your understanding of techniques that are difficult to convey in words and pictures.

Online Communities

Follow and interact with people whose work you admire, and join groups and discussion forums. Also seek out connections with people who are on the same journey as you are—they can provide excellent support. When you spend a lot of time online, it is easy to start comparing yourself and your work in a negative way to those with more experience, which can lead to a loss of confidence. Bear in mind that the most experienced sign painters were once beginners. Be inspired by them, not threatened or intimidated.

Practice, Practice, Practice

To succeed, commit to regular and focused practice, and don't be deterred when things do not go perfectly the first time. You will always be improving. Remember, no one learned to walk without falling over; what is important is getting up and trying again until you can do it confidently.

To practice lettering you can use paper or a primed and topcoated panel, but the best way, especially when you are starting out, is to use a piece of glass that can be painted, wiped clean (using a rag soaked with mineral spirits), and painted again endlessly. Make sure the glass is toughened and the edges polished, and handle it with care at all times. Practicing on glass allows you to place alphabets and printed sheets of practice strokes behind it to guide you. I developed my alphabet posters for precisely this purpose.

As the strokes begin to come more naturally, you will feel ready to take on simple projects—perhaps small pieces for friends and family. That allows you to continue experimenting and learning without the pressure of a fee-paying client. You will eventually feel ready to charge for a job, and then, as they say, the world is your oyster.

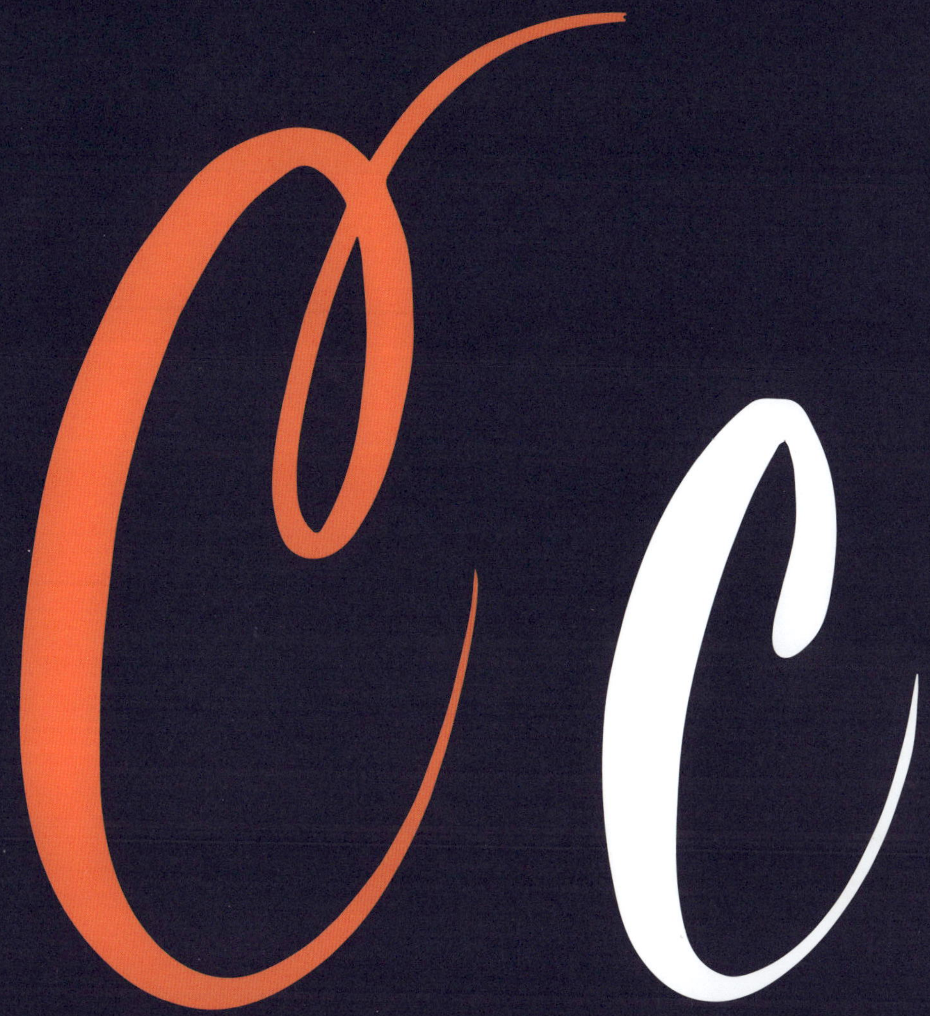

The Alphabets

Lettering by Barbara Enright, Dancing Script, see page 110

Elena Albertoni (La Letteria), Letterista Script

www.letteria.berlin | Instagram: @letterista

AaBbCcDdEe
FfGgHhIiJjKk
LlMmNnOoPp
QqRrSsTtUu
VvWwXxYyZz
!?1234567890&

Mike Meyer, Pottsmith

www.betterletters.co/workshops | Instagram: @mikemeyersignpainter

ABCDEF
GHIJKL
MNOPQRS
TUVWXYZ

abcdefghijk
lmnopqrstu
&?-vwxyz,.!

1234567890

Karen Cartwright (Red Truck Company), Vintage Neon

redtruckcompany.com | Instagram: @redtruckcompany

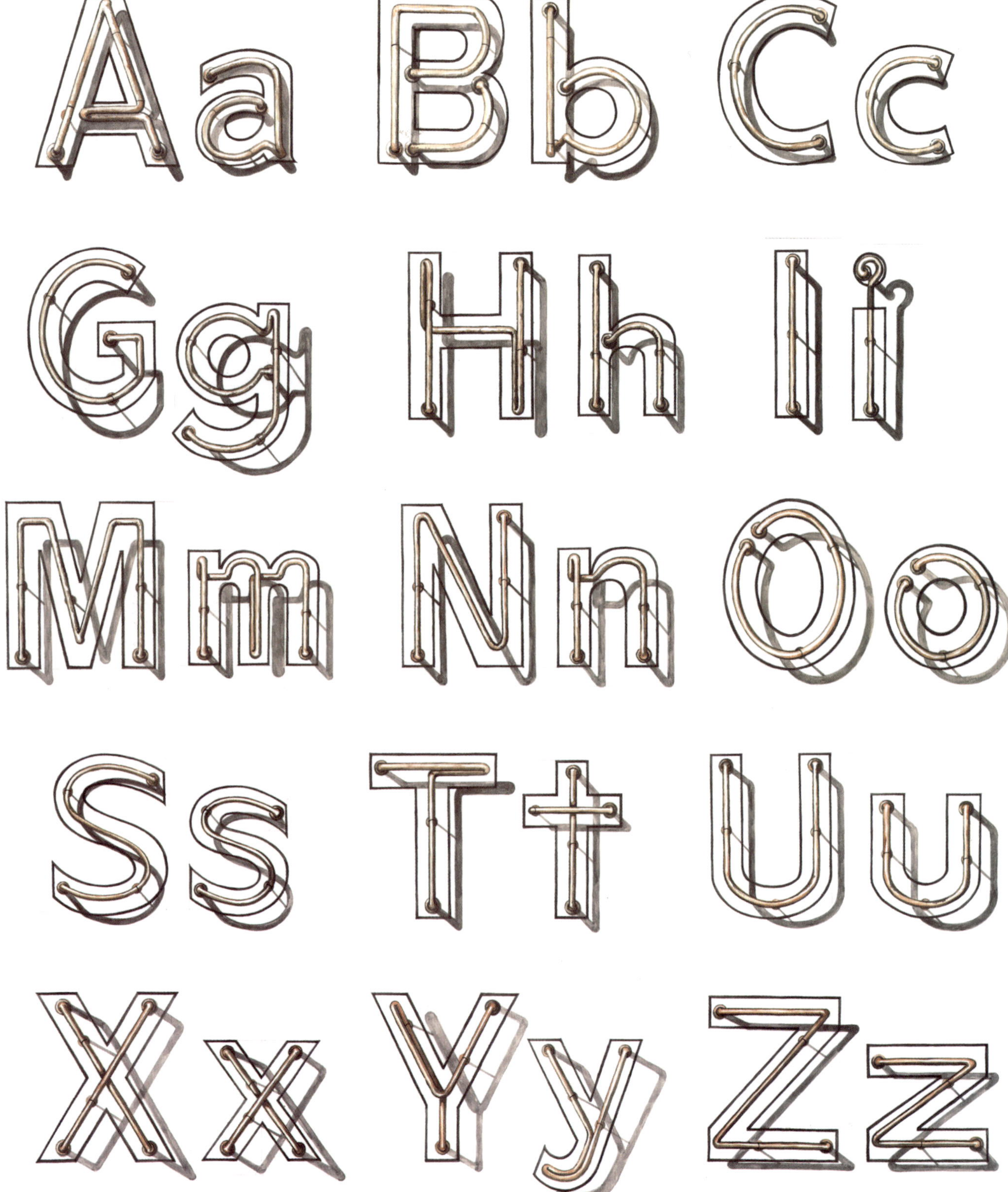

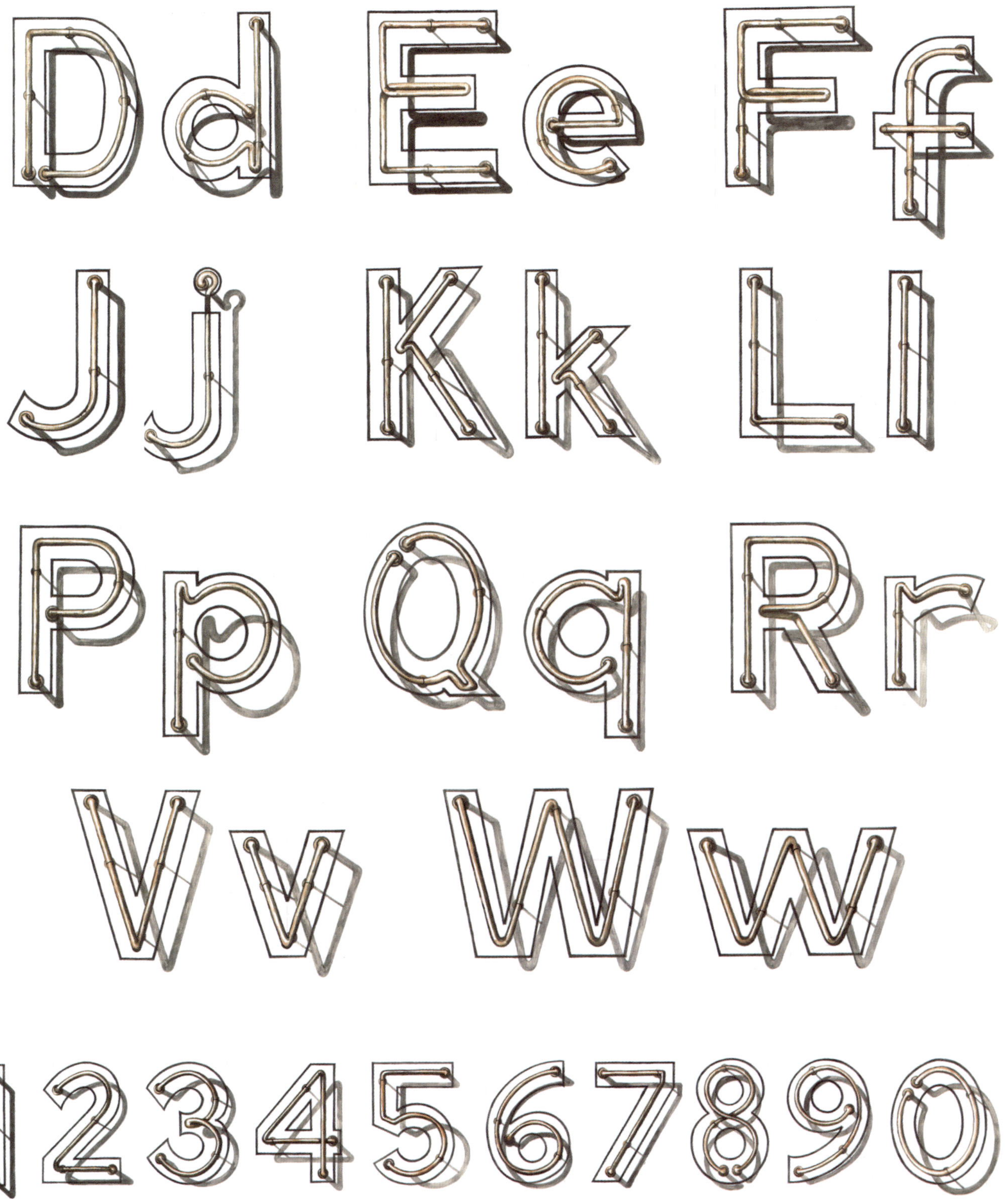

www.gastonthepainter.com | Instagram: @gastonthepainter

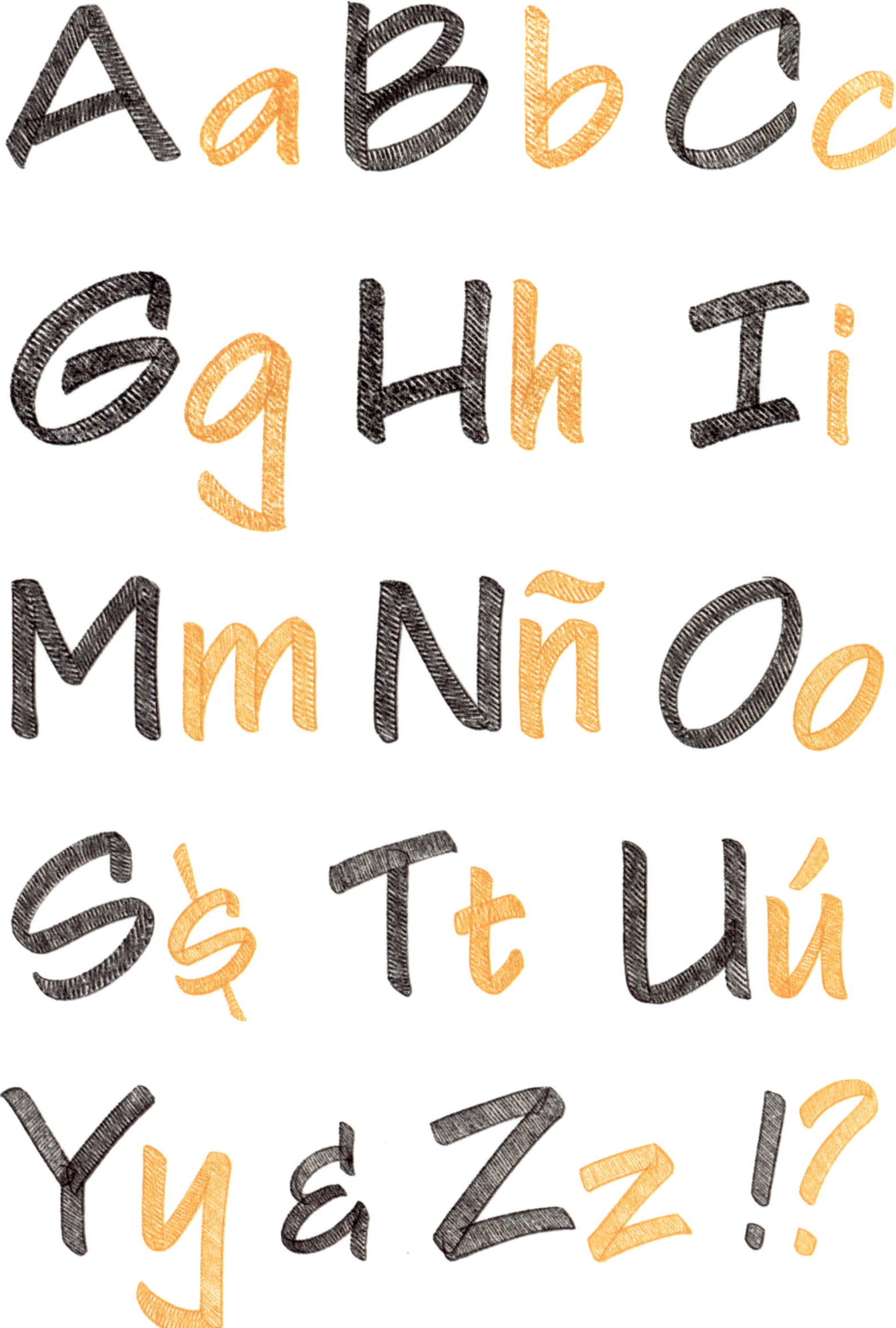

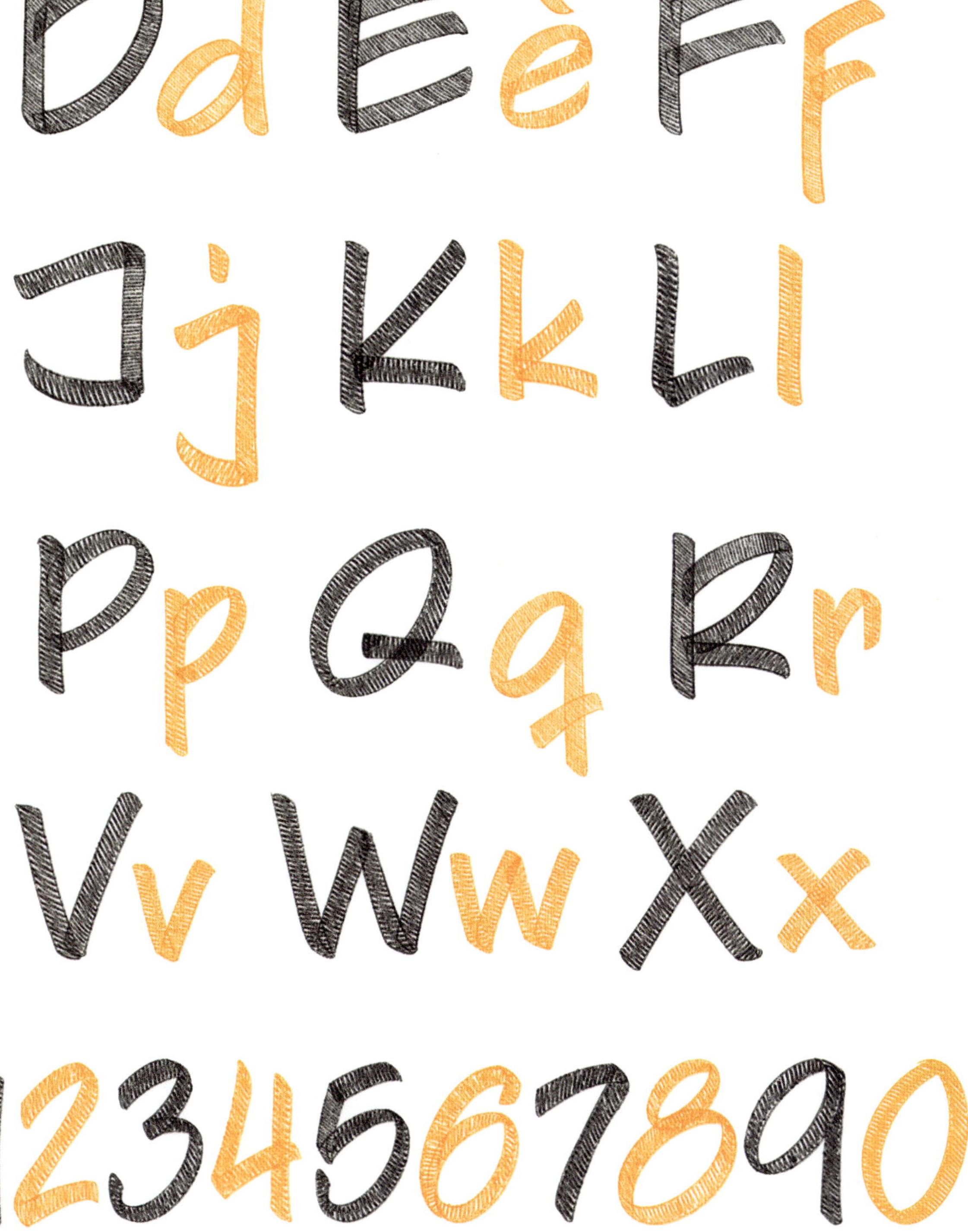

Ivan Castro, Cugat

www.ivancastro.es | Instagram: @ivancastrolettering

AaBbCc
GgHhIiJj
NnOoPp
UuVvWw
!?12345

DdEeFf
KkLlMm
QqRrSsTt
XxYy&Zz
67890%

Bob Behounek, Wauwatosa

www.chicagobrushmasters.com

104

Aa Bb Cc
Gg Hh Ii Jj
Nn Oo Pp
Uu Vv Ww
! ? 12345-

Dd Ee Ff

Kk Ll Mm

Qq Rr Ss Tt

Xx Yy Zz

67890 .,&

Aa Bb Cc
Gg Hh Ii Jj
Nn Oo Pp
& Tt Uu Vv
Zz 12345

Dd Ee Ff

Kk Ll Mm

Qq Rr Ss

Ww Xx Yy

67890?!

Aa Bb Cc

Gg Hh Ii Jj

Oo Pp Qq

Uu Vv Ww

12345678

Dd Ee Ff

Kk Ll Mm Nn

Rr Ss Tt

Xx Yy & Zz

90 !?$%#

Barbara Enright, Dancing Script

www.learnbrushlettering.com | Instagram: @barbaraenright

Aa Bb Cc
Gg Hh Ii Jj
Nn Oo Pp
Uu Vv Ww
123456

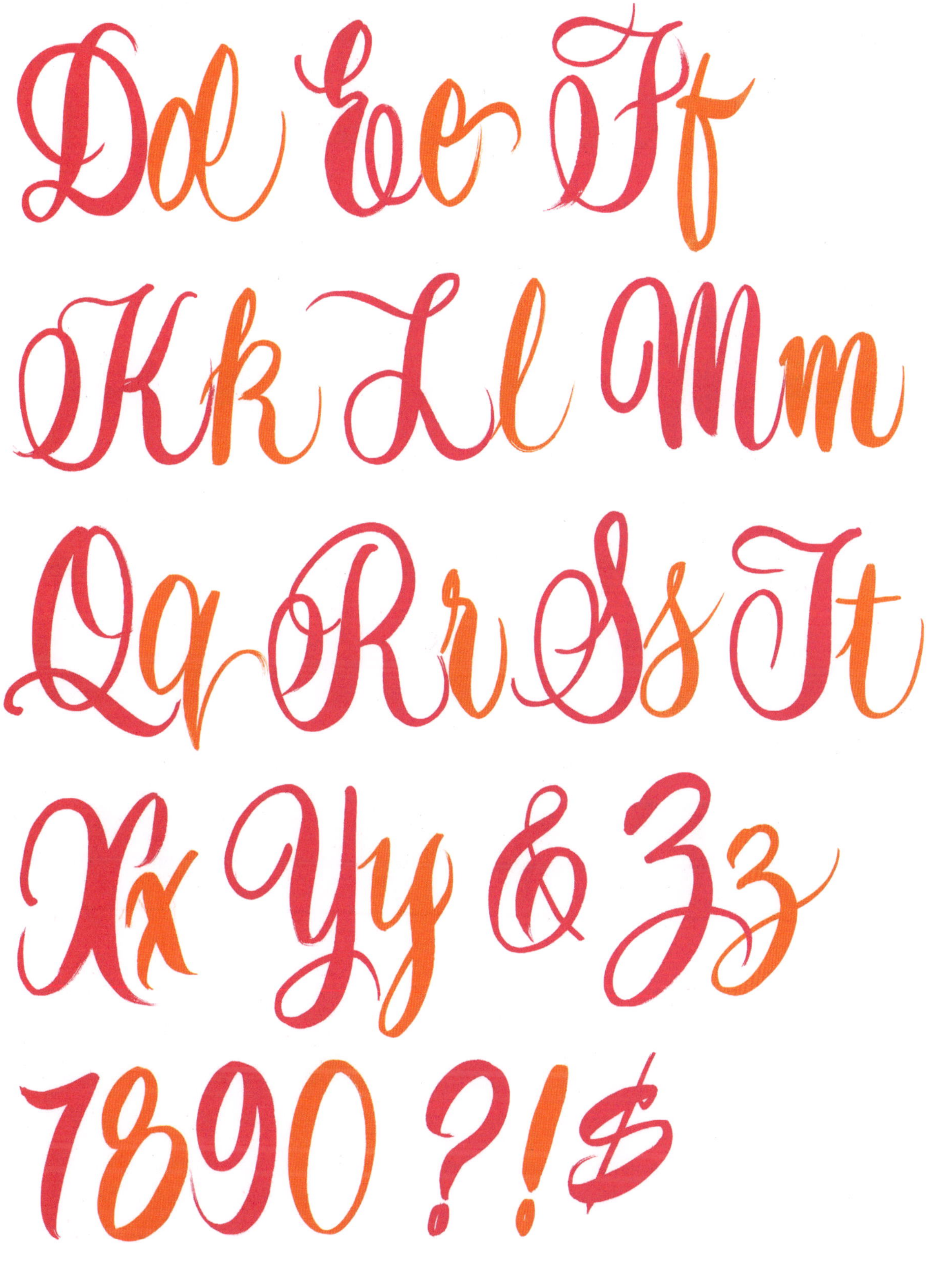

Dd Ee Ff
Kk Ll Mm
Qq Rr Ss Tt
Xx Yy & Zz
7890 ?!$

Gustavo Ferrari, Porteño

www.ferrarifileteados.com | Instagram: @ferrarifileteados

¡i Aá Bb Cc
Gg Hh Ii Jj
Nñ Oo Pp
Uu Vv Ww
¿? 1 2 3 4 5

Dd Ee Ff

Kk Ll Mm

Qq Rr Ss Tt

Xx Yy Zz !

67890 &

Aa Bb Cc
Gg Hh Ii Jj
Nn Oo Pp
Uu Vv Ww
1234567

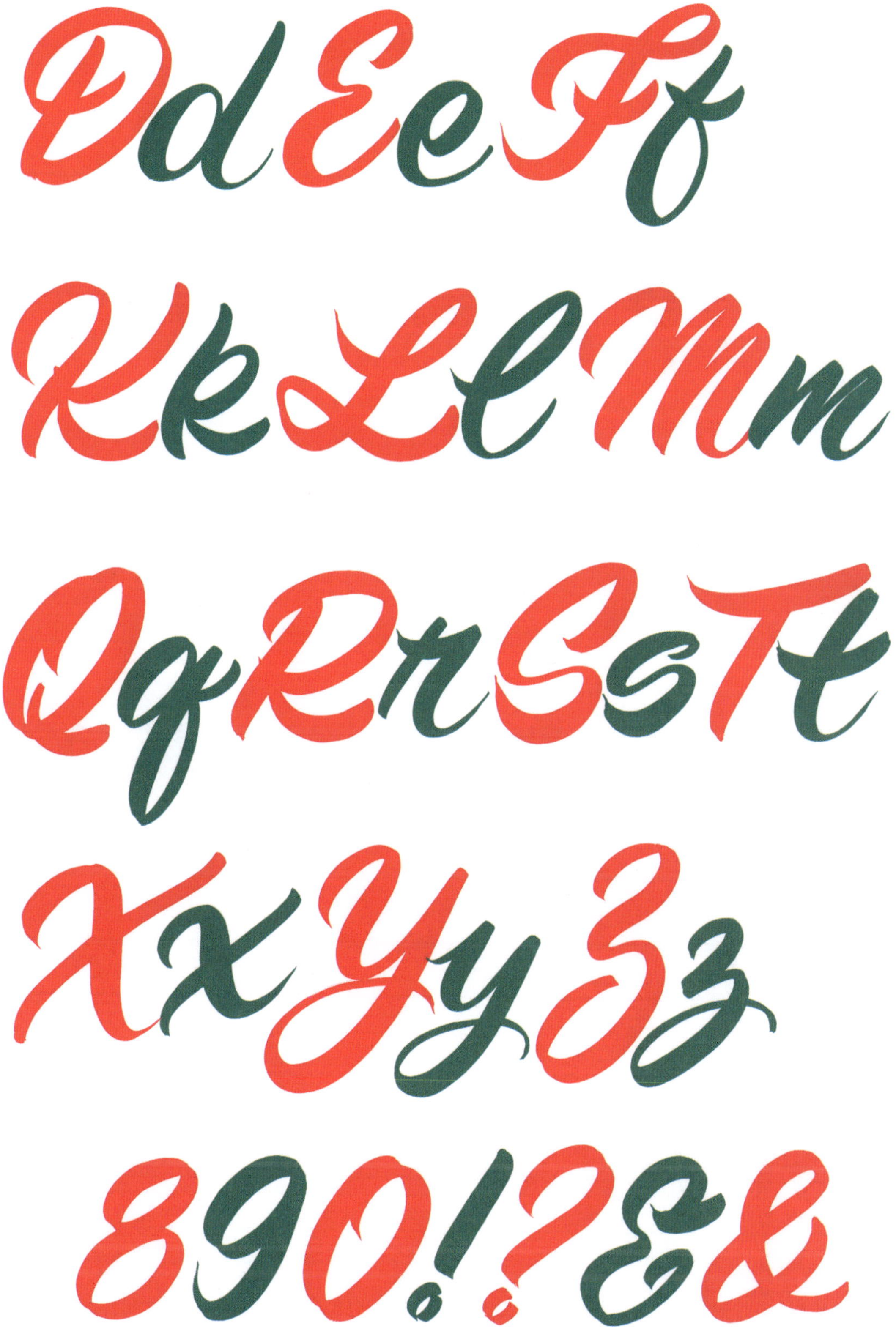

Dd Ee Ff
Kk Ll Ll Mm
Qq Rr Ss Tt
Xx Yy Zz
890 .!? &&

Alice Mazzilli, Jazz

www.alicemazzilli.com | Instagram: @alicemazzilli

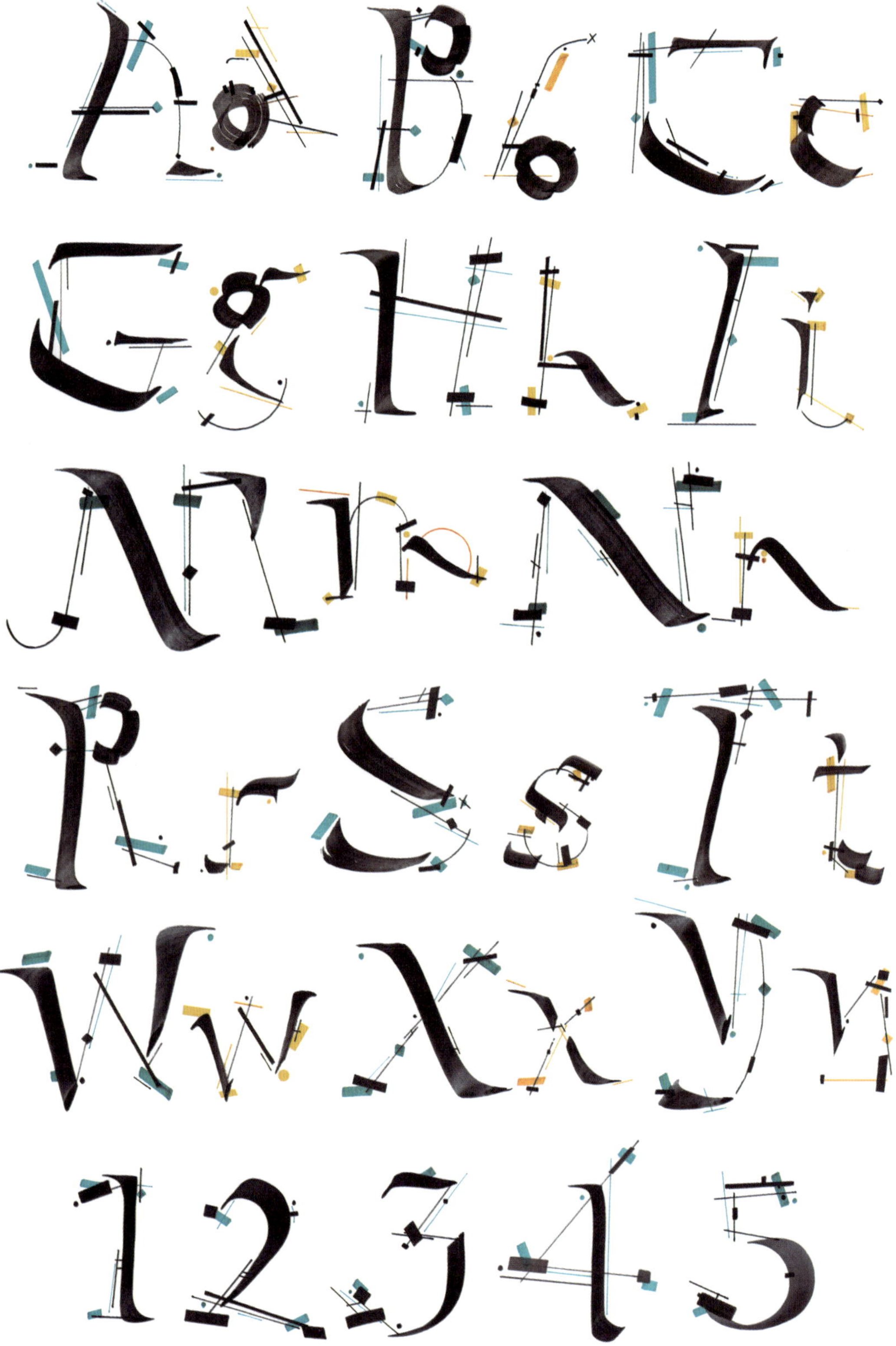

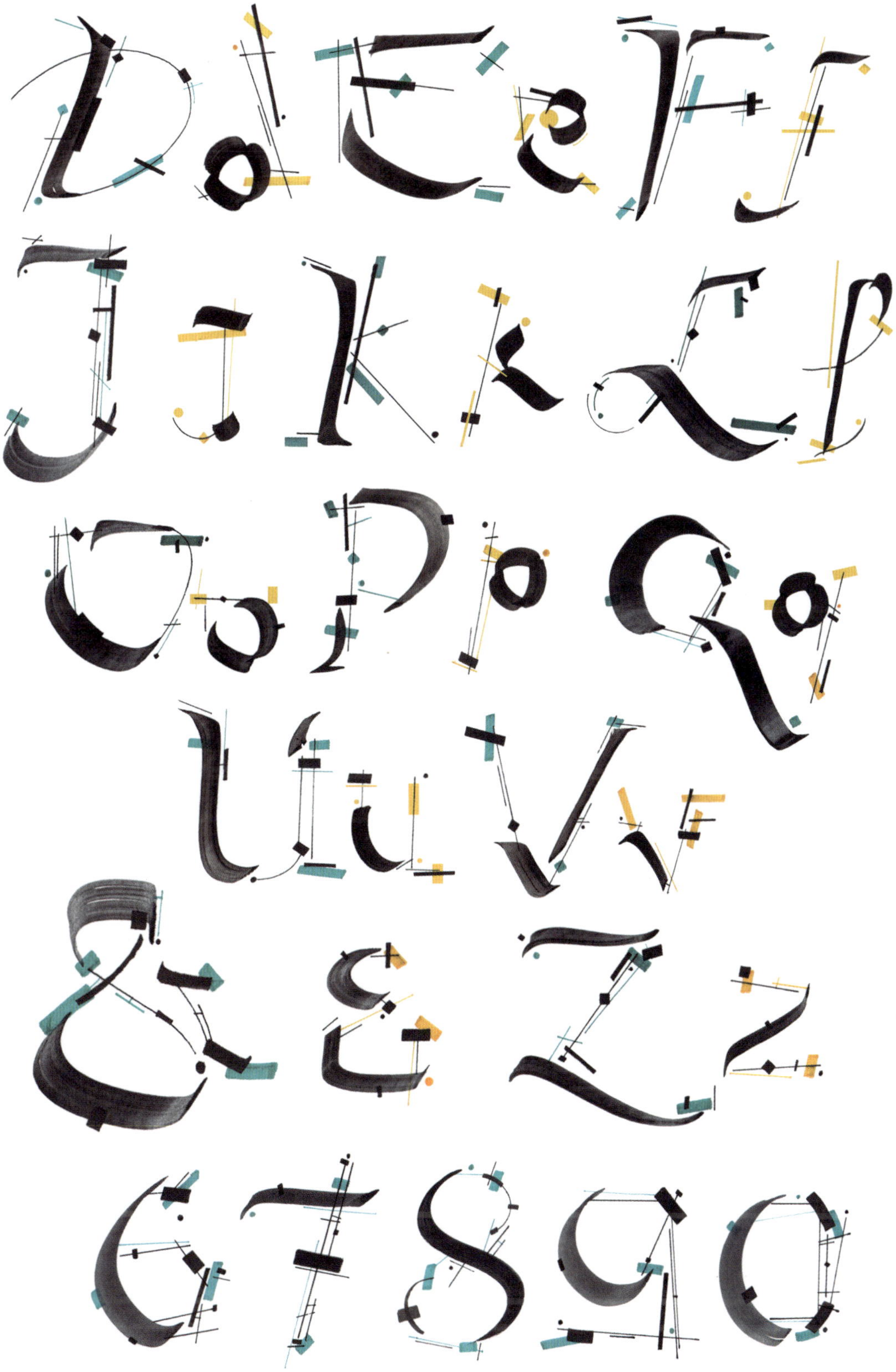

Fernando Mello, Touriga

www.fermello.org | Instagram: @fermello78

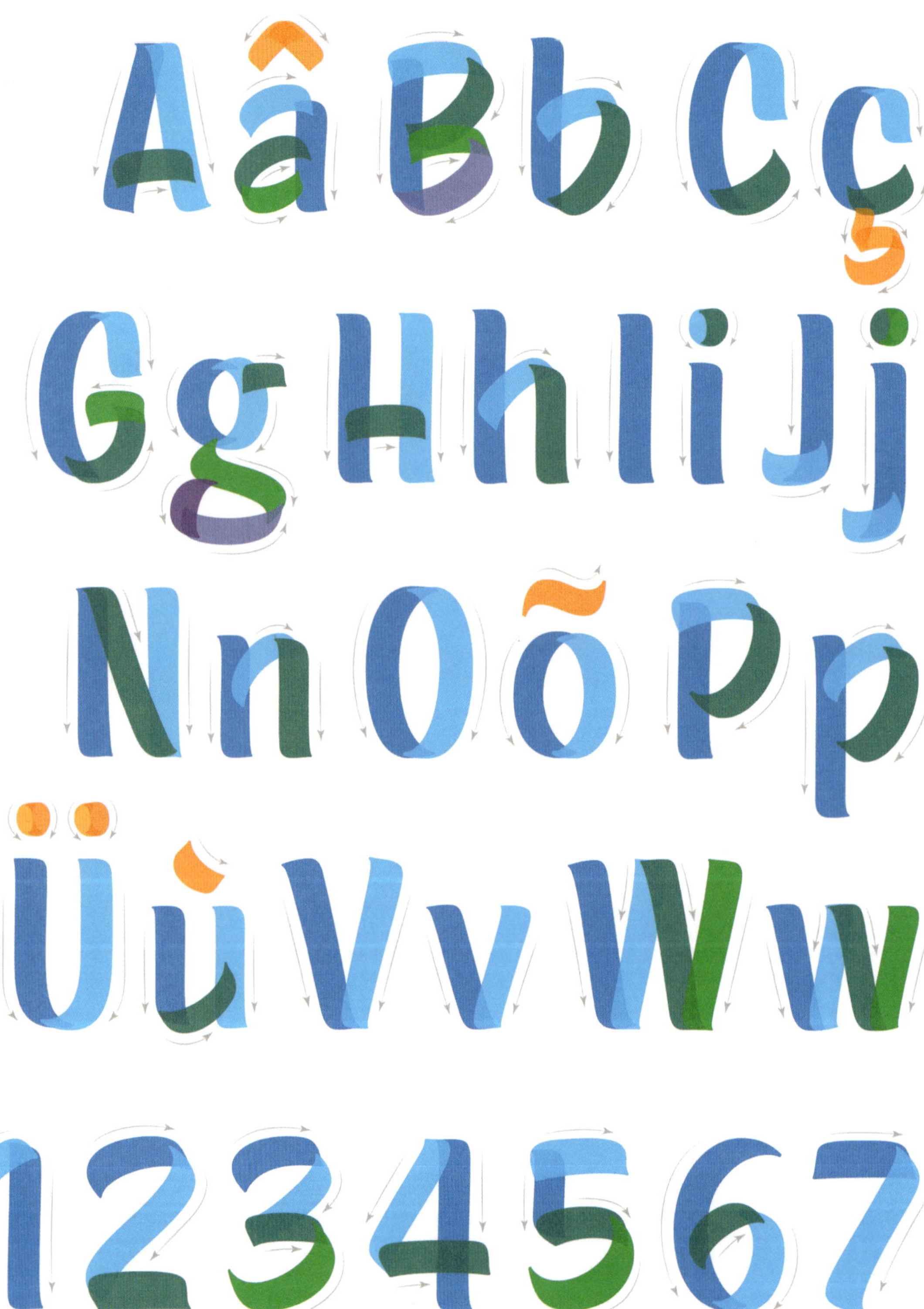

Dd Ee Ff
Kk Ll Mm
Qq Rr Ss Tt
Xx Yy & Zz
890 !? %

Adrián Pérez (El Deletrista), Sexy Bevels

www.deletrista.es | Instagram: @eldeletrista

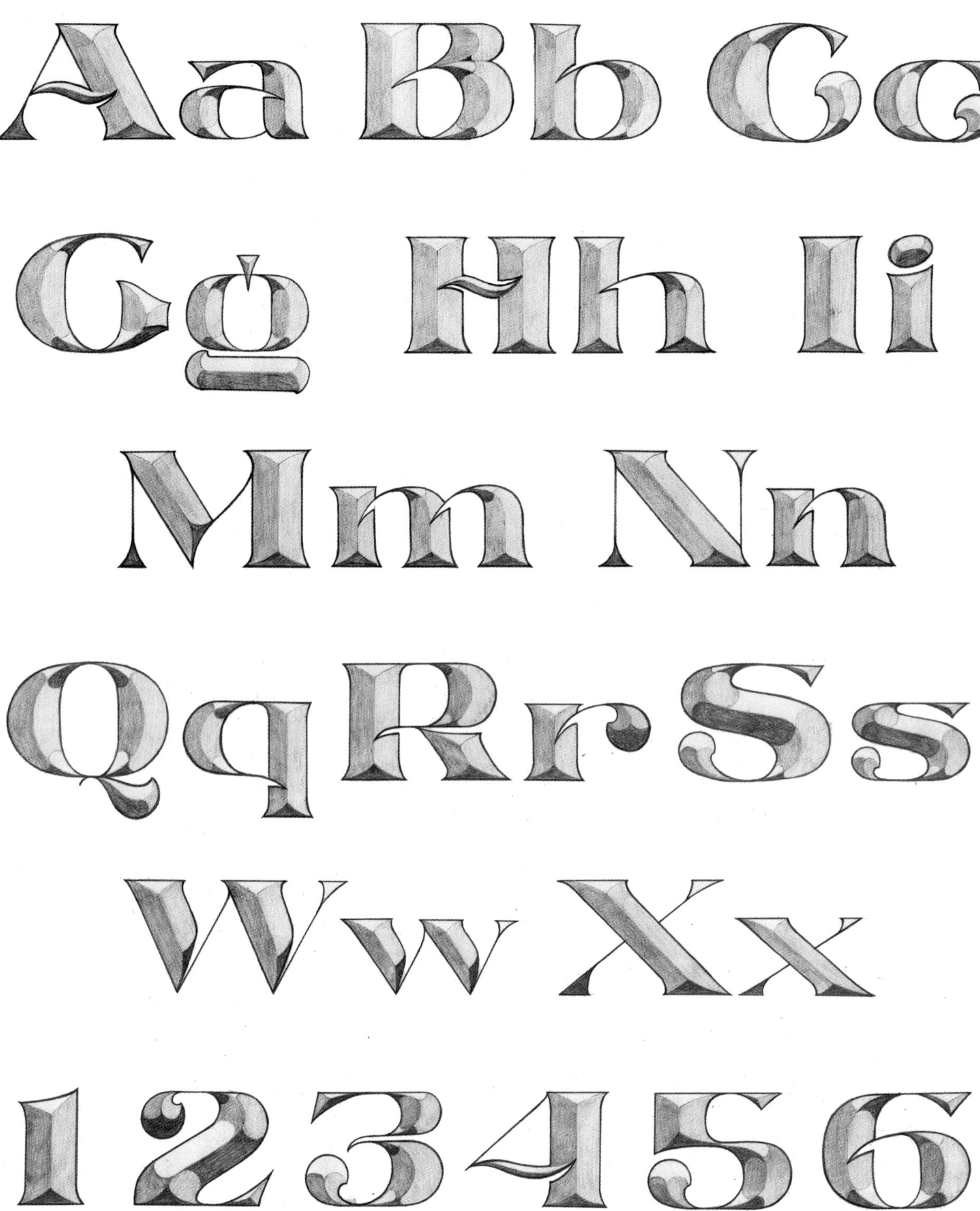

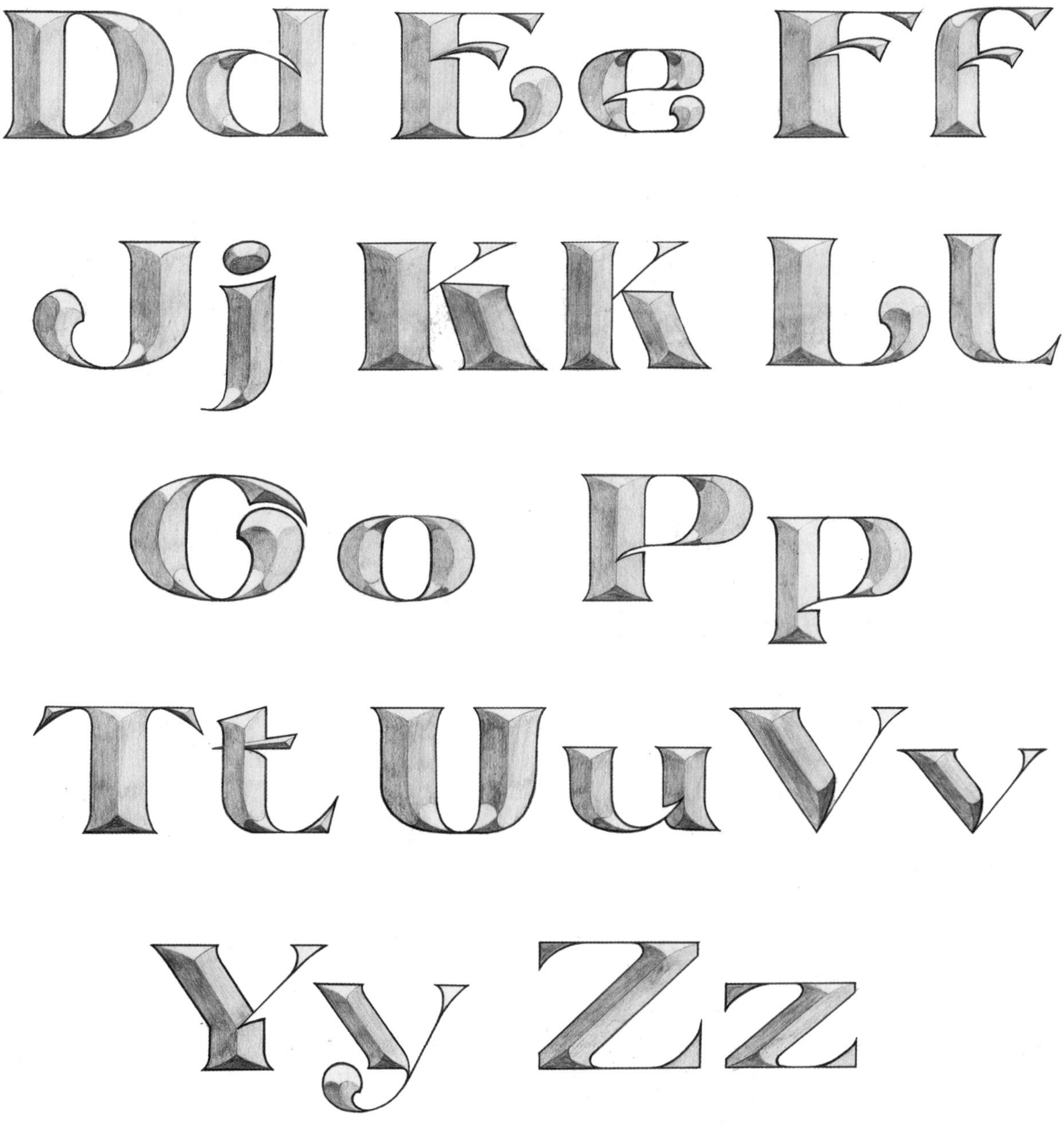

Dd Ee Ff
Jj Kk Ll
Oo Pp
Tt Uu Vv
Yy Zz
7 8 9 & O

Miss Merlot, Merletters

www.merlotism.com | Instagram: @merlotism

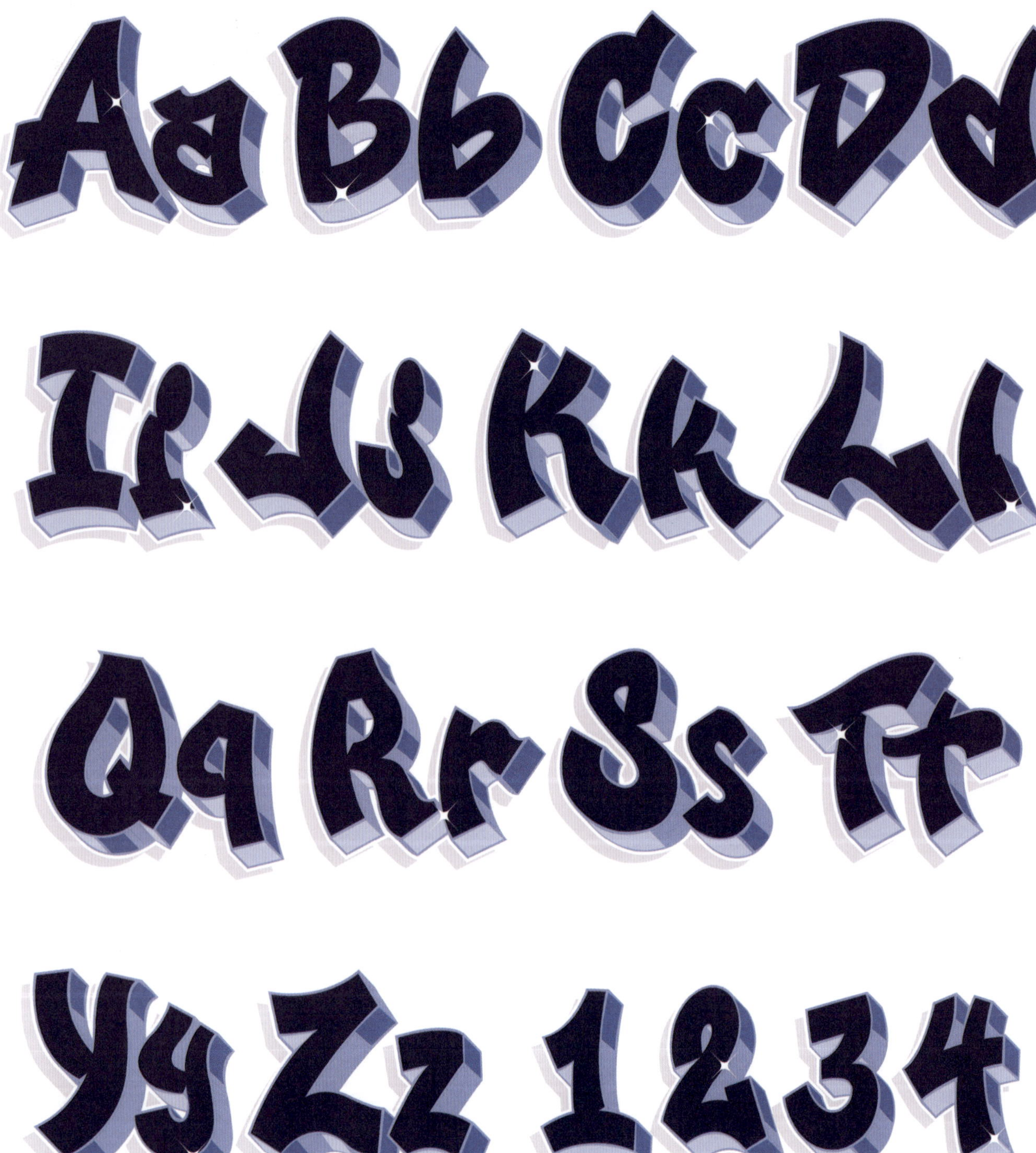

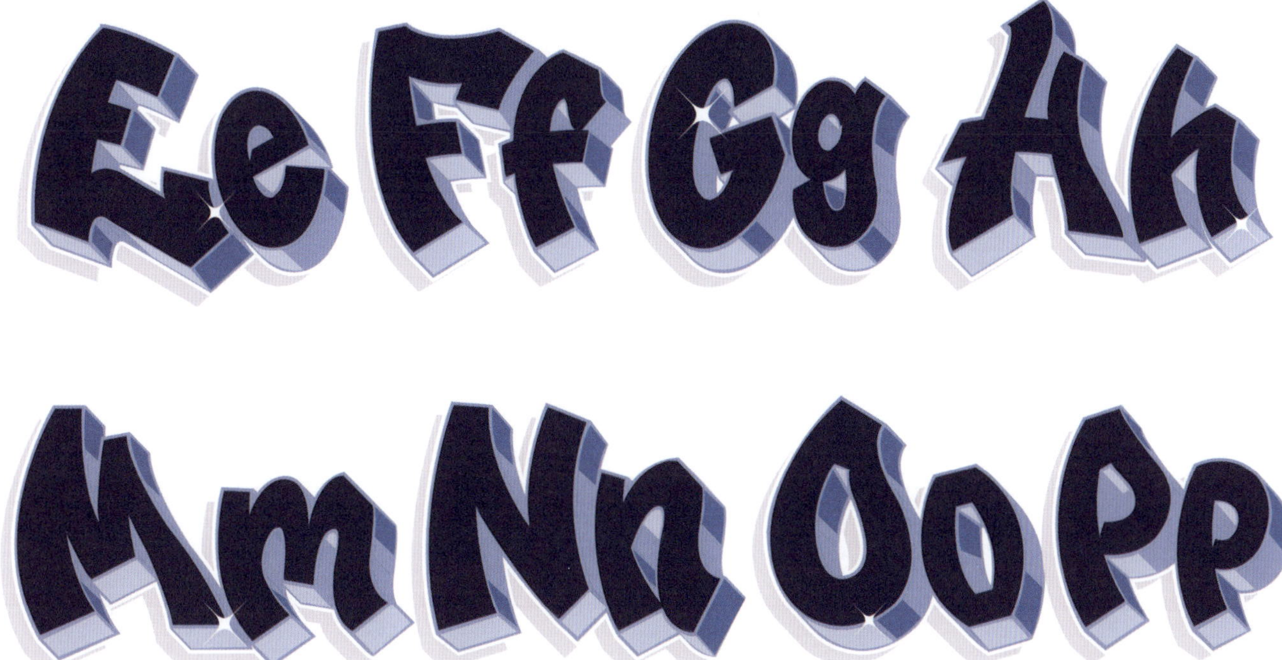

Ged Palmer (The Luminor Sign Company), Luminor Poster Block

www.luminorsignco.com | Instagram: @theluminorsignco

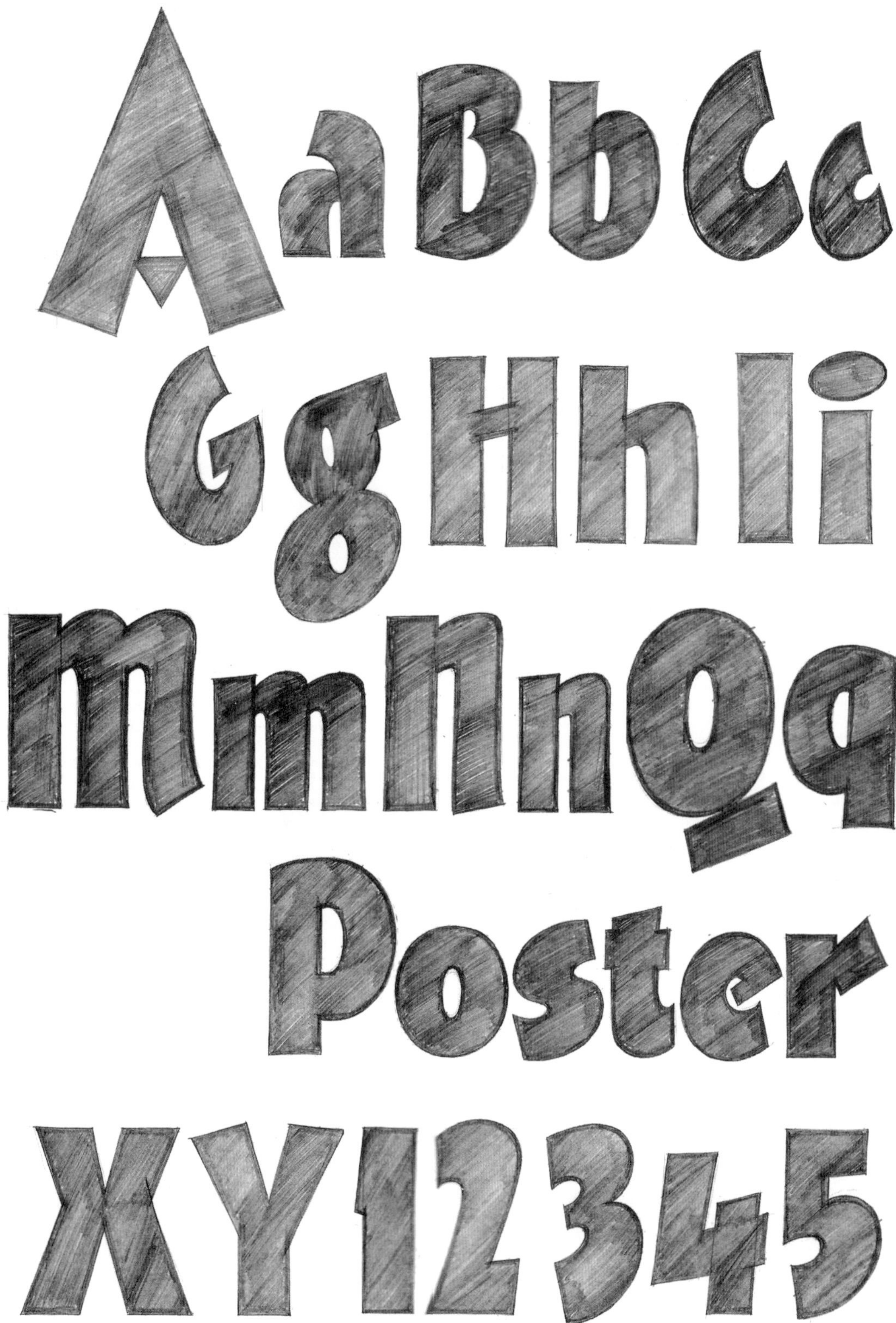

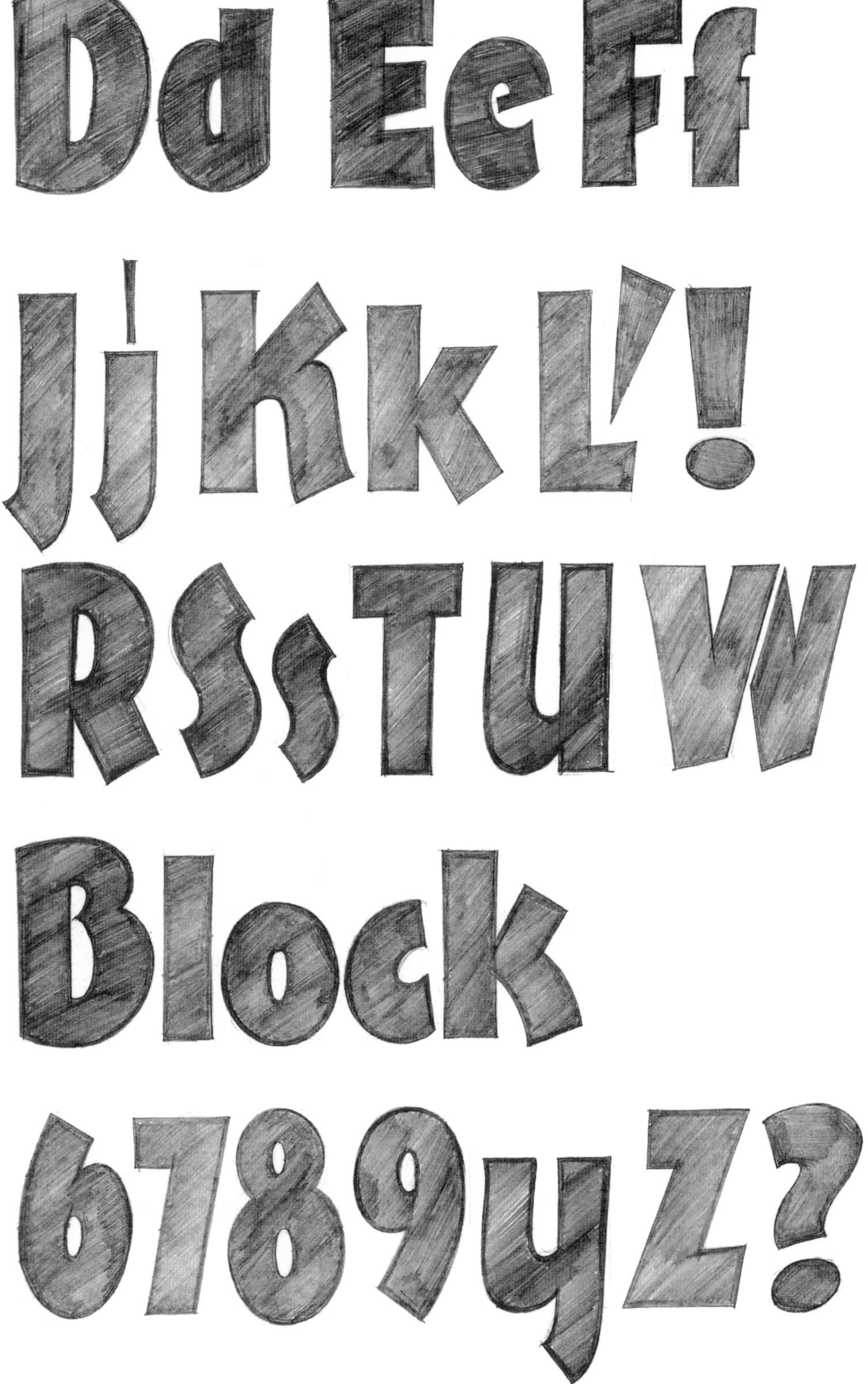

Dd Ee Ff
Ji Kk L' !
RSs TU W
Block
6789 yZ ?

Joan Quirós, Abrupt Serif

www.joanquiros.com | Instagram: @joanquiros

Aa Bb Cc Çç

Hh Ii Jj Kk

Ññ Oo Pp

Uu Vv Ww

1234567

Dd Ee Ff Gg

Ll Mm Nn

Qq Rr Ss Tt

Xx Yy & Zz

890 ¡!¿?%

Pieter van Tongeren (Mossy Giant), Mossy Letters

www.mossygiant.com | Instagram: @mossygiant

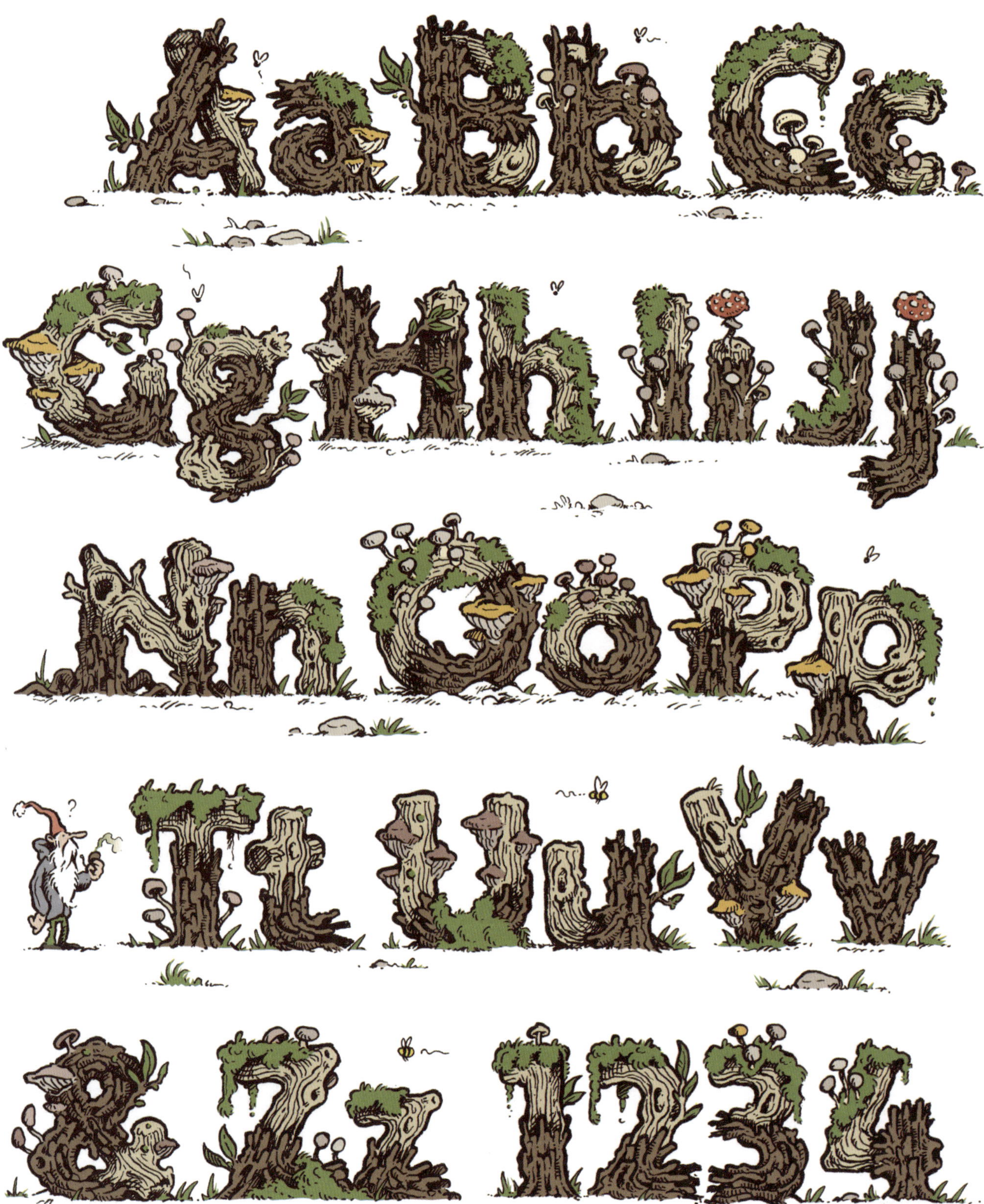

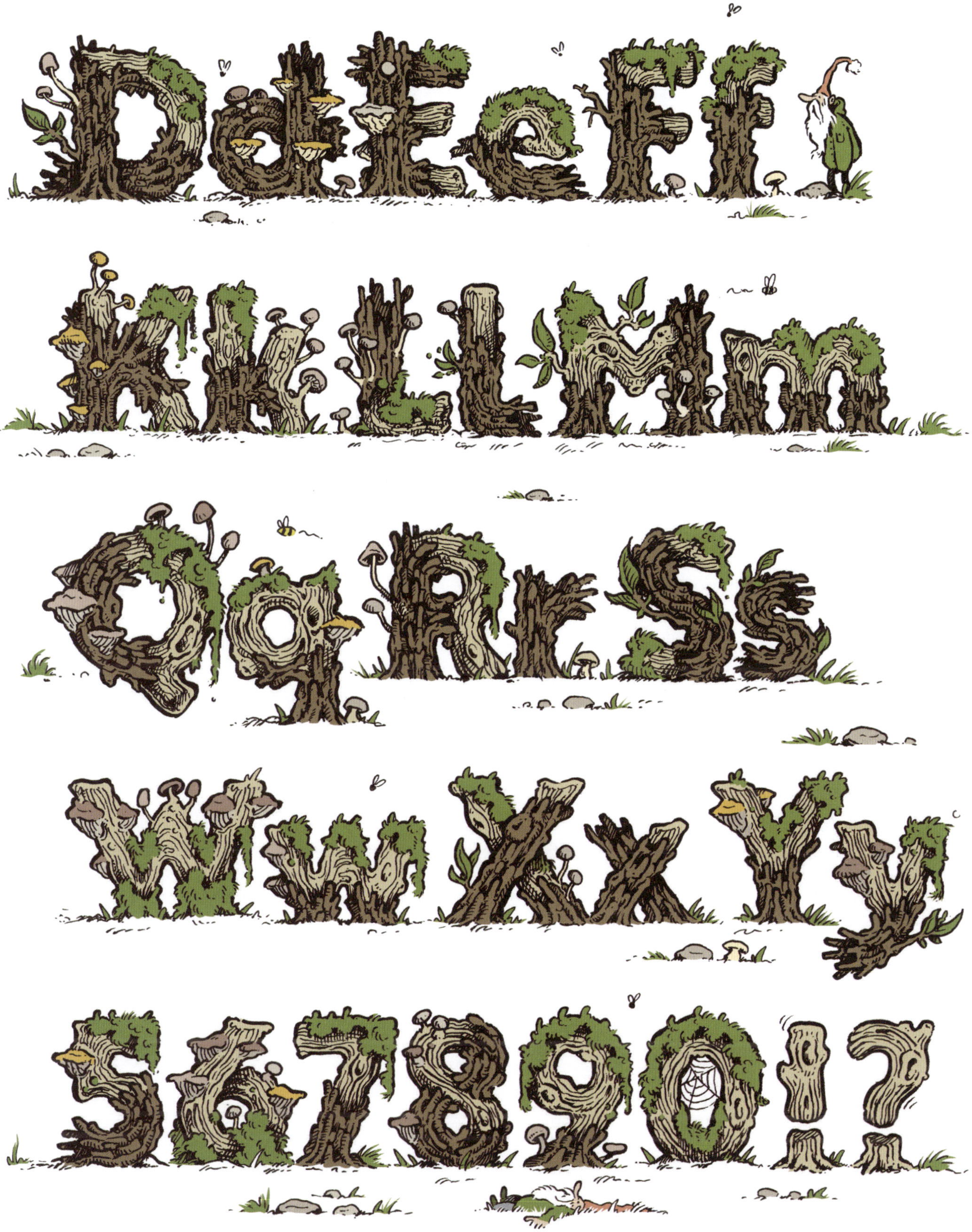

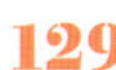

129

130

Aa Bb Cc

Gg Hh Ii Jj

Nn Oo Pp

Uu Vv Ww

~ & 12345

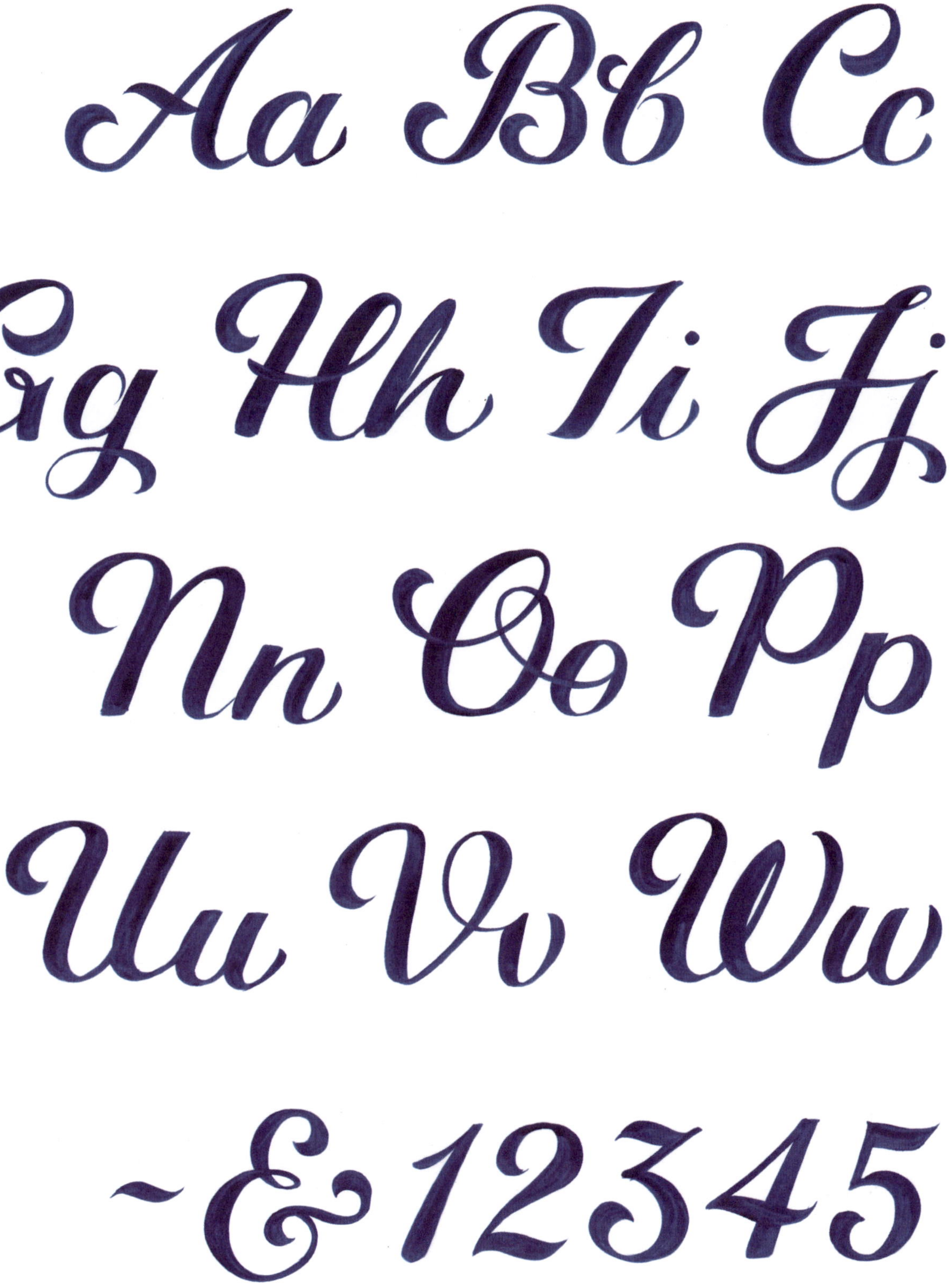

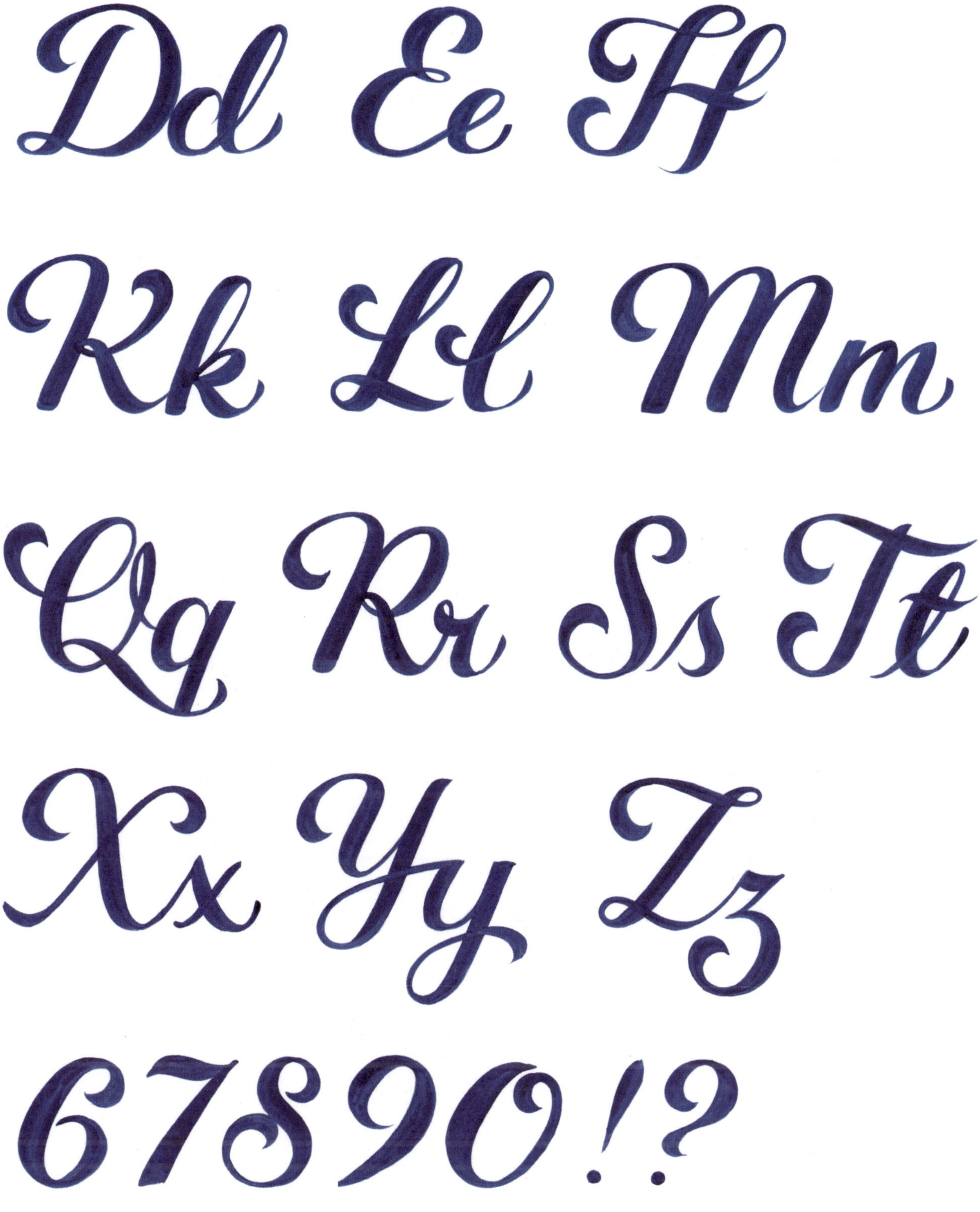

Dd Ee Ff

Kk Ll Mm

Qq Rr Ss Tt

Xx Yy Zz

67890!?

Ashley Willerton, Housemaster

www.ashleywillerton.com | Instagram: @ash_willerton

AaBbCc

GgHhIiJj

NnOoPp

UuVvWw

1234567

Dd Ee Ff Kk Ll Mm Oo Qq Rr Ss Tt Xx Yy & Zz 8 9 0 ! ? %

Aa Bb Cc

Cc Ge Hh Ii Jj

134

Nn Oo Pp

Uu Vv Ww

1 2 3 4 5 6

Dd Ee Ff
Kk Ll Mm
Qq Rr Ss Tt
Xx Yy Zz
7890!?&

Aa Bb Cc
Gg Hh Ii Jj
Nn Oo Pp
Uu Vv Ww
1234567

Dd Ee Ff

Kk Ll Mm

Qq Rr Ss Tt

Xx Yy Zz

890 ½ ¼ ? !

Dorota Letachowicz, Classic Serif

www.facebook.com/dorota.letachowicz | Instagram: @dorotaletachowicz

Aa Bb ! Cc

Gg Hh Ii Jj

Nn Oo Pp #

Uu Vv Ww

1 2 3 4 5 6 7 8

Dd Ee Ff ?

Kk Ll Mm

Qq Rr Ss Tt

Xx Yy & Zz

90 Ą Ę Ć Ł

Jean Desfeux, Poulpe

Instagram: @jean_desfeux

Aa Bb Cc
Gg Hh Ii Jj
Nn Oo Pp
& Tt Uu Vv
Zz ∴ 1 2 3 4 5

Dd Ee Ff

Kk Ll Mm

Qq Rr Ss

Ww Xx Yy

67890 ! ? :

142

Aaà Bb Cc

Gg Hh Iiì Jj

Nn Ooò Pp

Uuù Vv Ww

1234567

Dd Eeéè Ff

Kk Ll Mm

Oq Rr Ss Tt

Xx Yy & Zz

890 € ,.!?%

Mark Josling (Spectrum Signs), Carzorla Condensed

www.spectrumsignsuk.co.uk | Instagram: @spectrumsigns

Aa Bb Cc

Gg Hh Ii Jj

Nn Oo Pp

Uu Vv Ww

12345678

Dd Ee Ff

Kk Ll Mm

Qq Rr Ss Tt

Xx Yy Zz

90 !?&£$,

AaBbCc
GgHhIiJj
NnOoPp
UuVvWw
!?12345

DdEeFf
KkLlMm
QqRrSsTt
XxYyZz
67890&

James Cooper (Dapper Signs), Rheingold Rascal

www.dappersigns.co.uk | Instagram: @dappersigns

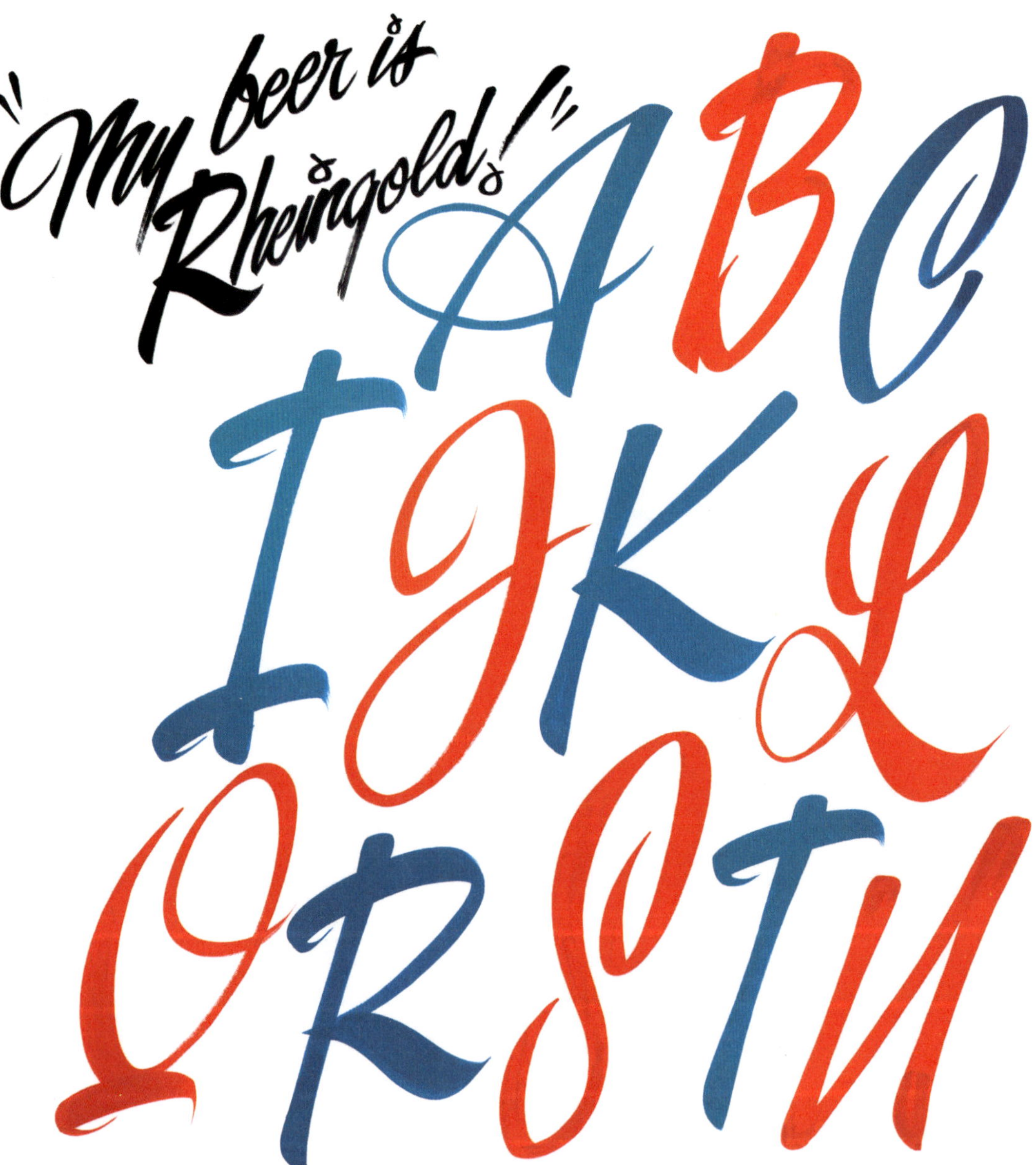

DE7GH
MNOP
VWXY
&3

"Wrap that Rascal!"

Astrid Oud, Magic Monkey

www.studiotoveraap.nl | Instagram @toveraap

AaBbCc
GgHhIi
MmNn
QqRrSs
WwXx
!?12345

DdEeFf
JjKkLl
OoPp
TtUuVv
YyZz
67890&

Ray Mawst, Amalgaration

www.raymawst.com | Instagram: @raymawst

Aa Bb Cc

Gg Hh Ii Jj

Nn Oo Pp

Uu Vv Ww

& 1 2 3 4 5 6

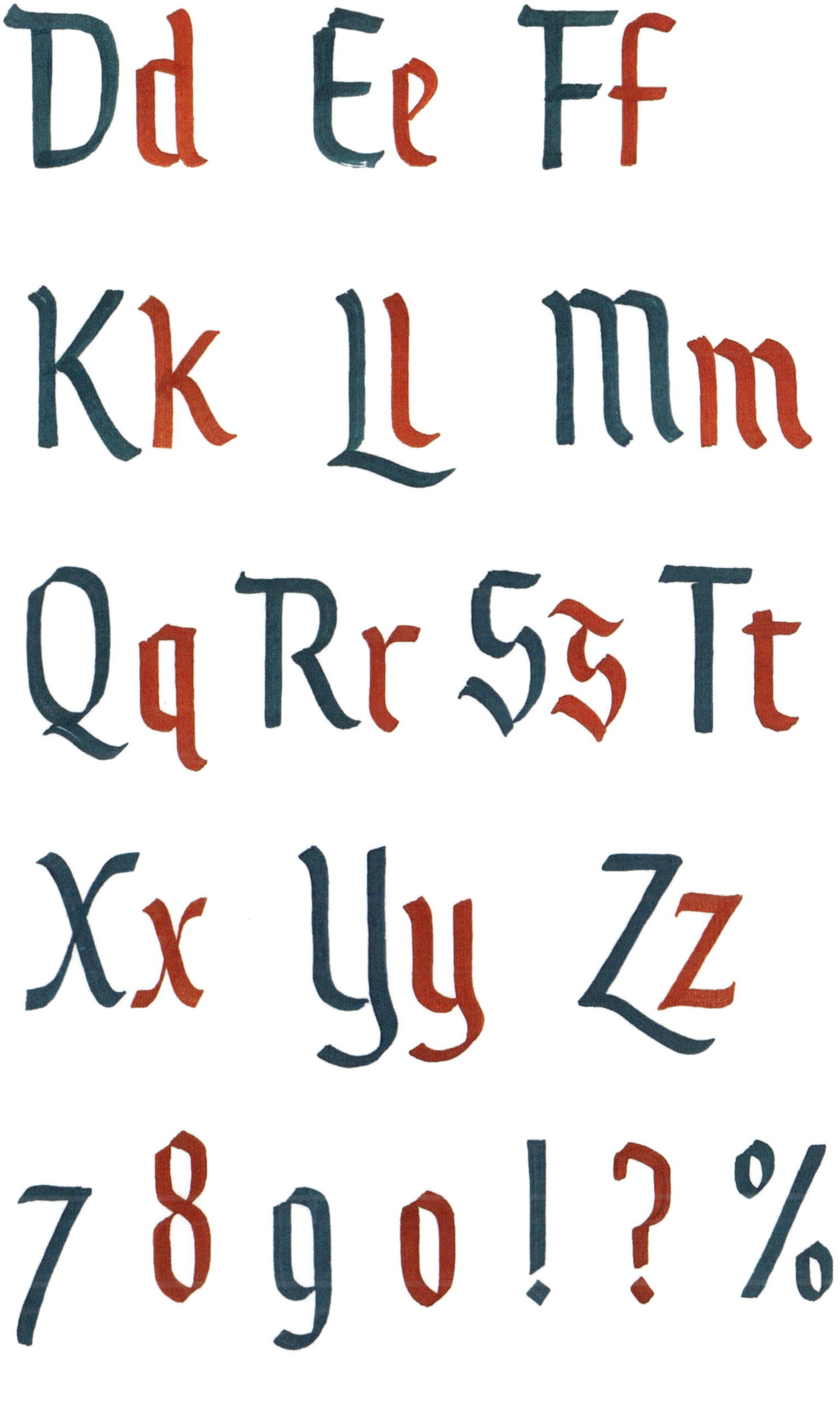

Dd Ee Ff

Kk Ll Mm

Qq Rr Ss Tt

Xx Yy Zz

7 8 9 0 ! ? %

Emily Balsley, Fill 'Er Up

www.emilybalsley.com | Instagram: @milybluestar

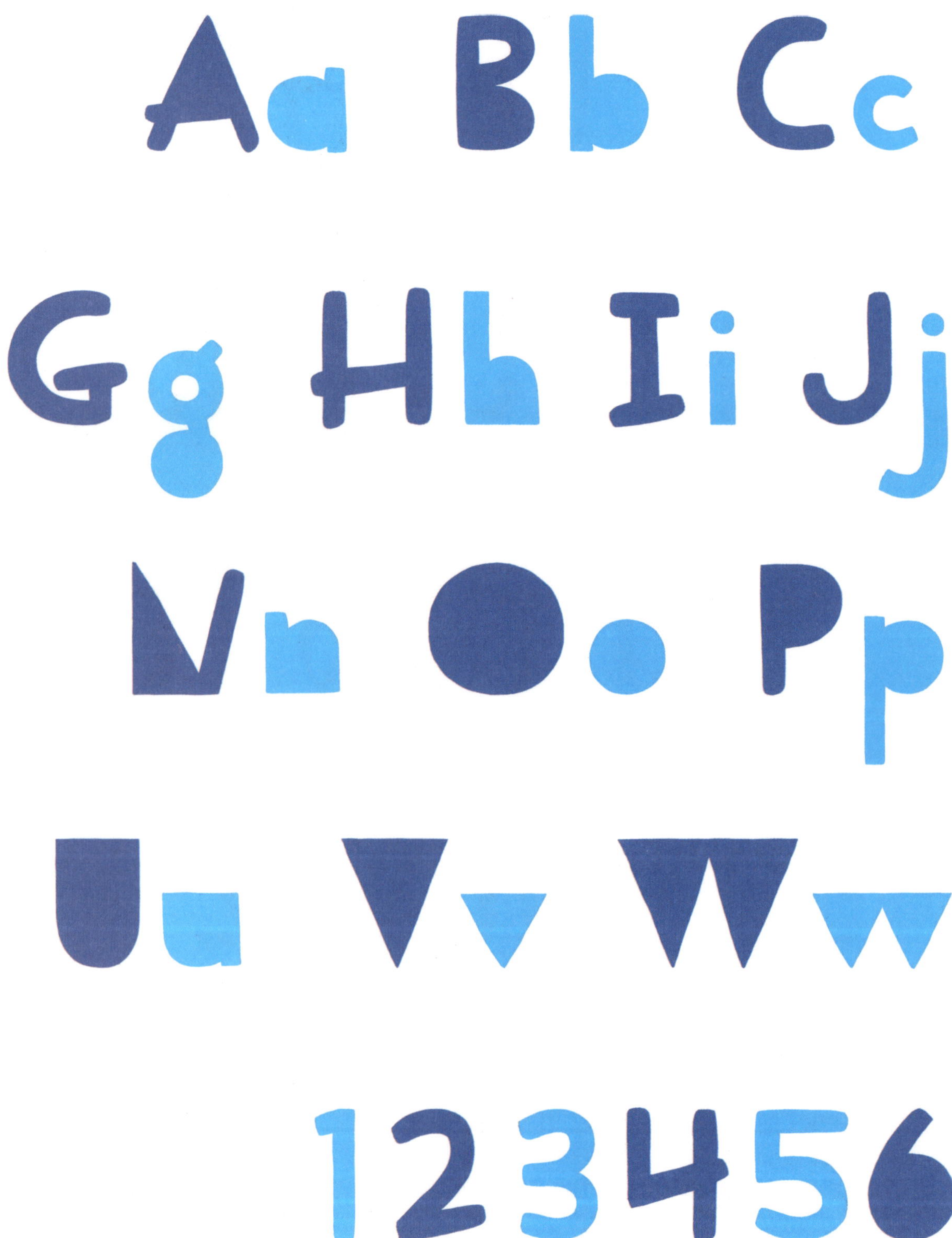

Dd Ee Ff

Kk Ll Mm

Qq Rr Ss Tt

Xx Yy & Zz

7890 !?@

Derek McDonald, Chisel Speed Stroke

www.goldenwestsignpainter.com | Instagram: @goldenwestsignarts

Aa Bb Cc
Gg Hh Ii Jj
Nn Oo Pp
Tt Uu Vv Ww
012345

Dd Ee Ff

Kk Ll Mm

Qq Rr Ss

Xx Yy & Zz

6789?!

Kendra Spanjer, Pinhead Script

www.kendraspanjer.com | Instagram: @kendystix

Aa Bb Cc Dd
Ii Jj Kk Ll
Qq Rr Ss Tt
Yy & Zz !? !?%

Ee Ff Gg Hh

Mm Nn Oo Pp

Uu Vv Ww Xx

1234567890

Jeroen Koning, King Script

www.amsterdamsignpainters.nl | Instagram: @jeroenkoning

Aa Bb Cc

Gg Hh Ii Jj

Nn Oo Pp

Uu Vv Ww

?!% 1 2 3 4 5 €

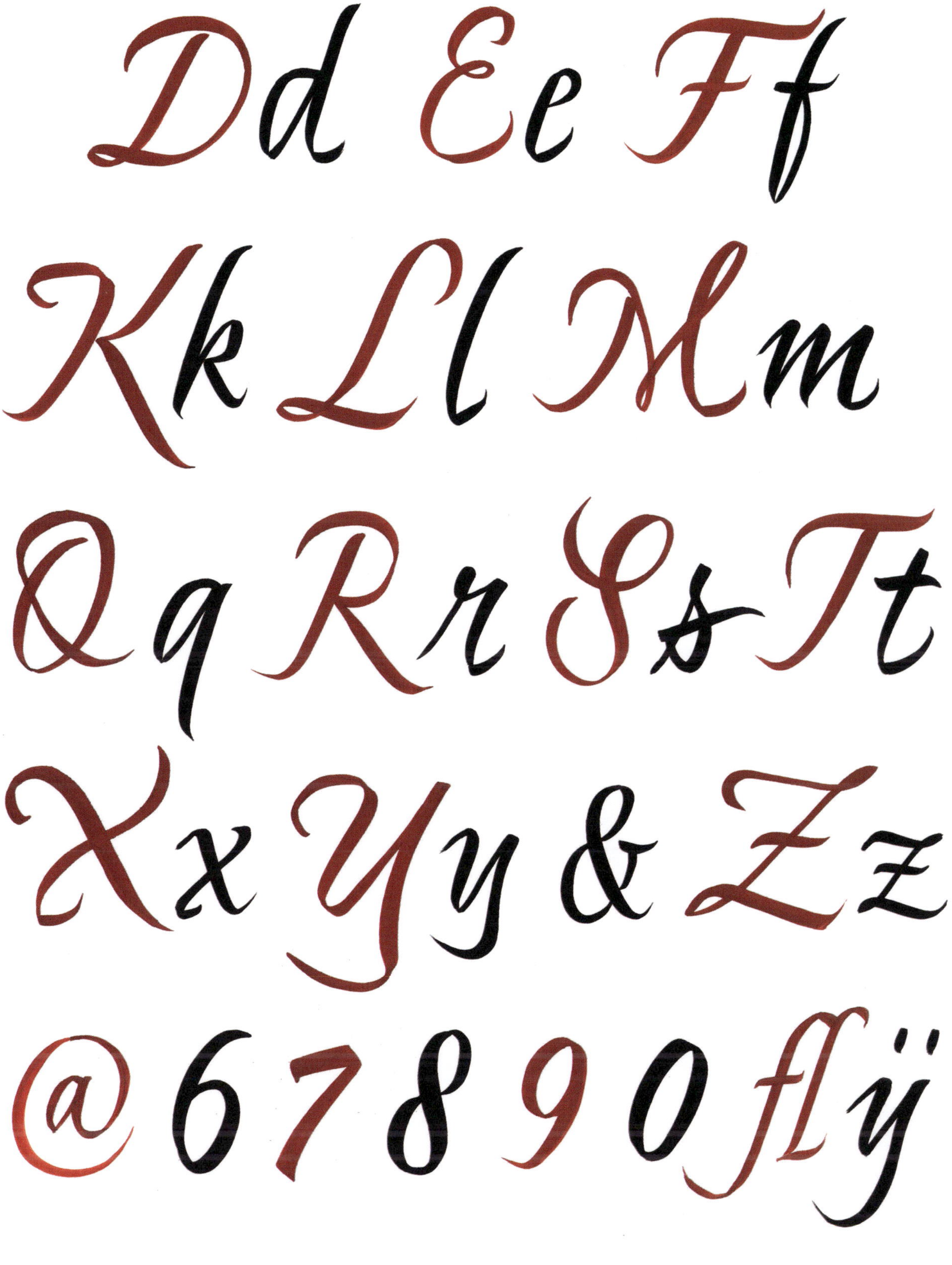

Dd Ee Ff
Kk Ll Mm
Qq Rr Ss Tt
Xx Yy & Zz
@ 6 7 8 9 0 flÿ

Jasper Andries, J's 26

www.amsterdamsignpainters.nl | Instagram: @amsterdamsignpainter_jasper

Aa Bb Cc Dd

Ee Ff Gg Hh

Ii Jj Kk Ll

Mm Nn Oo Pp

Qq Rr Ss Tt

Uu Vv Ww Xx

Yy *and* Zz

1234567890?!%

Pascale Arpin, Honeymoon in Cortez

www.pascalearpin.com | Instagram: @pascale_arpin

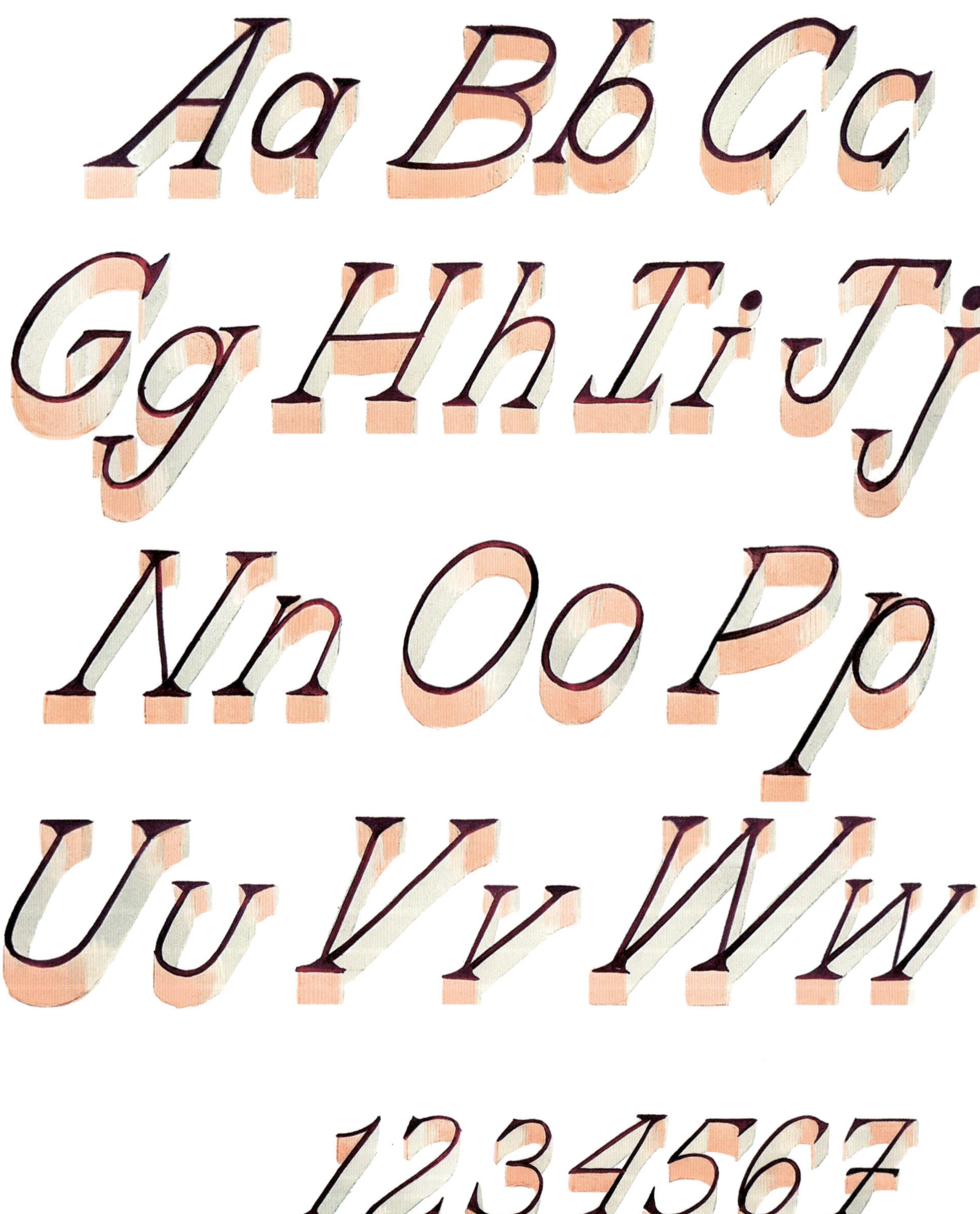

Dd Ee Ff

Kk Ll Mm

Qq Rr Ss Tt

Xx Yy Zz

890!&?%

Aa Bb Cc

Gg Hh Ii Jj

Nn Oo Pp

Uu Vv Ww

1234567

Dd Ee Ff

Kk Ll Mm

Qq Rr Ss Tt

Xx Yy & Zz

890 !?öß

Jakob Engberg (Copenhagen Signs), Copen Black Oblique

www.copenhagensigns.dk | Instagram: @copenhagensigns

AaBbCc
GgHhIiJj
NnOoPp
UuVvWw
& 123456

Dd Ee Ff

K·k Ll Mm

Qq Rr Ss Tt

X x Y y Z z

7 8 9 0 ? !

Carl Fredrik Angell (Frisso), Christiania

www.behance.net/christianiadesign | Instagram: @frisso151

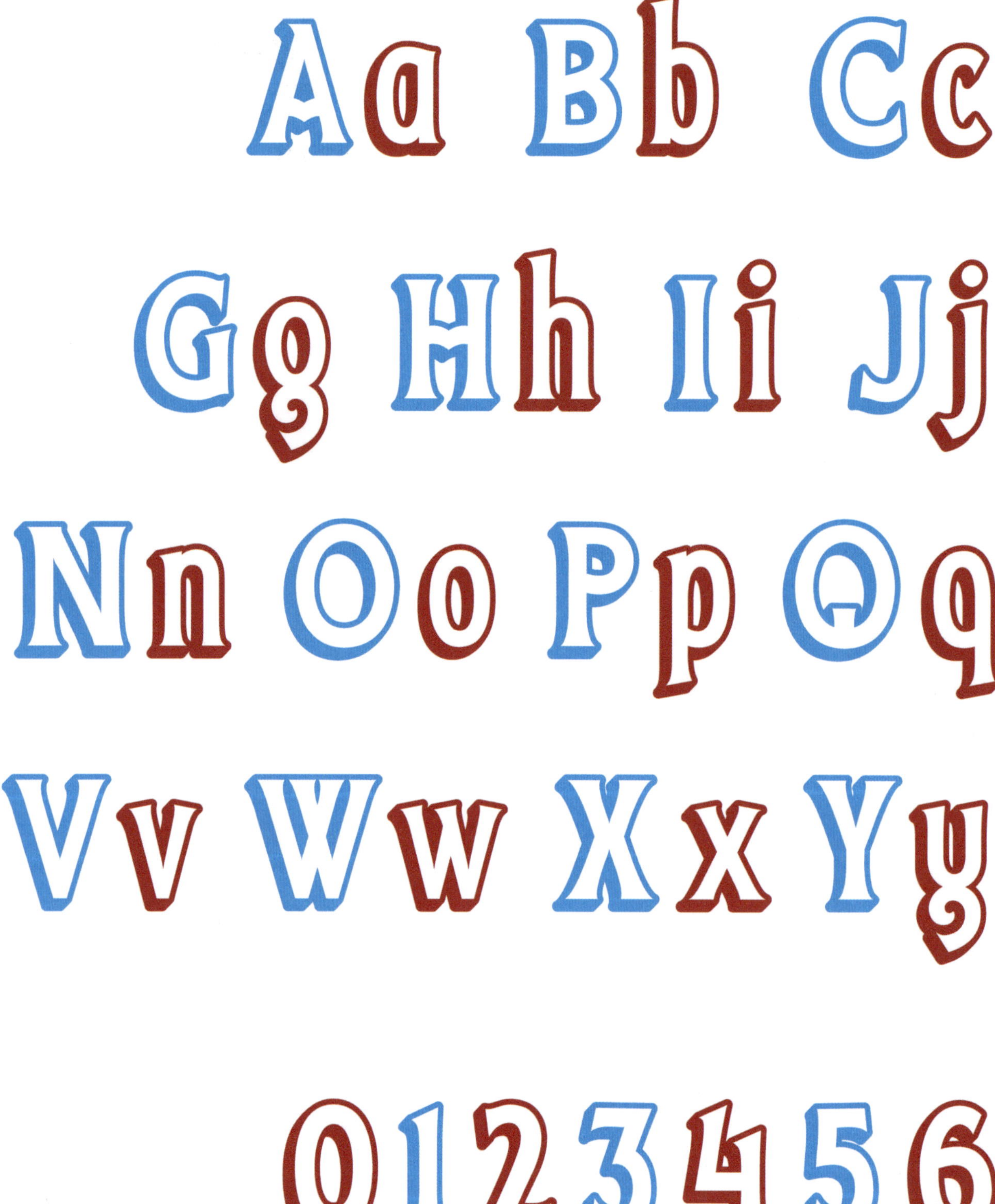

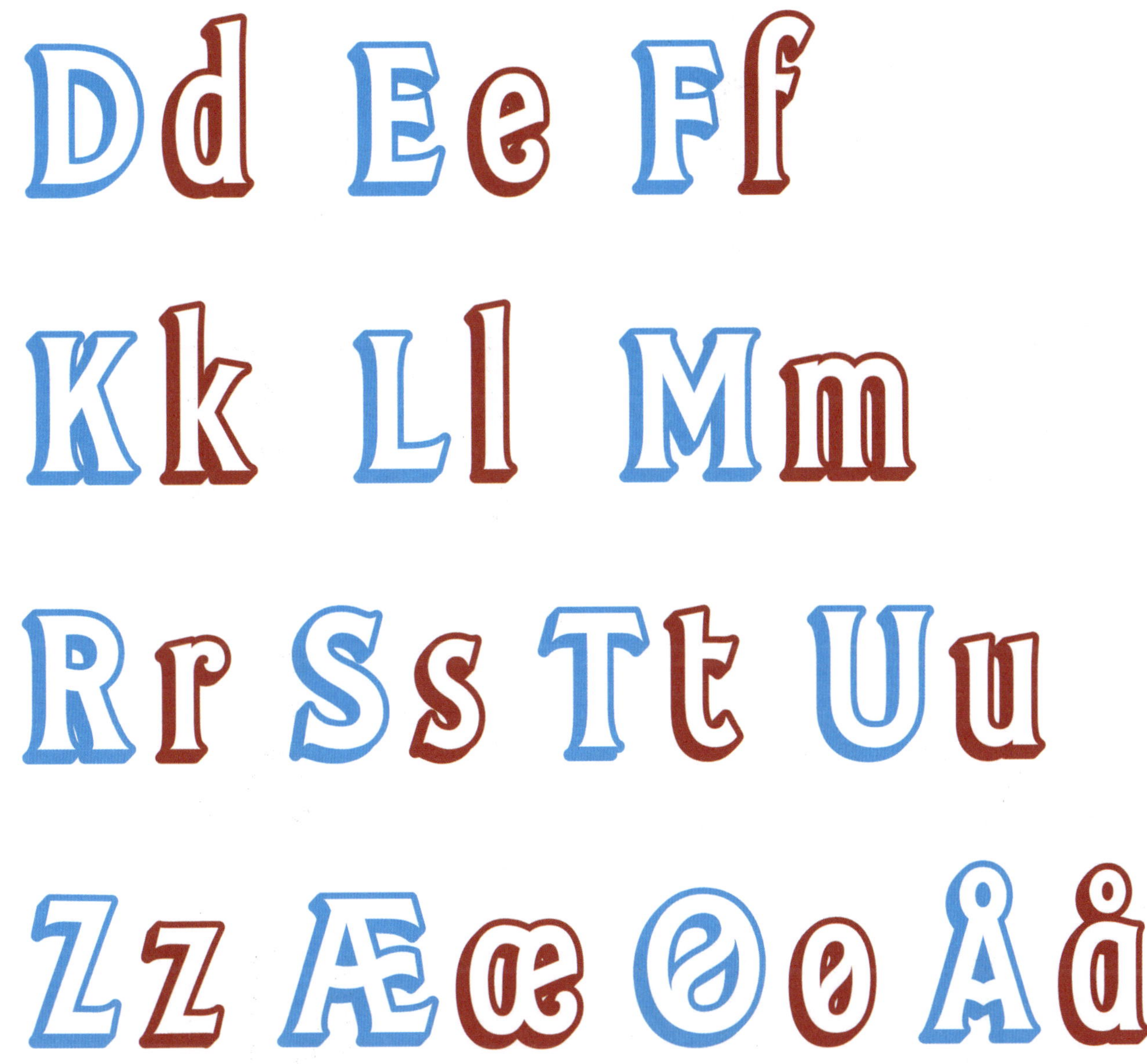

Dd Ee Ff
Kk Ll Mm
Rr Ss Tt Uu
Zz Æ Œ Øo Åå
7 8 9 & ? !

Miranda Ensink, Alfabetty

www.amsterdamsignpainters.nl | Instagram: @amsterdamsignpainter_miranda

Aa Bb Cc

Dd Ee Ff Gg

Hh Ii Jj Kk

Ll Mm Nn

1 2 3 4 5 6 7 8 9 0

Oo Pp Qq

Rr Ss Tt

Uu Vv Ww

Xx Yy Zz

& f € @ ÿ ; ! ?

Adam Romuald Klodecki (Theosone), Teotextura

www.scriptoriumberlin.com | Instagram: @theosone

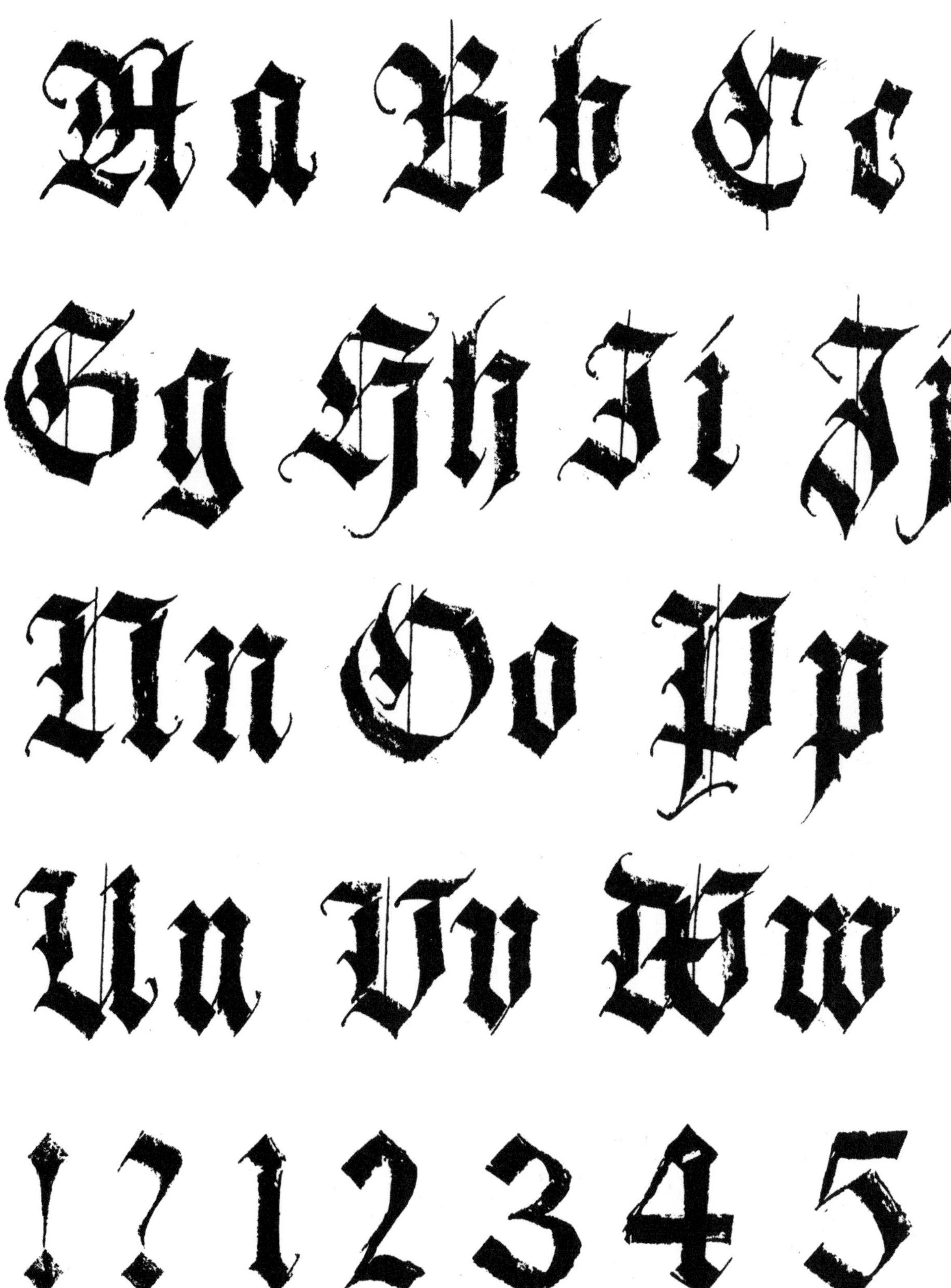

174

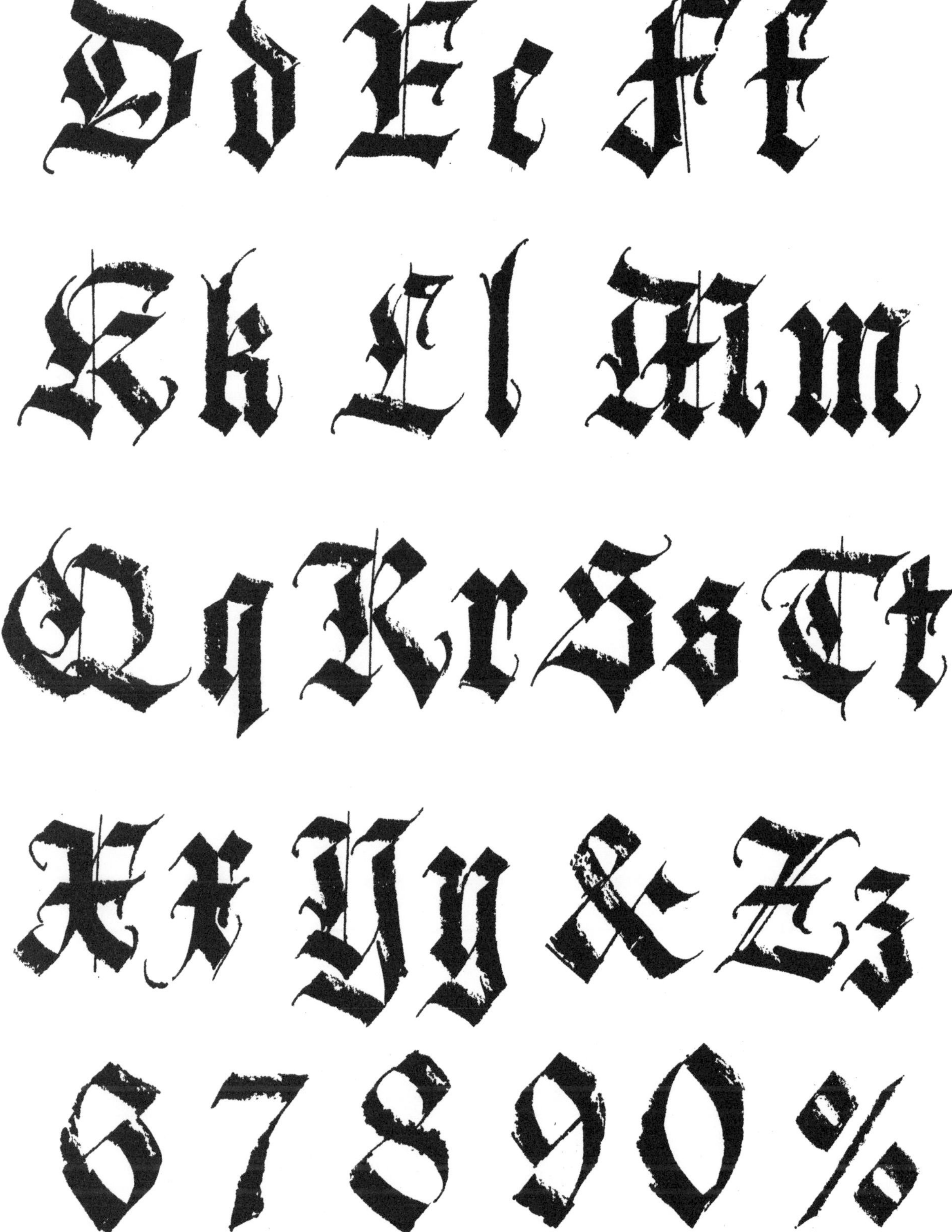

Matthieu Verlaine, Verlaine Script

www.matthieuverlaine.com | Instagram: @matthieuverlaine

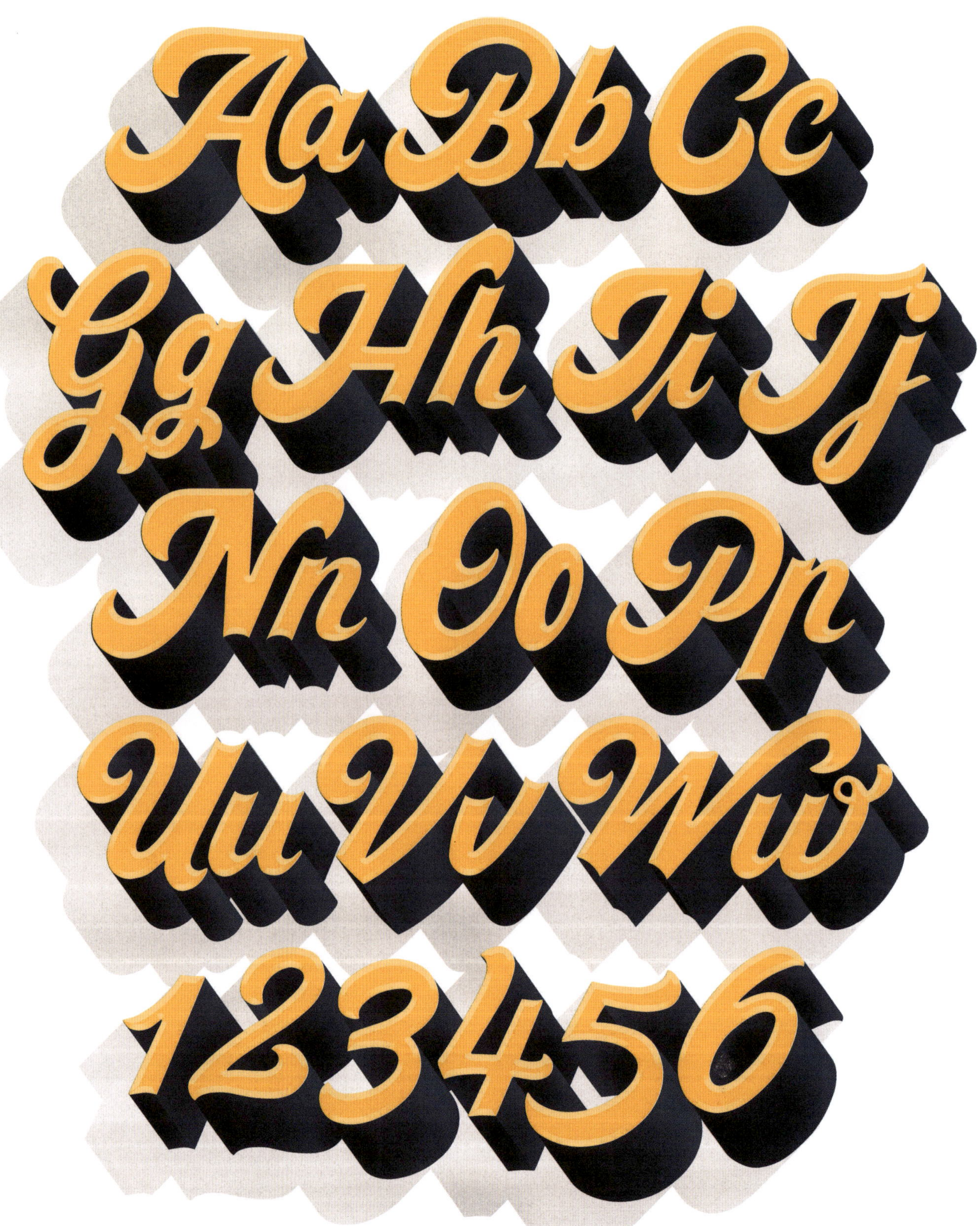

Dd Ee Ff
Kk Ll Ll Mm
Qq Rr Ss Tt
Xx Yy Zz
7890&!?
Verlaine.

Artist Profiles

The alphabets on pages 96 to 177 include a diversity of styles that can be used and adapted for all forms of sign work. It is a privilege to include contributions from old hands alongside many from those who are relatively new to the trade. These alphabets also double as a world tour in miniature, with contributions from Berlin to Buenos Aires, Melbourne to Minnesota, and Norway to The Netherlands. Please look up and follow every one of the contributors, and let them know when their work has inspired you.

Elena Albertoni

As an active member of the Berlin type scene Elena has organized numerous workshops, film screenings, and exhibitions. She runs a studio for sign painting, type design, and lettering called La Letteria. La Letteria is a play on the Italian word *latteria* (dairy), which well represents Elena's interest in designing everyday things and enhancing the ordinary. She enjoys the interaction with her neighborhood when making handcrafted signs for local shops, and finds inspiration for her lettering creations in the vernacular heritage of a particular place.

Jasper Andries

Jasper Andries worked as a commercial artist, mostly drawing storyboards for ad agencies and film directors. He got to know Mike Meyer personally when he organized Mike's first Amsterdam workshops. Since then, Jasper has committed to making hand-painted signs himself and co-founded Amsterdam Signpainters. Nowadays he adds pictorial work to his signs whenever he can.

Carl Fredrik Angell

Carl Fredrik Angell, a.k.a. "Frisso," is a graphic designer from Rykkinn, Norway, with a MA in Visual Communication from Kolding School of Design in Denmark. In 2013, he went to Boston for a three-month apprenticeship with Josh Luke and Meredith Kasabian of Best Dressed Signs to learn the craft of sign painting. Since then, he has applied what he learned from the world of sign painting to his design work. He designs custom handcrafted lettering wherever it is required with skill, passion, and a knowledge of typography.

Pascale Arpin

Pascale Arpin is a freelance creative from Ottawa, Canada, who was introduced to sign painting through working in film and television. She has since shifted her focus towards honing her sign-painting craft, notably by learning under Mike Meyer at one of his annual workshops in Mazeppa, Minnesota, which in turn led to becoming his assistant on a number of workshop tours in the USA. Alongside creating a new demand for traditional hand-painted signs in Ottawa, Pascale recently assisted film director Tim Burton with pieces for his art exhibition at the Neon Museum in Las Vegas and is currently illustrating *Phantomtits*, a graphic novel for noted Canadian artist Cara Tierney.

Emily Balsley

Emily Balsley is an illustrator from Madison, Wisconsin. Her work includes book and editorial illustration, games and puzzles, posters, maps, and murals. She is active in the creative community, participating in arts events, gallery shows, panel discussions, and occasionally leading workshops and camps. When she's not drawing, she loves biking, boxing, and hanging out with her friends and family.

Bob Behounek

Bob's passion for sign painting began in 1969 with an apprenticeship in Chicago with the local 830 Sign & Pictorial Union. He was Apprentice of the Year in 1972! He has been a contributing writer for *SignCraft* magazine since 1985 and apprentice instructor for the local union school since 1987. He published a sketchbook about truck signage in 1992. In 2007 he started a charitable group called The Chicago Brushmasters to use sign painters' passion to help others in need. He says it's been a great journey, and the best is yet to come.

Joby Carter

Joby Carter is an expert in traditional sign writing, fairground art, and fancy lettering. He started his apprenticeship at the age of 17 with the legendary signwriter Stan Wilkinson. As a vintage fairground owner and artist, Joby has showcased his sign-writing skills on the rides and attractions at Carters Steam Fair for the past 30 years. The rides date from the 1890s to the 1960s and have been restored using traditional techniques and designs. No computers, no tape, no cheating! Joby's aim is to make it look like new. He prides himself on maintaining these traditional skills and teaches sign-writing courses at his fairground yard in Maidenhead, England.

Karen Cartwright

Karen Cartwright is a lifelong artist with a passion for illustration using traditional pencil and paint. Since creating her first hand-painted sign in 2014, she's been hooked with an insatiable need to continue learning the craft and improve her lettering skills, including by attending workshops with Mike Meyer.

Gaston Castagnet

Gaston the Painter is an Australian–Uruguayan sign painter and lettering artist based in Melbourne, Australia. With a background in graffiti and graphic design, Gaston approaches the trade of sign painting with a fresh outlook. His style reflects the eclectic mix of disciplines he explores in his practice, fusing traditional styles and techniques with the modern tools and digital platforms of today. Swinging between analog and digital, traditional and experimental, Gaston intends to put a twist upon his sign painting, employing the craft in a contemporary and imaginative manner. He also designs logos, typefaces, and products, hosts type events, and teaches workshops around the world.

Ivan Castro

Ivan Castro is a graphic designer based in Barcelona, Spain, who specializes in calligraphy, lettering, and typography. His work involves everything from advertising to editorial, and from packaging to logo design and gig posters. Although Ivan claims to have no specific style, one could say that he has a strong respect for the history of popular culture. He has been working in the field for 20 years, and has been teaching calligraphy and lettering for about 15 years in the main design schools in Barcelona including Elisava and BAU. He travels frequently, holding workshops and giving lectures at design festivals and conferences. He is the author of *The ABC of Custom Lettering* and two online lettering courses on the Spanish platform Domestika.

Morgane Côme

Morgane Côme is a French sign painter and graphic designer based in Brittany, France. She discovered sign painting while on a trip to New York City (via ESPO and Colossal Media murals). A Better Letters workshop in London in 2014 ignited a passion for the craft, which she has worked hard at ever since. Since moving to Brittany in 2016, she has focused on offering bespoke hand-painted lettering to independent stores. Brittany retains a strong popular culture, which endures in costume, music, language, typography, and the conservation of nature and architecture; it's a place where sign painting can flourish.

James Cooper

James Cooper of Dapper Signs describes his entry into the world of sign painting as pure chance: "A bit over ten years ago I did some casual work for a mate who had a food tent and was doing loads of festivals during the summer. One evening it became apparent that there weren't any menus. I heroically volunteered to stop cleaning dirt off pans in order to scribble words on a blackboard with a Posca pen. When I got home I printed off a bunch of business cards that said 'James Cooper, Signwriter' as though I'd been doing it for twenty years and, ridiculously, I've not looked back since."

Dave Correll

Dave Correll is a 1985 graduate of The Detroit Lakes Area Vocational Technical School, Minnesota, in the Sign Lettering and Design program. After graduating, he moved to Milwaukee and worked at Kid Sign Co. as a sign painter. In 1988, he and his wife Ann started and operated Brushwork Signs, in Faribault, MN, and earned a reputation for a unique style of signature custom signs. He wrote several articles for trade magazines such as *SignCraft* and *Signs of the Times*, and gave seminars and workshops on sign-making techniques and design at various Letterheads meets. After 30 years in the sign business, Dave and Ann downsized Brushwork signs and now focus on creative, hand-lettered work. Dave's Casual is an alphabet that evolved over more than 30 years. It's also a font called by a different name, LHF Anna Banana, created by Dave, who is a contributing artist at Letterhead Fonts (www.letterheadfonts. com). What you see on pages 108 and 109 is slightly different and is hand lettered for this book.

Jean Desfeux

After two years studying graphic design, Jean was hired as an apprentice by Jean Michel Drolon, a sign painter who had been in business in Paris for 20 years. He learned on the job by painting every day, mainly for cafés and restaurants. He has now been sign painting for six years and is passionate about his craft.

Valentina Di Donato

Valentina Di Donato or Valdid is a web designer based in Bologna, Italy. She's passionate about graphic design, illustration, and everything around calligraphy, lettering, and typography. Laurel is her new alphabet, combining straight and curved, narrow and wide, especially in its uppercase version.

Jakob Engberg

The founder of Copenhagen Signs, Jakob Engberg has a background in graffiti, photography, and graphic design, and is one of the few full-time sign painters in Denmark. He specializes in custom lettering, gold-leaf work, and traditional sign writing, as well as mural art and logo design. Exploring lettering with a unique approach combined with old techniques, Jakob is well established on the international scene of sign painting and hand lettering.

Barbara Enright

Barbara studied showcard and ticket writing in 1967 and hasn't put down her brushes since. She was the first New South Wales female president and national co-ordinator of the Sign Association of Australia (now ASGA). Barbara owned and operated a successful sign studio for over two decades where she created by hand countless showcards, banners, display tickets, calligraphic invites, place cards, and many other job requests for clients all over Sydney. She has been a passionate teacher throughout her career and currently passes on her brush skills globally.

Miranda Ensink

Miranda Ensink was a graphic designer before dedicating herself to sign painting with Amsterdam Signpainters, a sign company in The Netherlands. Here she combines every aspect she loves into the workplace and deals with letters, images, painting, designing, drawing, organizing, and laughing every day.

Gustavo Ferrari

Gustavo Ferrari is an artist and historian from Buenos Aires, Argentina. He has worked as a Fileteador and a sign painter since 2001. Fileteado is a traditional art from Argentina that was declared by UNESCO to be an item of Intangible Cultural Heritage of Humanity in 2015. In the last decade Gustavo has showcased the Fileteado style around the world, at Letterheads meets, tango festivals, and various design events in the USA, Canada, Europe, and Asia. He has given demonstrations, lectures, and workshops in London, Paris, Berlin, Amsterdam, Oslo, St Petersburg, Toulouse, Warsaw, Moscow, São Paulo, Rio de Janeiro, Lima, and Tokyo.

Carla Hackett

Carla Hackett studied graphic design at university and worked at some of Australia's top agencies in Sydney before escaping to Berlin to nurture her love of lettering and artisan design. On returning to Australia, Carla set up a studio in Melbourne with the aim of bringing a warm, human element to a world dominated by digital fonts and design. She handcrafts lettering for a range of clients in creative industries, including fashion, music, food, branding, magazines, and books. She runs regular brush lettering workshops all over Australia with her mentor Barbara Enright. In 2016, they launched an online course teaching the skill to students around the globe. In the same year, Carla created an all-girl lettering group, The Letterettes, who pop up at events to create live lettering.

Mark Josling

Mark Josling gained a City & Guilds qualification in Signwork and began his career at a sign company in West London. In 1988 he started his own business, Spectrum Signs. He has gone from hand lettering to vinyl and digital and back to hand lettering, which is now his main source of work; he specializes in honors boards, gold leaf, and general hand-painted signs.

Adam Romuald Klodecki

Adam was born in Bialystok, Poland, in 1984. He is a calligrapher, industrial designer, and tattoo artist who is interested in illustration and street art. He studied product design and visual communication at the Fine Arts Academy in Gdansk. After moving to Berlin, he opened his own studio and art gallery, Scriptorium Berlin, with a focus on high-quality tattooing, workshops, and art exhibitions. Today Adam focuses on creating lettering tattoos, handcrafted logotypes, and paintings, and traveling with numerous workshops, street art projects, and tattoo conventions. Adam has worked for brands including Montblanc, Rolex, Lego, Cadillac, Citroën, BMW, Audi, Hennessy, Chivas, DC Shoes, and ESPN ExGames.

Jeroen Koning

Jeroen Koning studied Graphic Design in 's-Hertogenbosch in The Netherlands and worked for several design companies. In 2013 he finished the Expert Class Type Design at the Plantin Institute of Typography in Antwerp. He co-founded Amsterdam Signpainters in 2016.

Heather Leavitt Martinez

Heather has studied with master calligraphers, sign painters, and graffiti artists. She uses letters found in her environments in her work as a visual practitioner, writing with Neuland® markers on paper. She translated the casual script style Mike Meyer taught her for use with a brush marker and it is one of the main content lettering styles used in her work. She is the author of *Lettering Journey: Fast. Functional. Fun!* Neuland Hand was designed in 1923 by Rudolf Koch and has been interpreted by calligraphers as a bold, display lettering style. Heather learned Neuland Hand majuscules from Carol DuBosch in 2016 and developed a minuscule version by looking at a set of hand-cut stamps Carol showed her in 2019. When she saw an interpretation of Neuland Hand on the wall of Mike Meyer's studio she realized that sign painters use it too.

Dorota Letachowicz

Dorota is a calligrapher from Poland and one of the founders of the Warsaw House of Calligraphy. Taking part in workshops with Jakob Engberg, Mike Meyer, and Jeff Marshall was the beginning of her sign-painting adventure. During the last two years she has given calligraphy workshops and courses for children and adults. She loves Roman Capital proportions and the smell of turpentine.

Ray Mawst

Ray Mawst is a freelance artist who spends most of his time creating lettering and custom artwork for logotypes, hand-painted signage, and murals. His lettering practice is closely tied to his interest in and practice of calligraphy, in particular pen-written gothic scripts, formal italic, and brush-written Roman capitals. His goal is to honor previous generations of lettering artists by learning and practicing classic lettering styles, and bringing them into the future with a modern twist.

Alice Mazzilli

Alice Mazzilli is a calligrapher with a background in graffiti, sign painting, and graphic design. Her work is inspired by the history of writing; the journey from the symbol to the letter form. Her current exploration involves translating movement and rhythm into form, alongside street art and a consideration of the future and evolution of our writing systems. Her alphabet is called Jazz because the letters are inspired by the concepts behind that musical genre.

Derek McDonald

After running his own sign firm (Golden West Sign Arts) for over 10 years, Derek now works full time at the in-house sign shop at Disneyland in California. Derek's alphabet was worked super fast with no touch-ups; all imperfections are included. It is designed as an alternative to casuals when speed is needed, with the brush always held at a 45-degree angle. Chisel Speed Stroke is based on styles in showcard lettering manuals from the 1930s and 1940s.

Cheryl McLean

Cheryl McLean runs a successful blackboard art and sign business in Sydney, Australia. She started in the sign industry in 1993, when her sign-writing work overtook her school-teaching career. Formally trained as a showcard and ticket writer, she developed her blackboard art skills by never saying "no" to any new challenge. She runs blackboard art workshops all over the world, combining her love of travel with the absolute joy of passing on hand-lettering skills.

Fernando Mello

From São Paulo, Brazil, Fernando Mello studied type design in the UK, Belgium, and the USA. He has been a typeface designer at Fontsmith in London since 2008 and his typefaces have won several design prizes. His background in multiple visual areas—namely architecture, typography, graphic design, and illustration—guides his search for creating innovative and original typefaces. Fernando also has a keen interest in sign painting, specially in the casual script. Touriga is named after a grape variety used for making port wine.

Mike Meyer
Mike Meyer is a sign painter from Mazeppa, a small rural
town in Minnesota. He has run his own business since 1989
and regularly travels the world to attend and support
Letterheads sign-painter events, as well as hosting many
in his own shop. He is an ambassador for the sign-painting
business and, in 2012, his dedication was recognized through
an appearance in the internationally acclaimed film, *Sign
Painters*. In 2013 he held his first ever hand-lettering workshop
in Christchurch, New Zealand, and has now gone on to inspire
people in dozens of cities across Europe, the USA, Canada, and
Australia. In his own words, "Nothing can replace the 'power' of
what a brush in your hand can produce."

Miss Merlot
Graffiti artist Merlot—a Seattle native, currently based in
Chicago—constantly strives to push boundaries. Painting since
2007, Merlot strikes a balance between exploring new directions,
while paying homage to the traditional styles that form a
timeless, unmatched Americana foundation. Merlot's diverse
background in graphic design has instilled a fearlessness in
her experimentation with letter forms and her approach as a
whole. As an established creative director, she offers a mindful
attention to detail and an unmatched sight of the end result.

Astrid Oud
Astrid Oud is a designer/illustrator/muralist/letterhead living
in Amsterdam. She studied art at Amsterdam University of the
Arts. Her work is often based on nostalgia; the alphabet in this
book was inspired by the Belgian comic artist André Franquin,
whose work she read as a child. "Magic Monkey" translates to
"Toveraap," the name of her company.

Ged Palmer
Over the last fifteen years, Ged Palmer's fascination with letter
forms has led him into design, typography, calligraphy, mural
painting, sign painting, and gold-leaf signs. In 2015, inspired
by an old East London sign shop and letterworks that closed
in 1938, he launched his studio and shop, The Luminor Sign
Company. Hugely passionate about sharing his knowledge of
sign writing with the younger generation through workshops,
Ged and his work have been recognized by the International
Society of Typographic Designers, The Type Directors Club,
and various publications worldwide.

Adrián Pérez
Adrián Pérez (a.k.a El Deletrista) is a sign painter and
lettering designer based in Barcelona, Spain. He was born
into a family of tattoo artists and has always been obsessed
with letters, their forms, and counterforms. Growing up in
Madrid and Barcelona he fell in love with old signs and how
they become part of the landscape. He is self-taught, has
given workshops around the globe, and today makes a
living from this amazing craft.

Joan Quirós
Joan Quirós is a freelancer and teacher specializing in
calligraphy and lettering, based in València, Spain. He started
to be interested in letter forms during his teenage years, when
he got into the graffiti scene. Since 2012, he has increased
his knowledge and skills, learning from the most recognized
masters. He has great respect for the historical traditions
of lettering, paying special attention to the details of their
shapes, creating a nexus between the past and the present,
and applying his contemporary perspective to each project.

Kendra Spanjer
Kendra is a Colorado-based illustrator, pinstriper, letterer, and
graphic designer with an affinity for atomic-era Americana.
She's grateful to have found her paint family, and never lets
a day go by without learning something new.

Pieter van Tongeren
Pieter van Tongeren (Mossy Giant) is an Amsterdam-based
illustrator and graphic designer who practices his craft in
a small studio close to the city center. He takes tremendous
pride in his craft, always creating by hand while flirting with
the digital realm. Nature, man, beast, and machine are the
recurring themes at play within the creations of Mossy Giant.
Wizard-like hippies, jolly bears, and archaic transportation
devices are subjects that the giant loves to put on paper. The
alphabet in this book is inspired by the Brother 1816 font.

Matthieu Verlaine
After studying art direction and working in video games,
branding, and advertising, Matthieu Verlaine decided to
become a full-time artist to reconnect with his first love for
letters. His work is mostly inspired by 1980's visual codes,
big bold scripts, and Japanese culture, in a mix of tradition
and experimentation.

Hana Sunny Whaler
Hana Sunny Whaler is a sign painter based in London, where
she works for a wide variety of clients on projects ranging
from large-scale community murals to traditional pub signage.
A background rooted in drawing and a fascination with the
history of the sign-painting trade inform her traditional
decorative style—designed and drafted by hand, and often
attempting to avoid technology altogether! Hana always seeks
to learn from, collaborate with, and promote the sign-painting
community, and is a proud member of sign-gang Alphabetics
Anonymous, co-founder of Tactile Collective, and a regular
attendee at Letterheads meets worldwide.

Ashley Willerton
Ashley is a multi-disciplinary designer and craftsman with
a focus on hand lettering, traditional sign writing, and reverse
glass gilding. With a passion for design history and a particular
interest in the sign writing and gilding artistry of the Victorian
and Edwardian eras, Ashley has built a reputation for his
traditional approach, which wherever possible will employ the
same methods and materials that were used over a century
ago. His alphabet is inspired by the lettering used on a 1937
showcard for the play *Housemaster* by Ian Hay.

Glossary

ACP
See **Aluminum Composite Panel**.

Acrylic (Paint)
See **Emulsion (Paint)**.

Additive
Substances added to **paints** to affect their suitability for working, and also the final finish. Examples include **thinners, reducers, hardeners, driers,** and **retarders**.

Aluminum Composite Panel
Construction material consisting of a low-density core sandwiched between two thin sheets of aluminum.

Artwork
See **Design**.

Awl
See **Pounce Pin**.

Belly (Hair)
The middle part of the brush hairs that hold the bulk of the paint while working. For kolinsky **sable**, the belly is a bulge in the shape of the lower part of the hairs.

Binder (Paint)
The film-forming part of the **paint** that results in the solid state when **cured**.

Bodkin
See **Pounce Pin**.

Bon Ami
A mildly abrasive powder cleanser used with water to clean glass.

Brayer
A firm rubber roller with a handle used to apply pressure over a surface when sticking something down.

Bridge (Rest)
A raised length of wood, metal, or plastic used to keep the hand clear of the surface while working flat on painting.

Brush
Tool consisting of hairs joined to a handle used for the application of **paint** to **substrates**.

Bubble Level/Stick
See **Spirit Level**.

Bulletin Colors
Oil-based **paints** for temporary billboards, with **additives** that increase **flow** but reduce durability versus **enamels**.

Cap-Height (Letters)
Height of uppercase letters in an alphabet, and so equivalent to the top horizontal line for a line of lettering.

Carbon Paper
Coated paper that allows the transfer or copying of a **design** using pressure from a pencil, ballpoint pen, or similar hard tip. (Also see **Saral Transfer Paper**.)

Chalk Line
Long piece of nylon or string that is coated in chalk and "snapped" from a position of tension to create straight lines when **setting out** a sign.

Chamois Leather
Porous, non-abrasive, absorbent leather made from sheep or goat skin.

Chicken Scratch
Rough marking out of the position of letters, rather than setting them out in full, ahead of painting.

China Marker
See **Grease Pencil**.

Chinagraph Pencil
See **Grease Pencil**.

Chisel-Edge Writer (Brush)
Sign-painting **brush** with hair tips that form a flat chisel shape when the **heel** is pressed between thumb and forefinger.

Clear (Coat)
See **Varnish**.

Coach Liner (Brush)
See **Liner**.

Counter (Letter)
Enclosed space inside a letter (e.g. center of an O).

Crazing
Cracking of **paint** caused when a second coat is applied before the first has fully **cured**.

Cure (Paint)
Paint has cured when the binding process is complete, either through oxidation, polymerization, and/or the evaporation of all **solvents**.

Cutter (Brush)
See **Lining Fitch**.

Decal
A design on one material transferred onto another through adhesion. In the sign industry, usually adhesive vinyl signs.

Design
A design is a complete artwork for the creation of a sign or piece of lettering. It can be hand-drawn, digital, or printed from files.

Dibond
Brand of **Aluminum Composite Panel**.

Diluent
See **Solvent**.

Dippers
Small, usually round, metal cups used to hold paint and/or thinners and then clipped to a **palette** for working with.

Dowels
Cylindrical rods of wood, used as short pins to join other pieces of wood together.

Drawing
See **Design**.

Drier
Paint **additive** that speeds up the **curing** (drying) process.

Easel
Upright support structure used to position paper, boards, or other materials while painting.

Electro-Pounce
Electronic device used to burn tiny holes in paper to produce a **pounce pattern**.

Emulsion (Paint)
An emulsion is created by using an emulsifier to mix two liquids that would otherwise separate. In sign painting the term describes the family of **water-based paints** containing acrylic and/or latex **binders**.

Enamel (Paint)
Description of the high-gloss finish given by paints. Although usually used to describe **oil-based** sign **paints, water-based** enamels are also available.

Engine Grease
See **Engine Oil**.

Engine Oil
Oil used for car engines, which can also be used for preserving the hairs of **oil-based** sign-painting **brushes** when not in use.

Extender
See **Retarder**.

Ferrule
Metal tube used to fix the hairs of
a **brush** to the handle.

Filling
The hairs of a **brush**.

Film (Paint)
Solid covering created by the **binder**
in **paint** once it has **cured**.

Fine Line Tape
Family of vinyl tapes that can be used
for masking off lines of lettering, or
positioned in parallel to mask off the
painting of even lines and borders.

Fitch (Brush)
Brush with tough hairs, usually used for
painting rough **substrates** such as walls.

Flat (Brush)
Brush with a flattened **ferrule** that
positions the **filling** in a flat formation.

Flat (Paint)
See **Poster Paint**.

Flax Seed Oil
See **Linseed Oil**.

Flow (Paint)
The consistency of **paint** and the extent
to which it moves easily and consistently
from the **brush** to the **substrate**.

Foam Roller
See **Roller**.

Gaffer Tape
High-**tack** tape with strong fabric structure.

Ghost Sign
Faded painted sign, usually for a
redundant business.

Grease Pencil
Pencils made from hardened wax, well-
suited to marking glossy surfaces such as
glass and **Aluminum Composite Panel**.
Also referred to as wax pencils, china
markers, and chinagraph pencils.

Grit (Sandpaper)
Measurement standard that specifies
the average size of abrasive particles
used in manufacturing sandpaper.

GSM
Grams per square meter, used to
specify the "grammage" (density)
of paper and card stock.

Gum Arabic
Resin obtained from the sap of various
species of trees, typically the acacia tree,
used to protect the **filling** in **brushes**
after manufacturing but before use.

Handle (Brush)
Wooden or plastic stick joined to the
filling and held for painting.

Hardener
Additive for **oil-based paints** that
increases the hardness of the **cured film**.

Heel (Brush)
The portion of the **filling** closest to the
ferrule or **quill** on a **brush**.

Hiding Pigment
Colors with relatively high opacity,
caused by the **pigment** particles
effectively scattering light away
from the substrate.

High Tack (Tape)
See **Tack**.

Ink Roller
See **Brayer**.

Japan Colors
See **Poster Paint**.

Kit (Sign)
Name given to a box containing tools
and materials for sign painting.

Kolinsky Sable
See **Sable**.

Kraft Paper
Paper that has relatively high elasticity
and tear resistance. It is usually a brown
color, with a slight sheen on one side that
makes it excellent for practicing sign
painting. It also works well as paper for
pounce patterns.

Lacquer Thinners
High-strength **solvents**, usually used
to thin specialist automotive **paints**.

Latex (Paint)
See **Emulsion**.

Letterheads
Informal network of sign painters and
people in related trades from around the
world who share a passion for their craft
and a desire to learn from each other.
Can also describe a meet, which is a
gathering (of any size) of Letterheads
to share, learn, and have fun together.

Level
See **Spirit Level**.

Liner (Brush)
Long-haired **brush** that holds a lot of
paint for painting long lines.

Lining Fitch (Brush)
Coarse-haired **brush** used for working
on rough **substrates** or blending on
any substrate.

Linseed Oil (Boiled)
A drying oil obtained from the seeds of
the flax plant and which is used as the
binder in many types of **oil-based paints**.
It can also be used alone, or in combination with other substances, as a **retarder**
to keep paint **open**.

Low Tack (Tape)
See **Tack**.

Mahl Stick
Wooden, metal, or carbon fiber stick with
a padded end used to support the hand
while painting, or as the straight edge or
a pivot for straight lines and curves (from
the Dutch *maalstok*, from *malen*, meaning
"to paint," plus *stok*, meaning "stick").

Mask (Vinyl)
Vinyl cut so that areas to paint are left
exposed while areas that are not to be
painted are masked by the vinyl.

Masking Tape
Paper tape with an adhesive that allows
the tape to be removed without damaging
the surface underneath. In sign painting
it has many uses, including masking off
areas that must remain paint free.

Maulstick
See **Mahl Stick**.

Medium Density Overlay (MDO) Panel
Plywood with a resin overlay applied
to improve resistance to moisture and
weathering. It is far superior to regular
plywood and other timber for fabricating
sign boards.

Medium Tack (Tape)
See **Tack**.

Mineral Spirits
Clear liquid obtained as a by-product
in the process of crude oil refinery, used
in sign painting for cleaning **brushes**.

Mineral Turpentine
See **Mineral Spirits**.

Nap Roller
See **Roller**.

Neatsfoot Oil
Oil extracted from the shin and ankle
bones of cattle, usually used for the
conditioning of leather but also perfect
for working into the hairs of **oil-based
brushes** when not in use.

Oil-Based (Paint)
Family of **paints** that use drying oils
(e.g. **linseed oil**) as the **binder**.

One-Stroke (Brush)
See **Flat**.

Open (Paint)
Paint that has been applied but not yet
cured, and kept that way for working
further with it (e.g. blending).

Oxidization
Chemical reaction due to exposure
to oxygen. This is how **oil-based**
paints **cure**.

Paint
Liquid that **cures** to form a solid **film**
after application to a **substrate** for
decorative and/or protective purposes.
Consists of **binder**, **solvent**, **pigment**
(when colored), and **additives**.

Paint Match System
See **Pantone**®.

Painter's Tape
See **Masking Tape**.

Paint-Up-To Line
Horizontal line used in script lettering
to indicate the position above the
baseline where letters will be joined.

Palette
Flat, non-porous surface used to shape
sign-painting brushes (**paletting**)
while working, and to blend colors.

Palette Knife
Flat, blunt knife used to mix and
dispense **paint**.

Paletting
Shaping the brush once loaded with
paint, usually to a chisel shape as with
chisel-edge writers.

Panel Jam
Area in a **Letterheads** meet where
sign painters get creative, painting fun
panels to give away or sell in an auction
at the end of the event.

Pantone®
Color-matching standard used to specify
colors for inks and printing.

Pattern
Marked paper used to transfer a **design** to
a **substrate**, either by **pouncing** through
perforations or by pressure transfer.

Pattern Wheel
See **Pounce Wheel**.

PDF
Portable Document Format file that
allows consistent viewing of documents
regardless of the application used to
create them.

Pencil (Brush)
An older term for a **chisel-edge writer**.

Pencil (Graphite)
Regular pencil in various levels of hardness (H, 2H, etc.) and softness (B, 2B, etc.).

Pencil (Grease)
See **Grease Pencil**.

Petroleum Spirits
See **Mineral Spirits**.

Pigment
Solid material in **paints** that provides the
color. Can be organic, mineral, or synthetic
in origin. See also **hiding pigment**.

Pinstriping
Decorative art, usually on vehicles,
consisting of fine painted lines, either
alone or combined to form intricate,
often symmetrical patterns.

Plotter
Electronic hardware used to cut or
perforate vector graphics on paper
and vinyl.

Primer
Paint used to seal a **substrate** and make
it ready to receive further layers of paint,
including **topcoat** and lettering.

Pointer (Brush)
Sign-painting **brush** with hair that
naturally comes to a point.

Polymer
Large molecule made up of many repeat-
ing subunits (from the Greek *polumeros*,
meaning "having many parts").

Polymerization
Chemical process of **polymers** joining
together to form larger polymers, as
happens when **emulsion (latex) paint**
cures to form a solid film.

Poster Paint
Oil-based paints with larger quantities
of **driers** than **enamels**, which **cure**
to a flat matte finish. Can also refer to

distempers, or tempera paints, which are
not commonly used in sign painting.

Pounce Bag
Loose fabric bag filled with **pounce
powder** used to transfer **designs** to a
substrate via the **pouncing** technique.

Pounce Pad
Box with soft side that allows **pounce
powder** inside to come out when transferring **designs** to **substrates** using the
pouncing technique.

Pounce Pattern
Drawing with perforated outlines used
for transferring a **design** to a **substrate**
using the pounce technique.

Pounce Pin
A pointed metal tool with a handle that
can be used to perforate holes in a **design**
to create a **pounce pattern**. Similar tools
are referred to as **awls** and **bodkins**.

Pounce Powder
Fine powder made from chalk or charcoal
used with a **pounce bag or pad** to transfer
designs to **substrates**.

Pounce Wheel
Small rotating spiked metal wheel that
is used for perforating **pounce patterns**.
Larger sizes from the tailoring trade are
called pattern or tracing wheels.

Pouncing
Process of transferring a **design** to a
substrate using a **pounce pattern**,
pounce powder, and **pounce pad**.

Quill
Sign-painting **brush** in which the **filling**
is attached to the handle using a bird
quill or synthetic (plastic) substitute.
See also **ferrule**.

RAL
Color-matching standard used to specify
colors for **paints** in Europe.

Rattler
Flying-saucer-shaped piece of metal
placed inside a **paint** tin to help agitate
and distribute the **pigment** evenly
through the liquid when shaking.
Alternatives are large nuts and bolts.

Reducer
Liquid added to **paint** to increase or slow
down drying times in extreme cold (low-
temp) or hot (high-temp) conditions.

Retarder
Substance added to **paint** to slow the
curing process and keep it **open** for

longer, allowing work such as blending to be done.

Roller (Paint)
Handle and soft roller made of either foam (foam roller) or fibrous material (nap roller), used to apply paint to a substrate.

Sable
Hairs for **brush fillings** obtained from the Siberian weasel. Kolinsky sable hairs are from the more northerly species, and so thicker, while red sable is from animals that live further south.

Saral Transfer Paper
Wax-free transfer paper that works in the same way as **carbon paper** to transfer **designs** using pressure from a pencil or other hard point. Available in a variety of colors for working on different colored **substrates**.

Scotch Tape
Low-**tack** translucent tape.

Scumble
Glaze used with **water-based paints** to keep them **open** for longer to assist with blending.

Setting Out
Marking a sign with the outlines of lettering and other elements ahead of painting. It can be done directly on the **substrate**, or through the use of a transfer technique such as **pouncing**.

Showcard
Painted sign on paper or card, often used in shops, theaters, sports venues, and other locations to promote temporary products, services, and offers.

Skids
Beams with holes and movable **dowel** pieces that can be used to prop up sign boards for working at different heights.

Slant Liner (Brush)
See **Lining Fitch**.

Snap
The snap of a **brush** is the extent to which the hairs spring back into shape after being bent in one direction or another.

Solvent
Liquid that dissolves other substances. In sign painting it refers to **mineral spirits**, **turpentine**, water, and other liquids that are used to thin **paint** and clean **brushes**.

Solvent-Based (Paint)
See **Oil-Based**.

Spirit Level
Length of metal or wood with a small glass vial filled with spirit (usually alcohol) set in it. When the level of the liquid is aligned with the level marked on the vial, it shows that the length is perfectly horizontal or vertical.

Squeegee
Firm rubber or plastic strip fixed into a flat handle for applying **vinyl masks**.

Stitching Awl
See **Pounce Pin**.

Substrate
Any surface that is being used to paint a sign onto, including timber, metal, masonry, glass, paper, and fabric.

Synthetic (Brush)
Brushes made from non-natural hairs, usually polyester.

Tack (Tape)
The strength of the adhesive used on the tape, ranging from **low tack** (less sticky, used when you want to remove the tape quickly and easily) to **high tack** (more sticky, used for long-term adhesion).

Terminal (Letter)
End point of a stroke (line) of a letter that does not connect to any other part of the letter (e.g. top and bottom right of the letter L).

Thinner
See **Solvent**.

Ticket
Smaller paper or card sign giving the price of a particular product.

Tip
The very ends of the hairs on a **brush**.

Tip Out
Process of turning the **brush** at the end of a stroke in order to finish with a sharp point.

Tipping Off
Process of going over a painted board while still **curing** with a **roller** or **brush** to produce a smooth finish.

Topcoat
Layer of **paint** applied after the **primer** but before the lettering, and which will typically be partly visible on the final sign as the background, or the lettering if cutting in.

Tracing Paper
Translucent paper that can be laid on top of **designs** to allow copying (tracing).

Tracing Wheel
See **Pounce Wheel**.

Turpentine
Distilled resin from pine trees, used in sign painting as a **solvent**. Often called "turps" informally.

Turpentine Substitute
See **Mineral Spirits**.

Varnish
Non-pigmented **paint** used to provide a protective film on painted or unpainted surfaces.

Vinyl Mask
See **Mask (Vinyl)**.

Viscosity
A measure of the thickness of a liquid: the higher the viscosity, the thicker the liquid (e.g. honey has greater viscosity than water).

Water-Based (Paint)
Family of **paints** whose main **solvent** is water.

Wax Pencil
See **Grease Pencil**.

Weed (Vinyl)
Process of removing excess vinyl when applying as a **decal**, or for use as a **mask**.

Whale Tail
Informal name given to the chisel shape formed by a well-**paletted chisel-edge writer**.

White Spirit
See **Mineral Spirits**.

Whiting
Calcium carbonate (chalk) that has been powdered and washed.

x-Height (Letters)
Height of lowercase letters in an alphabet, specifically the height of the lowercase x.

Yardstick
Large ruler one yard (c.91cm) in length.

Stockists

Australia

1 Shot Paints Australia
141 Christmas Street, Fairfield,
Victoria 3078 +61 417 023 531
www.1shotaustralia.com
info@1shotaustralia.com

Airbrush Supply Network
1/14 Shelley Avenue, Kilsyth,
Victoria 3137 +61 1300 247 278
www.airbrushsupplynetwork.com.au
info@airbrushsupplynetwork.com.au

Bi-Wize Signage Supplies
4/161 Settlement Road Thomastown,
Victoria 3074 +61 3 9465 1233
www.bi-wize.com
sales@bi-wize.com

Viponds Paints
2 Norris Street, North Coburg,
Victoria 3058 +61 3 9350 4188
www.viponds.com.au
michael@viponds.com.au
or alan@viponds.com.au

Austria and Czech Republic

Airbrush-Shop
Husova 2833/87, 43003 Chomutov
+420 777 737 402
www.airbrush-shop.cz
info@airbrush-shop.cz

Belgium

Artobi
Mechelsesteenweg 119,
2860 Sint-Kateline-Waver
+32 15 55 61 97
www.artobi.be
artobi@scarlet.be

Canada

Canadian Signcrafters
4140 B Unit 8 Sladeview Crescent
Mississauga, L5L 6A1
+1 844 876 2130
www.signcraftersupply.com
orders.on@tggraphics.ca

Dragging the Line
+1 905 977 8023
www.draggingtheline.ca
draggingtheline1@gmail.com

ND Graphics
Stores across the country.
+1 888 634 7274
www.ndgraphics.com
customerservice@ndgraphics.com

Denmark

Airbrushshoppen
Industrivej 7, 4450 Jyderup
+45 2812 5270
www.airbrushshoppen.dk
info@customcolors.dk

Custom Colors
Industrivej 7, 4450 Jyderup
+45 28 11 02 23
www.customcolors.dk
proline@customcolors.dk

Finland

Pinstriping Finland
Valimontie 14A1, 60100 Seinäjoki
+358 500 265 324
www.pinstriping.fi
jussi.alasalmi@pinstriping.fi

France

Decor Plus
1 Place des Fêtes, 75019 Paris
+33 1 42 49 22 26
www.decorplus.fr
decor@decorplus.fr

STDS
12 Rue des Trois Saules,
77930 St Sauveur sur École
+33 1 60 65 94 30
www.stds.fr
contact@stds.fr

Germany

Airbrush4You
22A, Kettelerstraße,
97424 Schweinfurt
+49 9721 474 20 80
www.airbrush4you.de
info@herterich.biz

**JahPix Kustom Art
& Tattoo Gallery**
Elpersbüttelerdeich 15, 25704
Elpersbüttel +49 172 623 8956
www.kustomartgallery.com
info@kustomartgallery.com

Petzoldt's
Rehstr. 15, 58089 Hagen
+49 233 1788 7220
www.georg-petzoldt.de
shop@georg-petzoldt.de

Ireland

Cork Art Supplies
28 Princes Street, Cork
+353 21 427 7488
www.corkartsupplies.com
orders@corkartsupplies.com

Italy

Aerografando
Viale Cooperazione 19,
20095 Cusano Milanino (MI)
+39 26 13 12 73
www.aerografando.it
info@aerografando.it

Japan

Mooneyes
2-10 Honmoku-Miyahara,
Naka-ku, Yokohama,
Kanagawa 231-0804
+81 45 623 5999
www.mooneyes.co.jp
shop@mooneyes.co.jp

Netherlands

Airbrush Services Almere
Operetteweg 26, 1323 VA Almere
+31 365 331 531
www.airbrush-services-almere.nl
info@airbrush-services-almere.nl

Lion-Art
Smithweg 1.23, 4462 HC Goes
+31 113 785 147
www.lion-art.nl
info@lion-art.nl

New Zealand

Straightlinz
37 Skerten Avenue
Hornby, Christchurch 08042
+64 212 144 380
www.straightlinz.co.nz
enquiries@straightlinz.co.nz

Norway

Oslo Skiltmaler
Eilert Sundts gate 40,
0355 Oslo +47 40 59 88 95
shop.pinstriping.no
richard@skiltmaler.no

Poland

Deltaarts
Niepodlegosci 12A, Glubczyce, 48100
+48 695 874 169
www.deltaarts.pl
office@deltaarts.pl

Fine-Art
Salon Sprzedaz´y, 54-009
Wrocław ul. Serowarska 1B
+48 71 725 88 98
www.fine-art.com.pl
info@fine-art.com.pl

Spain

Racing Colors
Avenida Carrilet, 251, 08907
L'Hospitalet de Llobregat, Barcelona
+34 933 37 07 74
www.tiendaracingcolors.com
admin@racingcolors.com

Sweden

Highlights
Tjärhovsgatan 1, 116 25
Stockholm +46 8 642 81 90
www.hlstore.com
info@hlstore.com

Mooneyes Sweden
Vadsbro 5b, 774 99 By Kyrkby
+46 226 70480
www.mooneyessweden.com
info@mooneyessweden.com

Switzerland

Fabrikat
Militärstrasse 76, 8004 Zürich
+41 44 542 46 44
www.fabrikat.ch
shop@fabrikat.ch

UK

A.S. Handover
1 Farleigh Place, Farleigh Road,
London N16 7SX +44 20 7241 5877
www.handover.co.uk
info@handover.co.uk

Gold Leaf Supplies
Unit C, Ogmore Court,
Bridgend, CF32 9LW
+44 1656 720 566
www.goldleafsupplies.co.uk
info@goldleafsupplies.co.uk

Stuart R. Stevenson
68 Clerkenwell Road, London
EC1M 5QA +44 20 7253 1693
www.stuartstevenson.co.uk
info@stuartstevenson.co.uk

Wrights of Lymm
+44 1925 752 226
www.stonehouses.co.uk
info@wrightsoflymm.co.uk

USA

Alpha 6 Corporation
15336 Dale Street, Detroit, MI 48223
www.alpha6corporation.com

Blick
Stores across the country.
Mailing address: PO Box 1267, Galesburg,
IL 61402-1769 +1 309 343 6181 ext. 5402
www.dickblick.com
info@dickblick.com

Mack Brush
216 East Chicago Street, PO Box 157,
Jonesville, Michigan 49250
+1 517 849 9272
www.mackbrush.com
info@mackbrush.com

McLogan
21051 Superior Street, Chatsworth, CA
91311 +1 213 749 2262
www.mclogan.com

Michaels
Stores across the country.
Head office: 8000 Bent Branch Drive,
Irving, TX 85063
www.michaels.com

**Midwest Sign & Screen
Printing Supply Co.**
Stores across the country.
Head office: 45 Maryland Avenue East, St.
Paul, MN 55117
www.midwestsign.com
midwest@midwestsign.com

Ronan Paints
89 Taft Avenue, Newburgh, NY 12550
+1 800 307 7951
www.ronanpaints.com
info@ronanpaints.com

Further Reading

I am a big collector of books, and inspiration for many of my signs comes from these. I do not just buy specialist sign and lettering books, as I find material that can be studied and learned from in many different topics, from art and illustration to transport and architecture.

Rather than list all of these here, I have tried to highlight those books that I come back to again and again. Many of these are out of print, but can be found if you shop around on the used (secondhand) market. Many are available as free downloads via websites such as the Internet Archive (archive.org). For some of the rarer publications, have a look at the bundles and subscription service at Lettering Library (www.letteringlibrary.com).

In addition to books, I also search antique and thrift stores for vintage magazines and periodicals, mainly from the 1920s to the 1940s. I find that the hand-lettered, usually black-and-white advertisements in these provide endless inspiration for my own work, as collected in my own Morgue File publications. I recommend you start your own morgue file, clipping and keeping anything interesting you see for reference and as inspiration for future signs that you design and paint.

Sign Painting:

Practical Sign Shop Operation, by Bob Fitzgerald
Sign Painting Course, by E.C. Matthews
Sign Painting Techniques, by Ralph Gregory
Signwork, by Bill Stewart

Practical Lettering & Layout:

The ABC of Custom Lettering, by Ivan Castro
   (also see Ivan's alphabet in this book)
The ABC of Lettering, by Carl Holmes
The Golden Secrets of Lettering, by Martina Flor
House Industries Lettering Manual, by Ken Barber
In Progress, by Jessica Hische
Mastering Layout, by Mike Stevens
Speedball Textbook [24th edition ed. Angela Vangalis
   and Randall Hasson]
Studio Handbook, by Samuel Welo

Lettering Inspiration, History, & Theory:

The Art and Craft of Signwriting, by William Sutherland
The Curly Letter of Amsterdam, by Ramiro Espinoza
Designage, by Arnold Schwartzman
The Eternal Letter, ed. Paul Shaw
Fascia Lettering in the British Isles, by Alan Bartram
Fileteado Porteño, by Alfredo Genovese
*From Asam to Zrenner: Tracing the Legacy of the
   Munich Sign Painter Karl Blaschke*, by Oliver Linke
Ghost Signs, by William Stage
Ghostletters Vienna, by Tom Koch
Gràfica de les Rambles: The Signs of Barcelona, by
   Louise Fili
Graphique de la Rue: The Signs of Paris, by Louise Fili
A History of Lettering, by Nicolete Gray
Morgue File Book 1, by Mike Meyer
The Origin of the Serif, by Edward Catich
Scripts, by Steven Heller and Louise Fili
Shadow Type, by Steven Heller and Louise Fili
Sign Painters, by Faythe Levine and Sam Macon
   (also a feature-length documentary film available
   online: www.signpaintersfilm.com)
A Signpainter's Sketch Book, by Noel B. Weber
Signs of Italy, by James Clough
Signwritten Art, by A.J. Lewery
Slab Serif Type, by Steven Heller and Louise Fili
Stencil Type, by Steven Heller and Louise Fili

Index

Page numbers in *italics* refer to
illustrations.

A

abrasives 48
ACP (aluminum composite
    panels) 57
acrylic paints 14
alphabets 95–177
  Abrupt Serif 126–7
  Alfabetty 172–3
  Amalgaration 152–3
  Architect Casuals 100–1
  Blackboard Casual 136–7
  Bread and Butter Block 146–7
  Bretagne Block 106–7
  Carte-Deco 134–5
  Carzorla Condensed 144–5
  Chisel Speed Stroke 156–7
  Christiania 170–1
  Classic Serif 138–9
  Copen Black Oblique 168–9
  Cugat 102–3
  Dancing Script 110–11
  Dave's Casual 108–9
  Fill 'Er Up 154–5
  Fruity Script 114–15
  Honeymoon in Cortez 164–5
  Housemaster 132–3
  Jazz 116–17
  J's 26 162–3
  King Script 160–1
  Laurel 142–3
  Letterista Script 96
  Luminor Poster Block 124–5
  Magic Monkey 150–1
  Merletters 122–3
  Mossy Letters 128–9
  Neuland Hand Translated 166–7
  Pinhead Script 158–9
  Porteño 112–13
  Pottsmith 97
  Poulpe 140–1
  Rheingold Rascal 148–9
  Sexy Bevels 120–1
  Sunny Script 130–1
  Teotextura 174–5
  Touriga 118–19
  Verlaine Script 176–7
  Vintage Neon 98–9
  Wauwatosa 104–5
aluminum composite panels (ACP) 57
aluminum substrates 57–8, 72
application tools
  brayers (ink rollers) 46, 55

squeegees 46, 68–9
apprenticeships 92, 94
arcs 75
artist profiles 178–81
artwork 63, 73

B

banners *see* fabric banners
bibliography 188
binders (paint) 11
blades 47
block (alphabet) 80–5, *81*
bodkins 43
Bon Ami 48, 60
books 94, 188
box cutters 47
box stools 51
brayers (ink rollers) 46
brick walls 58–60, 72
bridges (hand rests) 45
brush boxes 37
brush cleaners 40
brush grip and angle 76–7
brush strokes 80–5
  block and thick 'n' thin 80–5, *81*
  casual 85–9, *86*
  script 89–91, *90*
brushes
  avoiding contamination 32, 36
  care of 32–6, 40
  cleaning 12, 33, 34–5, 36, 40
  construction 23
  drying 33
  ferrules and fillings 24–7
  markings on 23
  new, preparing 33
  for oil-based paints 33–5
  oiling 33
  preparing for painting 34
  preventing from drying out 34
  quill names 24
  sizes 23, 24
  starter kit 31
  storing 32, 35, 37, 40
  types 28–31
  for water-based paints 36
bulletin colors 13

C

"camel" 27
card substrate 62, 72
casual (alphabet) 85–9, *86*
chairs, low-down 51
chalk 40–1, 72
chalk lines 42, 71

charcoal 40–1, 72
"chicken scratch" 85
china markers *see* grease pencils
chisel-edge writers 28
cleaning *see* brushes, cleaning
clear angles 42
clear coats 54, 57
clips and fixers 47
color (pigments) 11
color fading *11*
color mixing 16–17, 60
color reference numbers 17
compasses 41
composition of paint 10–11
concrete walls 58–60
copying a sign 70
curing (paint) 11, 12, 56
cutters (blades) 47
cutters (brushes) *see* lining fitches

D

decals 68–9
design 63, 73
digital designs 63, 68
dippers 38–9, 79
direct markup *see* marking-up
drawing boards 49
drawings 63, 73
driers (paints) 19–20
drying planks 51

E

easels 49
electro-pounces and plotters 43–4, 64–5
emulsion paints 14
enamel paints 12–13
equipment (*see also* tools)
  basic starter kit 52
  brush starter kit 31
  hardware 49–51

F

fabric banners 43, 62, 72
fading of colors 11
ferrules 24
fillings (brushes) 24–7
film formers 11
fine line tape 46
finishing off 54
  fabric and vinyl banners 62
  glass 61
  timber and aluminum 56–7
  vehicles 61
  walls: brick, concrete, and plaster
    59–60

fitches (brushes) *see* lining fitches
flash (alphabet) 85–9, *86*
flats (brushes) 29
flats (paint) 13
flow (brushes) 25
fluorescent colors 60

G
gaffer tape 46
gilding 60, 61
glass cleaners 48, 60
glass substrates 60–1, 72, 76
glasspaper 48
glossary 182–5
grease pencils 40
grid lines 73

H
hair (brush fillings) 25–7
hand over hand technique 78
hand rests 45, 78
hardeners (paints) 19, 20
hardware 49–51
health and safety 10
hiding pigment 11
hog (bristle) 25, 27
horizontal lines 74–5

I
indoor applications 13
ink rollers *see* brayers (ink rollers)

J
Japan colors 13–14

K
kolinsky sable 25, 26
kraft papers 63

L
laser levels 72
latex paints 14
laying out *see* setting out
learning opportunities 92–4
Letterheads 92, *93*
lettering enamels 12–13
levels *see* spirit levels
liners (brushes) 30
lining fitches 30, 59, 77
low-tack tape 46

M
mahl sticks 45, 78
marker pens 41
marking-out tools 40–2, 72
marking-up 70–5
  arcs 75
  chalk lines 71

horizontal lines 74
materials 72
positioning 72
ruler pull method 74
scaling up 73
shadow lines 74, 75
masking tape 46
masks *see* vinyl masks
matte finish 13
MDO (medium density overlay) 54, 55
murals 58, 63

N
neatsfoot oil 40

O
oil-based paints 11–12
  brushes for 33–5
  driers 19–20
  hardeners 19
  reducers 18–19
  retarders (extenders) 19
  thinners 18
one-stroke brushes *see* flats (brushes)
online communities 94
opacity (paint) 11
ox hair 25, 27

P
paint (*see also* oil-based paints; water-based paints)
  additives 11, 17–20
  color mixing 16–17
  composition 10–11
  decanting 16
  mixing (shaking/stirring) 15
  "skinned over" 15
  storage 15, 16
  transferring to container 16
  types 11–15
paint application
  aluminum substrates 57–8
  fabric and vinyl banners 62
  glass substrates 60–1
  paper and card 62
  timber substrates 55–6
  vehicles 61
  walls: brick, concrete, and plaster 58–60
paint brushes *see* brushes
paint containers 16, 38–9
paint cups 16, 39, 78, 79
paint dippers 38–9, 79
paint hold (brushes) 25
paint palettes & dippers 38–9
paint rollers 31, 55
paint shakers and stirrers 15

paint tin openers, stirrers, and rattlers 38
paint trolleys 50
painting technique 76–91
  brush grip & angle 76–7
  brush strokes 80–91
  palettes/paletting 38, 79
  posture & positioning 76
  rests 45, 78–9
"paint-up-to line" 89
palettes/paletting 38, 79
Pantone® references 17
paper and card substrate 62, 72
paper dispensers 50
paper patterns 63, 66
pencils 40, 72
pencils (writers) *see* chisel-edge writers
pigments 11
pinkie down 79
pinstriping 30
plaster 58–60
plotters 64–5
plywood 54
pointers (brushes) 29
poster paints 13–14
posture and positioning 76–7
pouncing 64–6
pouncing tools/materials 43–4, 64
powder cleaners 48, 60
practicing 94
preparing for painting 54
  aluminum 57
  fabric and vinyl banners 62
  glass 60
  timber 55
  vehicles 61
  walls: brick, concrete, and plaster 58
pressure transfer 66–7
primers 15, 55
priming (undercoating) 54, 55
printing digital designs 63
projecting (setting out) 67–8

Q
quill names 24

R
RAL color standard 17
rattlers 38
red sable 25, 26
reducers (paints) 18–19
rests 45, 78–9
retarders (extenders) 19, 20
rollers *see* brayers (ink rollers); paint rollers
ruler pull method 74
rulers and measures 41–2

S

Sableline 27

safety *see* health and safety

sandpaper 48

sans serif *see* block (alphabet)

scaling up 73

scalpels 47

Scotch tape 46

scourers 48

scrapers 47

script (alphabet) 89–91, *90*

scuff pads 48

scuffing substrates 54

setting out *see* marking-up;
    transferring designs

shadow lines 74, 75

sign enamels 12–13

sign kits 37

skids 50

slant liners 30

slapdash (alphabet) 85–9, *86*

slash (alphabet) 85–9, *86*

snap (brushes) 25

solvent-based paints *see* oil-based
    paints

solvents 11, 12

spirit levels 42

squeegees 46, 68–9

squirrel hair 25, 26–7

Stanley knives 47

starter kit 52

steel wool 48

stock patterns 63

stockists 186–7

storing brushes 32, 35, 37, 40

storing paint 15

substrates 54–62

  aluminum 57–8, 72

  brick, concrete, and plaster
      58–60, 72

  existing board 55

  fabric and vinyl banners 62, 72

  glass 60–1, 72, 76

  marking-out tool suitability 72

  paper and card 62, 63, 72

  preparing and finishing 54–62

  timber 54–7, 72

sword liners 30

synthetic brushes 27

T

tapes 46, 70

terminology 182–5

thick 'n' thin (alphabet) 80–5, *81*

thinners (paints) 18, 20

timber substrates 54–7, 72

"tip out" 82

"tipping off" 55

tool boxes 37

tools

  blades 47

  brayers (ink rollers) 46

  clips and fixers 47

  marking-out 40–2

  paint handling 38

  palettes & dippers 38–9

  pouncing 43–4

  rests 45

  squeegee 46

  tapes 46

tracing paper 63, 70

tracing wheels 43, 64

training 92–4

transfer paper 66

transferring designs 63–9 (*see also*
    marking-up)

  copying 70

  positioning 63

  pouncing 64–6

  pressure transfer 66–7

projecting 67–8

using tape 70

vinyl masks 68–9

U

ultraviolet (UV) protection 11

V

varnishes 10

varnishing 54, 57

vehicles 61, 72

videos 94

vinyl banners 62, 72

vinyl masks 68–9

W

walls 58–60, 72

water-based paints 12, 20

  avoiding contamination 40

  brushes for 36

  emulsion paints 14

  enamels 12

  hardeners 20

  retarders (extenders) 20

  thinners 20

watercolors 11

wax pencil *see* grease pencils

weed (vinyl) 68

"whale tail" 79

whiting 48, 60

windows 60–1

wire brushes 48

wire wool 48

workshops 92

writers (brushes) *see* chisel-edge
    writers

Y

yardsticks 41–2

Acknowledgments

This book would not have been possible without the support of thousands of people that I have met throughout my life and work. I was going to try listing everyone and then realized that I'd only forget a few hundred, so instead I'd like to throw a big thank you blanket over the head of anyone and everyone who happens to be reading this. You *have* made a contribution, even if it is showing me how *not* to do things!

In terms of the practical aspects of bringing the book together, I would like to thank Sam Roberts who has helped to turn my thoughts into words, Jasper Andries who has illustrated these beautifully, Darius Zomorodian of A.S. Handover whose photography has helped to demystify many of the tools and materials discussed in these pages, and, last but not least, the talented contributors whose alphabets have provided me, and countless others, with no end of creative inspiration.

I have also benefited from the specialist knowledge, time, and resources of some of the best suppliers in the world, including Chris Fast at Mack Brush; James Kwiatkowski at Alpha 6 Corp; Michael Macre at 1 Shot Paints; Craig Morton, Rachel Neilson, Michael Venus, and Charlotte Wormley-Healing at A.S. Handover; and Matt Panuska at Ronan Paints.

And, finally, I would like to give the biggest thanks of all to my wife Ayleen and son Caleb who have supported my life's work and travels through thick and thin. (Shouldn't that be Thick 'n' Thin?) I wouldn't be where I am today without you.

Photography Credits

Colin Allen (www.colinallenphography.com), page 93, bottom
Jonathan Cherry (www.jonathancherry.net) page 21, below
Krista Lindahl (colossalmedia.com) page 93, top
Mike Hardwick pages 2, above and 6, both
Norman Hayes (www.wastestudio.com) page 37, left
Edwin Stoop (www.sketchingmaniacs.com) page 2, below
Goof Vermeulen (www.goofz.nl) page 61
Darius Zomorodian (www.handover.co.uk)

All alphabets on pages 96 to 177 are © the artists.